CiTY·SMaRT™
GUIDEBOOK

Calgary

Frances Purslow
Dining Chapter by Jacqueline Louie

John Muir Publications
Santa Fe, New Mexico

Acknowledgments

For my family: Teresa, Todd, Joel, Grant, and especially Neil, for their patience, support, and encouragement.

John Muir Publications, P. O. Box 613, Santa Fe, New Mexico 87504

Printed in the United States of America.
First edition. First printing February 1998.

ISBN 1-56261-322-7
ISSN 1095-7987

Editors: Krista Lyons-Gould, Elizabeth Wolf, Chris Hayhurst
Graphics Editor: Tom Gaukel
Production: Marie Vigil
Design: Janine Lehmann
Cover Design: Suzanne Rush
Typesetting: Ruth Anne Velasquez
Maps: Julie Felton
Printer: Publishers Press
Front cover photo: Fridmar Damm/Leo de Wys
Back cover photo: © Gerald Vander Pyl

Distributed to the book trade by
Publishers Group West
Emeryville, California

While every effort has been made to provide accurate, up-to-date information, the author and publisher accept no responsibility for loss, injury, or inconvenience sustained by any person using this book.

CONTENTS

MAP CONTENTS

HOW TO USE THIS BOOK

Whether you're a visitor, a new resident, or a Calgary native, you'll find the *City•Smart Guidebook: Calgary* indispensable. Authors Frances Purslow and Jacqueline Louie bring you an insider's view of the best Calgary has to offer.

This book presents the city in five geographic zones. The zone divisions are listed at the bottom of this page and shown on the map on the following pages. Look for a zone designation in each listing and use it to help you locate that listing. To help you find your way around, there are Public Transportation maps in Chapter 2; maps of the Downtown and Greater Calgary areas in Chapters 3, 4, 5; and a Calgary region map in Chapter 13.

Example:
CALGARY TOWER
101 - 9th Ave. SW, Calgary
403/266-7171   DT

Zone abbreviation = DT
The Calgary Tower is located on the Downtown Area map unless otherwise noted.

Calgary Zones

DT—Downtown Calgary
This area is bordered on the north by the Bow River and the east by the Elbow River. It extends south to the railway tracks (between 9th and 10th Avenues) and west to 11 Street, SW.

SE—Southeast Calgary
This area extends east of Centre Street and Macleod Trail and south of Centre Avenue and Memorial Drive (excluding the Downtown area described above).

SW—Southwest Calgary
This area extends west of Centre Street and Macleod Trail and south of the Bow River and Trans Canada Highway (excluding the Downtown area described above).

NE—Northeast Calgary
This area extends east of Centre Street and north of the Bow River, Centre Avenue, and Memorial Drive (which is an extension of Centre Avenue).

NW—Northwest Calgary
This area extends west of Centre Street and north of the Bow River until it intersects the Trans Canada Highway. Then Trans Canada Highway becomes the dividing line between NW and SW.

CALGARY ZONES

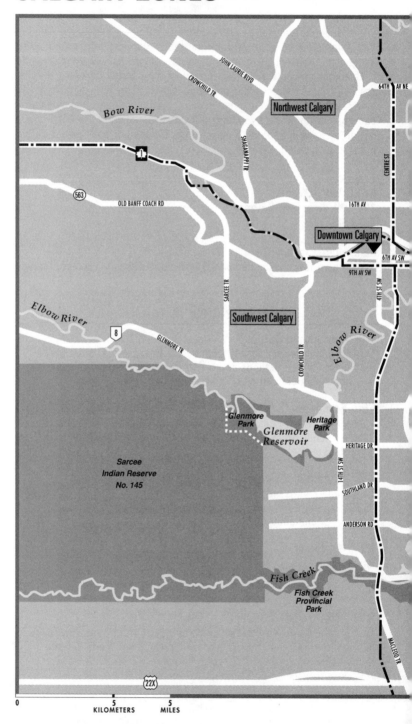

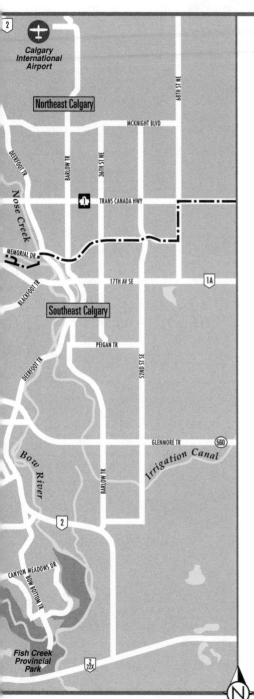

CALGARY ZONES

DT—Downtown Calgary
Bordered on the north by the Bow River and the east by the Elbow River, it extends south to the railway tracks (between 9th and 10th Avenues) and west to 11 Street, SW.

SE—Southeast Calgary
Extends east of Centre Street and Macleod Trail and south of Centre Avenue and Memorial Drive (excluding Downtown Calgary).

SW—Southwest Calgary
Extends west of Centre Street and Macleod Trail and south of the Bow River and Trans Canada Highway (excluding Downtown Calgary).

NE—Northeast Calgary
Extends east of Centre Street and north of the Bow River, Centre Avenue, and Memorial Drive (an extension of Centre Avenue).

NW—Northwest Calgary
Extends west of Centre Street and north of the Bow River until it intersects the Trans Canada Highway. Trans Canada Highway becomes the dividing line between NW and SW.

1

WELCOME TO CALGARY

A city of contrasts, Calgary's downtown projects its fingers of glass and steel skyward from the golden prairie. Thousands of commuters fill the city's core, dodging kamikaze bicycle couriers while bustling to work. Nearby, couples stroll leisurely along the pathways of Prince's Island Park, past fishermen casting for their dinners.

Also known as Cowtown, the gateway to the Canadian Rockies, the home of the Calgary Exhibition and Stampede, and the land of blue skies, green river corridors, and white Stetsons, Calgary is a young, vibrant city with a western flavour. The third-fastest-growing city in Canada, Calgary is the country's energy capital as well as one of the top centres for corporate head offices. Dynamic and cosmopolitan, Calgary is renowned for its entrepreneurial spirit.

Though a sophisticated urban centre, Calgary never strays far from its frontier heritage. Having achieved a metropolitan profile, it still retains a small-town friendliness and casual western demeanour where residents rate quality of life as its strongest attribute. Clean air, few traffic problems, modest housing costs, low crime rates, over 300 kilometers (190 miles) of pathways, and the city's proximity to the Rocky Mountains all contribute to Calgary's reputation as Canada's most livable city.

History of Calgary

Alberta's booming energy industry owes its success to geology. Millions of years ago, as marine plants and animals died, decomposed, and were buried under geological deposits, heat and pressure slowly changed the

Royal Canadian Mounted Police

organic material into coal, oil, and gas. Meanwhile, to the west, monumental subterranean forces formed the Rocky Mountains. Later, Ice Age glaciers did some sculpting of their own, their meltwater carving through the mountains to create the channels of the Bow River. Some remnants of these glaciers can still be seen in the Rockies today.

In the ensuing years, the area's climate gradually changed, and the resulting fertile lands attracted enormous herds of grazing bison. The bison supplied the native peoples with meat, skins for clothing and shelter, bones for tools and utensils, and sinew for thread and rope. But over time the bison numbers dwindled until, by the 1880s, they had all but vanished from the plains and settlers took over the vast prairies for farming.

In 1875, a detachment of red-coated North West Mounted Police (later renamed the Royal Canadian Mounted Police, or "Mounties") arrived in what is now Alberta to spread law and order and to establish a fort on the south shore at the confluence of the Bow and Elbow Rivers. Commanding officer Inspector Brisebois named the fort after himself, but the title proved unpopular and was later changed to Fort Calgary by NWMP Commissioner Macleod (see Trivia below).

TRIVIA

Calgary gets its name from the ancestral estate of NWMP Col. J. F. Macleod on the Isle of Mull in the Hebrides in Scotland. It is a Gaelic word meaning "bay farm."

By 1881 there were 75 people living in Fort Calgary. That same year, a herd of 3,000 cattle arrived, and the area's world-famous ranching industry was born. Later, in 1883, the Canadian Pacific Railway arrived. As the fort's population grew, the original site expanded west across the Elbow River to be near the railway station, and in 1884, incorporated as a town. Full passenger rail service followed soon after in 1886.

It was also in 1886—the year of the Great Fire—that the fledgling community experienced its first disaster. The fire destroyed 14 wooden buildings in the town's core. Although devastating at the time, the town turned its misfortune to its advantage. To preclude the fire's recurrence, sandstone was used in the town's reconstruction for its fireproof properties and for the ease with which it could be quarried and carved. Sandstone quarries sprang up throughout the Calgary area, transforming the sparcely populated pioneer settlement into an urban centre known as the "Sandstone City of the West." The solid and substantial appearance of the golden stone gave Calgary's streets an aura of prosperity which in turn attracted business and new residents.

In January 1894, with a population of 3,900, Calgary was officially declared a city. By the early 1900s, Calgarians began to enjoy the advantages of their rapidly growing home, and in 1911, city government took a firm stand when construction was finished on an imposing sandstone city hall with a clock tower 30.5 meters (100 feet) tall.

The Calgary Stampede was held for the first time in 1912, emphasizing Calgary's economic dependence on agriculture and ranching. This dependence was alleviated, however, when oil was discovered in Turner Valley in 1914. The only major oil field in Canada, Turner Valley solidified Calgary's emerging status as the nation's energy capital.

At the end of World War II, Alberta fell into recession due to the depressed agricultural economy, and residents moved elsewhere. Fortunately, Leduc Oil Field was discovered in 1947, launching Calgary into renewed prosperity.

Calgary, Alberta: Quick Facts

Population: *750,000*

Location: *51° N latitude, 114° W longitude, in the foothills of the Rocky Mountains at the junction of the Bow and Elbow Rivers*

Elevation: *1,139 m (3,740 ft) above sea level*

Area: *721 square kilometers (279 square miles); second-largest city in Canada by area*

Calgary Time Line

1875	Calgary is founded when the North West Mounted Police (NWMP) build a fort and establish trading posts at the confluence of the Bow and Elbow Rivers.
1881	Calgary's world-famous ranching industry begins with the arrival of the first herd, 3,000 cattle. The fort's population is 75.
1883	The *Calgary Herald* publishes its first edition.
1884	Calgary incorporates as a town.
1886	Sir John A. Macdonald, Prime Minister of Canada, sweeps through town on the first transcontinental passenger train heading west.
1892	Train service links Alberta's two major cities, Calgary and Edmonton.
1894	Calgary incorporates as a city.
1905	Alberta joins Confederation.
1905	1905–1908 Calgary's population doubles and building booms.
1909	Early in the year, lots sell for between $100 and $800, but by the end of 1909 skyrocket to $1,750 per foot frontage.
1911	City Hall opens.
1912	Calgary Stampede is held for the first time.
1919	The Prince of Wales visits Calgary and buys EP Ranch, south of the city.
1923	The popularity of the Calgary Stampede encourages organizers to make it an annual attraction.
1930	Calgary lawyer R. B. Bennett becomes Prime Minister of Canada.
1939	King George VI visits Calgary.
1947	The discovery of the Leduc Oil Field reaffirms Calgary's position as the energy capital of Canada.
1948	The Calgary Stampeders win the Grey Cup.
1950	Calgary Transit switches from streetcars to buses.
1951	Princess Elizabeth and Prince Philip visit.
1955	Alberta celebrates 50 years as a province.
1957	Southern Alberta Jubilee Auditorium opens its doors.

The University of Alberta opens a campus in the city's northwest.	**1960**
Heritage Park Historical Village opens.	**1964**
Oil prices soar, leading to frenzied growth and construction in Calgary.	**1973**
Calgary celebrates its centennial.	**1975**
In the midst of the city's boom, Calgary sets a new record of $1.1 billion for the construction value of building permits.	**1978**
A banner year! The Calgary Flames bring the NHL to the city's doorstep while Calgary wins bid to host XV Olympic Winter Games. The C-Train (light rail transit system) begins operation.	**1981**
The Olympic Oval—the first covered speed skating oval in the world to be used for Olympic competition—is officially declared open.	**1987**
The world watches as Calgary hosts the XV Olympic Winter Games.	**1988**
The Calgary Flames win the Stanley Cup. Calgary's film industry scores a coup with the $16 million shoot of the Japanese epic *Heaven and Earth*, the largest production ever organized in Canada.	**1989**
The city begins its residential recycling program.	**1990**
City's smoking bylaw establishes non-smoking as the norm in public places, and fluoridation of the city's water supply commences.	**1991**
Calgary ex-mayor Ralph Klein is named Premier of Alberta.	**1992**
Calgary hosts the Grey Cup.	**1993**
Calgary celebrates its centennial of incorporation.	**1994**
Calgary hosts World Police/Fire Games.	**1997**

Between 1947 and 1965, Calgary's population exploded from 100,000 to 325,000. In 1968, as if to signify the city's financial comeback, the Husky Tower (later renamed the Calgary Tower) raised its head over all other downtown buildings. Soaring 190 meters (623 feet) into the sky, this familiar landmark graces the intersection of Centre Street and 9th Avenue SW.

The 1970s were the boom years. Jobs were plentiful and housing scarce. At the decade's peak, 3,000 people flowed into Calgary every week; the construction value of building permits was valued at over $1 billion per year. And, in the midst of it all, the city celebrated its first centennial.

Then the 80s arrived, and the successes of the previous decade were met head on by another recession. Layoffs forced people to leave the province in droves. But Calgarians refused to be discouraged and rallied around the city's brightest hope: hosting the XV Olympic Winter Games. Their optimism never flagged, even in 1986 when the bottom fell out on the price of oil and still more jobs were eliminated.

Since then, Calgary's economy has diversified—manufacturing, tourism, and retail trade have elbowed in to take their places next to the oil industry. The city's location, well-educated workforce, high computer literacy rate, and entrepreneurial attitude have created new opportunities. While Calgary is still an energy-based city, this diversification has broadened its economic base, and currently Calgarians enjoy the lowest unemployment rate of any major centre in the country.

Now they look ahead to their province's centennial in the year 2005.

The People of Calgary

If there is a predominant mood in Calgary, it's that anything can happen. With a median age of 31 years, the typical Calgarian is full of big ideas and optimism, an attitude evident in both community and business.

In Canada's most educated city, 58 percent of adults—11 percent above the national average—have some post-secondary education. Residents also rank fourth in the nation for personal disposable income.

While the majority of Calgarians are British in descent, the next largest ethnic groups are German and Chinese. A quick look at the list of restaurants in town gives an idea of Calgary's cultural makeup. Italian,

TIP

History buffs will enjoy self-guided heritage walking tours of the downtown area. Booklets and maps of the tours are available at City Hall. See Chapter 5, "Sights and Attractions," for more information.

German, French, Ukrainian, Japanese, Chinese, Vietnamese, and Greek immigrants have poured into the city to shape and influence the cultural landscape and enrich Calgary's cosmopolitan ambiance.

Business and Economy

Calgary's beginnings are rooted in the agriculture industry, which still thrives around this city of the Rocky Mountain foothills. Most agricultural revenue is derived from three commodities: cattle, wheat, and small grains. Though Calgary is not the producer of these goods, it benefits from a wide range of agriculturally based industries and services.

Additionally, as Canada's energy capital, 87 percent of the country's oil and gas producers and 64 percent of coal companies are headquartered here. Consequently, Calgary is home to a large concentration of expertise in oil and gas technologies, petrochemical engineering, natural gas compression, and heavy oil development and engineering. The city is also home to much of Canada's energy service industry, including many firms specializing in engineering, geology, and data processing. The production of coal, natural gas, and unconventional sources of oil, such as the oil sands, will ensure that Calgary remains an energy centre as conventional sources of oil are depleted.

Cattle, one of the Calgary area commodities

The city's strategic location on major air, rail, and highway corridors renders it Western Canada's most important transportation hub. It has also attracted top ranking business leaders and finance companies and has positioned Calgary as the financial capital of the West.

Calgary's cooperative, entrepreneurial-minded business community has encouraged many major companies to locate here. Firms like

Calgary CVB/Chris Large

Top Ten Calgary Features
by Glenn Tibbles
Managing Director of the Calgary Chamber of Commerce

1. Calgary's volunteerism and community spirit.
2. The city's entrepreneurial nature.
3. The system of bicycle trails and pathways along the river.
4. The Rocky Mountains.
5. Calgary Exhibition and Stampede.
6. Winter chinooks.
7. Prince's Island Park.
8. Calgary International Airport.
9. Spruce Meadows.
10. Calgary's heritage buildings and houses.

TransCanada Pipelines, Shell Canada Inc., Amoco Canada Petroleum Ltd., Petro-Canada Inc., and Nova Corporation have headquarters in the city.

Traditionally, the Calgary business community has been dominated by the resource sector, but this is changing as the city's economy continues to diversify. The headquarters of CP Rail, Suncor Inc., Shaw Communications, Canadian Tire, and Dow Chemicals are just a few of the companies to join Calgary's business scene. This diversification will ensure a stable future for the city's economy. New areas of growth are telecommunications, manufacturing, retail trade, tourism, and, most recently, high technology. As one of the first global InfoPorts, Calgary is a worldwide supplier of information technology, products, and services. InfoPort Calgary has attracted more than 700 advanced technology companies specializing in telecommunications and wireless equipment development, software development, geographic information systems, and knowledge-intensive services.

TRIVIA

To convert Canadian dollars to U.S. dollars, use the following formula: 1.42 Canadian dollars = 1 U.S. dollar (at time of printing).

Calgary's pro-business reputation—including the relatively low costs associated with running a business here—has made it the city of choice for many new businesses. Forecasts predict Calgary will lead the country in growth and job creation through 2005.

Calgary's robust economy is reflected in the abundance of houses being built, companies moving in, and new jobs being created. Approximately half of Calgary employers are paying incentive compensation on top of salaries, while employees in the city are receiving salary increases among the highest in Canada. Bonuses and profit-sharing based on company/division and individual performance are the favoured forms of incentive plans.

Alberta is the only Canadian province without a sales tax. It has no payroll or capital tax and touts low corporate taxes. Alberta recently decreased its aviation fuel tax and is looking at doing the same for railway fuel.

Low taxes combined with favourable U.S. exchange rates, spectacular scenery, long hours of sunshine in summer, and experienced crews have made Calgary an ideal location for movies, television shows, and commercials. Indeed, the entertainment industry flourishes here.

Housing

The effects of Calgary's bustling corporate and industrial activity are in turn increasing housing starts and used-home sales. Calgary has a 1.5 percent apartment vacancy rate and, per capita, is experiencing the most single-family housing starts of any large Canadian city. Low interest rates, strong job creation, and immigration have also contributed to the upbeat mood in the housing industry.
Approximately 7,800 homes are built annually in the city, with an average selling price of $172,000. On the resale side, more than 17,000 used homes were sold in 1996 for an average price of $135,000.

Calgary night skyline

Calgary CVB/John Sharpe

Resale Housing Market
Under $120,000—45.7%
$120,000 to $150,000—27.5%
$150,000 to $200,000—17.1%
$200,000 to $300,000—8.1%
Over $300,000—1.6%

For those interested in a home near the water, there are a number of trout-stocked lakes in Calgary with access restricted to community residents. Home owners pay between $100 and $400 annually for the privilege of using the lakes.

Schools

Calgary embraces two public school systems: the Calgary Board of Education, with approximately 95,000 students in 219 schools; and the Calgary Roman Catholic Separate School district, with approximately 37,000 students in 83 schools. Both systems are generally structured as follows: kindergarten; elementary school to grade 6; junior high (grades 7 to 9); and senior high (grades 10 to 12).

There are alternative programs of study offered by three charter schools in Calgary—Global Learning Academy, Action for Bright Children (ABC), and Almadina Charter School—as well as numerous private schools.

Post-secondary education is available at several local institutions, including Alberta College of Art and Design, Alberta Vocational College, Mount Royal College, Southern Alberta Institute of Technology (SAIT), and the University of Calgary.

Calgary's Weather

	Avg. High Temps (°C)	Avg. Low Temps (°C)	Avg. mm Rain	Avg. mm Snow
January	-3.6	-15.7	0.2	18.0
February	-0.5	-12.3	0.2	14.9
March	3.3	-8.4	1.5	18.7
April	10.6	-2.4	9.2	20.4
May	16.4	3.0	43.9	10.2
June	20.6	7.4	76.7	0.3
July	23.2	9.5	69.9	0.0
August	22.7	8.6	48.7	0.0
September	17.4	3.8	42.7	6.4
October	12.6	-1.2	6.4	11.5
November	2.9	-9.0	0.6	16.0
December	-2.3	-14.4	0.1	19.0

Source: Atmospheric Environment Services—Calgary Weather Office

Taxes

Alberta has no provincial sales tax, but there is a federal Goods and Services Tax (GST) of 7 percent which applies to most goods and services. Alberta also has a 5 percent hotel tax.

Property taxes, depending on location, are in the vicinity of $3,600 for a 2,400-square-foot house.

Cost of Living

Daily newspaper: 50 cents
Dinner for one: $15
Movie admission: $8
Hotel double room: $70
5-mile cab ride: $8
Jumbo hot dog and drink from downtown vendor: $2
Annual heating costs for 1,200- to 1,400-square-foot bungalow: $600

Calgary Weather

Alberta receives more hours of sunshine yearly than any other province in Canada, and Calgary follows suit. The city is known for its sunny skies and a moderate four-season climate with substantial variations in temperature between seasons. Summer days are usually warm and dry with cool evenings due to the altitude and proximity to the mountains. July sees the most thunderstorm and hail activity.

The greatest rainfall occurs during the spring months while winters are characterized by moderate snowfall and chinooks. Precipitation averages 424 mm (16.7 in.), of which 150 mm (6 in.) falls as snow. Chinooks—Pacific-warmed, dry winds that develop over the Rockies and can raise temperatures more than 20°C in a few hours—turn winter into spring. Typically, Calgarians welcome 20 to 25 chinooks per year, though those with respiratory problems or a predisposition to migraines sometimes find them a nuisance.

TIP

Temperatures are measured by the Celsius temperature scale, where the freezing point is 0°C. To convert Celsius to degrees Fahrenheit, use the following formula: °F = $\frac{9}{5}$ x °C + 32.

When to Visit

Calgary is blessed with some of the finest natural areas within a Canadian municipality. This fact, coupled with proximity to the mountains, fosters outdoor pursuits at all times of the year.

The advent of warm weather in spring encourages flowering trees and shrubs to don their pink and yellow blossoms, lifting the spirits of Calgarians anxious to see plant life awaken after months of dormancy. Another colourful season is autumn, when leaves change to scarlet, orange, and gold in an arresting display before the snow flies.

Calgary Stampede Parade

While each season in Calgary has its own appeal, winter and summer months overflow with things to do and see. Once Ol' Man Winter makes an appearance, outdoor enthusiasts flock to Calgary to partake in the pleasures of ice skating, tobogganing, and skiing (cross-country and downhill), or to participate in the various winter festivals in the area. Summer weather lures those who prefer canoeing, sailing, hiking, cycling, ballooning, golfing, or in-line skating. And of course, the world-famous Calgary Stampede attracts over a million visitors annually when it takes over the city for ten days in July.

Calendar of Events

JANUARY
PlayRites Festival (January and February, 403/294-7402)—Alberta Theatre Projects' annual festival of new plays presented at the Martha Cohen Theatre of the Calgary Centre for Performing Arts; Harness racing opens at Stampede Park.

FEBRUARY
Calgary Winter Festival (403/543-5480)—Ice sculpture and other winter fun abounds at the downtown Festival Fun Zone and Winter Playground at Canada Olympic Park; **Canada's Cowboy Festival** (403/777-0000)— Calgary Convention Centre celebrates the authentic cowboy lifestyle with western exhibits, music, poetry, art, and Native dancing.

MARCH
Rodeo Royale (403/777-0000)—Annual indoor rodeo featuring saddle bronc, bareback, bull riding, calf roping, and steer wrestling at the Stampede

Corral; Thoroughbred racing opens at Stampede Park; **Cabane à Sucre** (403/571-4000)—Join a French Canadian celebration with a special brunch, sleigh rides, and maple syrup taffy at the Trans-Canada Highway and Springbank Road.

APRIL

Cannons triple-A baseball season opens (403/284-1111)—See Chapter 10 for more info; **Calgary Kiwanis Music Festival** (403/283-6009)—20,000 amateur musicians and speech performers compete for scholarships and are judged by national and international adjudicators at Jubilee Auditorium and SAIT Orpheus Theatre.

MAY

Calgary International Children's Festival (403/294-7414)—One of Canada's top festivals with performers entertaining the young set at several downtown venues; see Chapter 6 for details; **Fourth Street Lilac Festival** (403/228-0902)—noontime parade followed by unique crafts, music, entertainment, food, and fun surrounded by the sight and smell of lilacs on 4th Street SW; **Heritage Park** season opens (403/259-1900)—A living historical village with costumed interpreters and Canadian heritage and cultural displays; **Calaway Park** opens (403/240-3822)—Western Canada's largest family amusement park, with rides, food, games, and a petting zoo; **"The National"** (403/974-4200)—Top riders from across Canada compete in equestrian show jumping events at Spruce Meadows.

JUNE

Calgary Summer Antique Show (800/667-0619)—Over 150 antique dealers display their wares at Canada Olympic Park; Calgary Stampeders CFL Football season opens (289-0205)—See Chapter 10 for details; **CariFest** (403/292-0310)—Steel drum bands and colourful dancers kick off this Caribbean Festival with a popular parade through the downtown core followed by a week of activities, music, films, and cuisine; **Calgary International Jazz Festival** (403/259-8080)—Leading jazz musicians celebrate big band, be-bop, blues, gospel, swing, salsa, summer, and song at various venues with some free concerts downtown; harness racing opens

T I P

Check out the City of Calgary Web site at http://www.gov.calgary.ab.ca/ for up-to-the-minute info on events and attractions as well as other helpful visitor information.

at Stampede Park; **Kite Day**—For colourful action check out the sky above South Glenmore Park on Father's Day; **Native Awareness Week** (403/296-2227)—Pow-wows, Native cuisine, arts and crafts, films, lectures, and free performances at Olympic Plaza; **Banff Festival of the Arts** (800/413-8368)—This summer-long event brings together Canadian and international artists in music, opera, theatre, dance, and visual arts.

JULY

Canada Day celebrations (403/259-1900)—Native performers, family games and races, birthday cake, multicultural events, parades, and fireworks on Prince's Island and Heritage Park; **"The North American"** (403/974-4200)—Show jumping riders from Canada, the United States, and Mexico compete at Spruce Meadows; **Calgary Exhibition and Stampede** (403/269-9822 or 800/661-1767)—Dress western and enjoy the bull-riding, chuckwagon races, carnival rides, and more at the Stampede Grounds and the "Greatest Outdoor Show on Earth"; **Calgary Folk Music Festival** (403/243-7253, ext. 2363)—Acts from around the world perform at Olympic Plaza and Prince's Island Park. Enjoy continuous music, buskers, kid stuff, specialty food booths, and a beer garden.

AUGUST

Heritage Day Festival (403/259-1900)—Family events at Heritage Park and Prince's Island with music, food, and fun; **Bluesfest**—Annual blues festival with some free concerts; **International Native Arts Festival** (403/233-0022)—Native artists gather at several downtown venues to share their culture and heritage through daily tipi raisings, dancing and entertainment, and art shows and sales; **Afrikadey!** (403/283-7119)—A five-day festival of African arts and culture at various venues; **BBQ on the Bow** (403/225-1913)—Championship barbecue competition and family fun day at Prince's Island Park; **Alberta Dragon Boat Race** (403/255-2993)—Watch the colourful boats and listen to the drummers as they pace the teams of paddlers along Glenmore Reservoir.

City of Calgary crest

SEPTEMBER

"Masters" (403/974-4200)—International equestrian show jumping competition at Spruce Meadows; Philharmonic and theatre seasons open—See Chapter 11 for more info; **Artweek** (403/297-8687)—Open house at local art galleries, special exhibitions, take a trek through Calgary's visual art world with Artwalk;

Calgary Symbols

The upper third of Calgary's official crest depicts the setting sun above a mural crown (symbol of loyalty) and the Rocky Mountains. The lower two-thirds bears the red Cross of St. George and the Canadian maple leaf inset with a bull buffalo, all supported by a horse and a steer. Below the shield are the Leek of Wales, the Rose of England, the Thistle of Scotland, and the Shamrock of Ireland, which represent the ancestry of most of Calgary's early settlers. On the scroll is Calgary's motto, "Onward," between the dates of incorporation as a town (1884) and as a city (1894). Under the scroll are the Union Jack (signifying the city's relationship with the British Commonwealth) and the Canadian Ensign (the former national flag). Calgary's official flag incorporates a white Stetson with the letter C. The flag is white and red, which Calgary adopted as its colours in 1984.

Calgary's official floral emblem is the Anemone pulsatilla rubra, or Red Pasque Flower. This perennial plant is an early bloomer with bright red flowers appearing around mid-April.

Thoroughbred racing opens at Stampede Park; **Old-time Fall Fair** (403/259-1900)—Fresh vegetable and fruit sales, competitions, family games, and entertainment at Heritage Park.

OCTOBER
Calgary Flames NHL hockey season opens (403/777-2177)—See Chapter 10 for details.

NOVEMBER
Ski resorts open; **Esther Honens International Piano Competition and Festival** (403/299-0130)—Competition to find the best piano player in the world, held every four years; the next one is in 2000; **Twelve Days of Christmas** (weekends only Nov and Dec, 403/259-1900)—Crafts, carolers, and sleigh rides at Heritage Park, and brunch at the Wainwright Hotel.

DECEMBER
Festival of Trees display—Visit the indoor forest of decorated trees, with choirs, craft shop, and gingerbread village, all at the Convention Centre;

First Night Festival (403/243-7253, ext. 2222)—A variety of downtown events celebrate New Year's Eve.

Dressing In Calgary

Be ready for anything. Snow has fallen in August while chinooks have raised temperatures in February to 17°C (63°F).

Generally speaking, in spring and fall bring a warm jacket and clothing that can be layered. During winter months, don a ski jacket, boots, gloves, and a hat. Summer requires a light jacket or sweater for evenings or inclement weather and, if activities in the mountains are planned, hiking boots and warm clothing that can be layered.

City wear is generally casual except for business or formal occasions. Few restaurants have strict dress codes. Suits and ties for men are de rigeur in most offices, with comparable wear for women. Fridays are casual dress days throughout much of the city's business sector. During Stampede Week (early July) everyone turns into an urban cowboy and western wear reigns supreme. Jeans, denim skirts, cowboy hats and boots, and big, silver belt buckles are the order of the day.

Calgary CVB/Gerald Vander Pyl

2

GETTING AROUND CALGARY

City Layout

Calgary is a very easy city to get around once you understand the layout. Designed on a grid, its avenues run east to west and streets run north to south, with numbers radiating out from Centre Street and the Bow River. All include quadrant designation. Streets in the downtown and surrounding area are numbered, so the address "850 - 16th Avenue SW" tells you that the location is near 8th Street on 16th Avenue in the southwest quadrant of the city.

In many communities, streets begin with the same letter as the community (e.g., Midpark Boulevard in Midnapore) and many names are similar, so it's important to know whether you are looking for Midpark Drive, Midpark Place, or Midpark Crescent.

There are 203 kilometers (126 miles) of expressways within the city, and most of their names end in Trail.

Downtown

Calgary is a big city without big-city problems. It has the safest downtown of any city in North America; in fact, crime has declined in the downtown area for the past five years. The hustle and bustle of downtown Calgary is a counterpoint to the peace and quiet of the pathways alongside the rivers flowing through the city's core. Fishermen cast for trout within sight of glass office towers. Elegant shops share space with fresh food markets. Fitness buffs jog in Prince's Island Park or work out at the Eau Claire YMCA.

Unlike some cities, downtown Calgary hums with activity seven days a week. Shoppers venture downtown on weekends to sample the more than

500 retail shops and services that make it Calgary's largest retail shopping centre. Then they relax with a culinary treat at one of the region's fine dining establishments and perhaps end their day enjoying a production at the Calgary Centre for Performing Arts. Chinatown, which borders downtown at Centre Street between the Bow River and 4th Avenue SE, offers unusual shops featuring everything Chinese from antiques to food.

The vibrant downtown area has many one-way streets to aid traffic flow, and 7th Avenue S is closed to all vehicles except emergency and transit vehicles. As well, 8th Avenue S is a downtown pedestrian walkway between Olympic Plaza (1st Street SE) and 3rd Street SW (Barclay Mall). This is the Stephen Avenue Mall, an outdoor mall lined with some of Calgary's oldest buildings from pioneer days.

The most distinctive landmark of the downtown area is the Calgary Tower, standing 190 meters (623 feet) high at the corner of Centre Street and 9th Avenue S.

Southeast

Southeast Calgary is generally considered the industrial quadrant of the city although there are award-winning residential lake communities further south. This area is also characterized by Fish Creek Provincial Park, the largest urban park in Canada, as well as Stampede Park, which is not a park in the usual sense of the word but the venue for the Calgary Exhibition and Stampede and home to the Canadian Airlines Saddledome, where NHL Calgary Flames and WHL Calgary Hitmen host visiting teams. The Big Four Building houses the Stampede Casino, while myriad trade shows and exhibitions frequent the Round-Up Centre.

Antique hunters seek out the treasure-filled shops of historic Inglewood.

Southwest

Calgary's southwest quadrant is largely residential, with some pockets of nightspots, coffeehouses, and shopping districts along 11th and 17th Avenues. Some of the popular, established areas in this quadrant offer a quiet lifestyle within ten minutes of downtown. Others further south afford spectacular views of the mountains.

Also of note in the southwest is Heritage Park Historical Village, which you won't want to miss. Canada's largest living historical village, it recreates the sights and sounds of life in pre-1915 Western Canada.

Northeast

The most notable northeast landmark (and the one many people see first) is the Calgary International Airport. Ranked number one in Canada in terms of overall customer convenience, it is the gateway to Western Canada for 7 million people annually.

Deerfoot Mall, Franklin Mall, Sunridge Mall, Marlborough Mall, and Northgate Village attract droves of visitors, as does the Crossroads Market, Calgary's largest farmers' market and flea market.

The residential areas in the northeast offer a varied mix of housing styles and prices and reflect the city's cultural diversity in the many ethnic restaurants and shops.

Northwest

When lit up for night skiing, Canada Olympic Park (COP) glitters on a hillside in the northwest quadrant of the city. COP was the site of luge, bobsleigh, ski jumping, and freestyle competitions during the 1988 Olympic Winter Games. Today visitors can try out some of these sports or take a tour of the Olympic Hall of Fame and Museum, but most people come to COP for a day of skiing or snowboarding.

Trans-Canada Highway

Calgary CVB/Alberta Economic Development & Tourism

The northwest, which has seen rapid development over the last few years, is home to some of the city's hilliest residential areas as well as the trendiest boutiques and coffeehouses. Kensington (especially between Kensington Road and 10th Street NW) has been a favorite hangout for Calgarians for decades.

Bowness Park is a popular spot for year-round outdoor recreation.

Highways

There are two major highways leading into Calgary. The Trans-Canada Highway (also known as Highway 1) serves east-west destinations and, as its name suggests, stretches from one end of the country to the other. Once inside the city limits, it becomes 16th Avenue N. Use the Trans-Canada to get to Banff National Park.

The other major highway is Highway 2, which leads north to Edmonton and south to the U.S. border. It becomes Macleod Trail/Deerfoot Trail when it enters the city.

Public Transportation

Buses and Light Rail Transit

Veteran transit riders, the average Calgarian makes 73 transit trips per year. Some ride the transit every day to work while others use it only as a hassle-free means of getting to and from special events like Stampeder or Flames games.

While the car remains the dominant mode of city transport for Calgarians, investment in transit has resulted in a higher level of service and

Driving Distances via Primary Highways

Calgary to:	km (mi)
Airdrie	25 (16)
Banff	125 (75)
Cochrane	35 (22)
Edmonton	297 (185)
High River	56 (35)
Lethbridge	218 (135)
Medicine Hat	302 (188)
Okotoks	36 (22)
Red Deer	131 (81)

usage. Calgary's efficient and economical transit system consists of buses and the light rail transit (a.k.a. LRT or C-Train). The C-Train is an above-ground rapid transit system that eases congestion and provides a fast and efficient alternative for travelers. Bus service feeds from the C-Train to residential and commercial areas. The fleet in its entirety consists of 488 regular buses, 90 low-floor buses, 34 community shuttle buses, and 85 light rail vehicles, covering a total of 2,540 kilometers (1,578 miles) on 123 routes.

Calgary Transit has taken steps to improve accessibility of regular transit services for people with reduced mobility. The centre door on each C-Train car is marked with a wheelchair decal because the vertical grab bar in the doorway is bent to allow wheelchair access. As well, priority seating adjacent to doors is designated for persons with limited mobility. All C-Train platforms and stations are wheelchair accessible. Introduced to the fleet in 1995, low-floor buses have no steps and feature a retractable ramp allowing convenient access for travelers who use mobility aids.

For the visitor to Calgary, the transit offers a low-cost option for touring the city. Because the C-Train is not an underground rail system, it

TIP

You can ride the light rail transit (LRT or C-Train) at no cost in the Free Fare Zone downtown on 7th Avenue between the 10th Street SW Station and the 3rd Street SE Station.

C-TRAIN

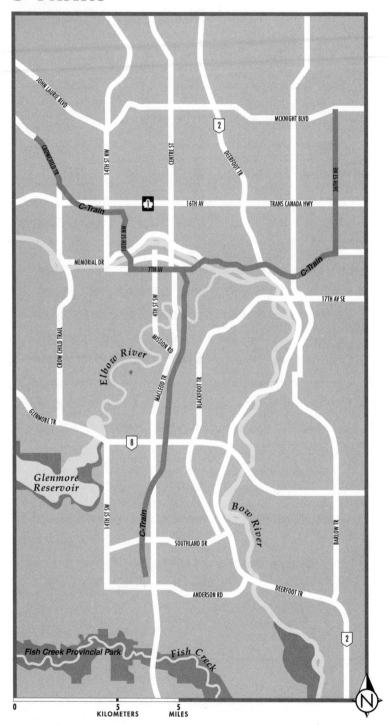

Transit Fare Options

	Adult	Child (6–14)
Single ticket or cash	$ 1.60	$1.00
Book of 5 tickets	$ 7.25	N/A
Book of 10 tickets	$13.50	$8.50
Day pass	$ 5.00	$3.00

$48-Adult/$34-youth monthly passes are also available. Children under 6 ride free.

Tickets and passes are interchangeable between buses and the C-Train. When boarding the bus, deposit tickets or cash in the fare box or show the driver your pass. When riding the C-Train, you must purchase or validate your ticket or day pass at the ticket-dispensing machines located at each station. Note that these machines require exact change. While individual tickets may be purchased at the ticket machines, passes or books of tickets are available at C-Train Concessions (at Anderson, Southland, Heritage, Chinook, Bridgeland/Memorial, Franklin, Marlborough, Rundle, Whitehorn, University, and Brentwood Stations), 7-Eleven Food Stores, Canada Safeway, Calgary Co-op, Mac's Convenience Stores, and some other independent vendors throughout the city.

Remember to keep your ticket for the duration of the trip. While tickets are bought on an honor system, authorities do occasional spot checks and fines are levied for failure to show a validated ticket or pass.

If starting your trip by bus, obtain a transfer from the driver. If transferring to a bus from the C-Train, present your C-Train ticket to the driver of the bus. If transferring from one C-Train to another, retain your ticket. Transfers allow you to travel across the city no matter how many transit vehicles are required. Transfers are valid for one trip in one direction, without stop-overs. If you have a lot of stops planned on a single day, you'd be better off purchasing a day pass.

There are three branches of the C-Train, all routed through downtown. If you want to travel the 12.9-kilometer (8-mile) south leg of the light rail transit, catch the C-Train that says "Anderson" on it. It provides service to the Canadian Airlines Saddledome, the Stampede grounds, Chinook Centre, and Spruce Meadows (when bus shuttle is running during events). The Whitehorn C-Train follows the northeast leg to Max Bell Arena and the Calgary Zoo before continuing on its 9.8-kilometer (6-mile) route. For a 6.6-kilometer (4-mile) trip to the northwest, look for the Brentwood train, which carries you to Kensington, the University of Calgary/Olympic Oval, Burns Stadium, Southern Alberta Institute of Technology (SAIT), Alberta College of Art and Design, and the Southern Alberta Jubilee Auditorium. Most, but not all, of the stations have parking lots so you can park and ride.

Security on the C-Train consists of intercoms and help phones in all C-Train stations and cars. In addition, train stations are under 24-hour video surveillance.

allows you to enjoy the sights while traveling in clean, comfortable surroundings. On the C-Train, you can breeze around the city with a pocketful of change and an hour or two of your time.

Taxis

There are 1,150 cabs in Calgary, operated by five major companies and numerous smaller ones. Rates are $2.10 for the first 210 meters (690 feet) and 20 cents for each additional 210 meters. Expect to pay about $5 to get around downtown and $20 from the airport to most downtown locations.

C-Train

While there are taxi stands at the airport and major hotels or shopping malls, you can also reserve by phone. Call Associated Cabs (403/299-1111), Calgary Cab Co. (403/777-2222), Checker Cabs (403/299-9999), Mayfair Taxi (403/255-6555), or Yellow Cab (403/974-1111).

Limousines

If pampering is what you're after, limo services provide transportation with style and elegance. Limo rates are typically between $75 and $100 per hour. Pay extra and they'll provide champagne and flowers.

Driving in Calgary

Visitors from other cities often remark on the ease of driving around Calgary. There is less congestion in Calgary than in other metropolitan cities due to its smaller population and greater area. In 1995, the city council adopted the $4 million Calgary Transportation Plan, or Go Plan, that maps out a 30-year plan for managing growth and transportation within the city.

T I P

For transit route information, call Calgary Transit at 403/262-1000 Monday through Friday 6 a.m. to 11 p.m. and Saturday and Sunday 8 a.m. to 9:30 p.m. For a transit map, visit the main office downtown at 240 - 7th Avenue SW, Monday through Friday 8:30 a.m. to 5 p.m.

TIP

The Calf Robe Bridge, on Deerfoot Trail just north of Glenmore Trail, is a particularly treacherous spot in winter. Icing and fog are frequent problems on this bridge due to the Bow River flowing underneath and effluent from the Bonnybrook Sewage Treatment Facility being released into the river near the bridge.

The expressways allow drivers to travel from one end of the city to the other in 40 minutes or less. The Deerfoot Trail, the city's major freeway, runs 40 kilometers (24 miles) north to south with a speed limit of 100 km/h (60 mph). There are also 203 kilometers (126 miles) of expressways that run east, north, west, and south with 389 kilometers (242 miles) of major roads feeding traffic from communities to expressways. Lastly, 2,828 kilometers (1,757 miles) of local roads in communities function as collectors for major roads.

Morning rush hour lasts from 7:15 to 8:15 while afternoon traffic peaks from 4:45 to 5:45. Of the 90,000 people who work downtown, about 61 percent drive to work and, despite public education on the environmental impact of automobiles, four out of five cars heading for the city core are still occupied by just the driver.

All radio stations give traffic reports during rush hours, so tune in to avoid trouble spots.

Metric Conversion

Canada uses the metric system for weights, measures, and distances. Gasoline is sold by the liter (3.8 liters = 1 U.S. gallon). Distance and speed are measured in kilometers (1 kilometer (km) = .6 mile). To convert from kilometers to miles, multiply the kilometers by .6 (e.g., 100 km/h on speed limit signs = 60 mph). To convert from miles to kilometers, multiply miles x 1.6 (e.g., if your speedometer reads 50 mph, you're going roughly 80 km/h).

There are some exceptions to Canadians' use of the metric system. For example, the housing industry refers to square feet rather than square meters. In this guide the Imperial equivalent appears in parentheses following the metric.

Parking Rates

Parking meters in the city accept $1 and $2 coins (often referred to as "loonies" and "twoonies"). A twoonie buys you varying amounts of time depending on the area and day of the week:
- *One hour and 20 minutes in the retail sections of downtown*
- *One hour and 36 minutes in the Beltline*
- *Two hours in Kensington*
- *Two hours in Inglewood*
- *Two hours in Uptown 17th*
- *Four hours on Saturday*

Street parking is free on Sunday.

Car Rentals

Expect to pay roughly $50 a day to rent a compact to mid-range vehicle, although many agencies have weekend specials. To rent a car in Calgary you'll need a major credit card and a valid driver's license and you must be at least 21 years of age. Book ahead for Stampede week.

Main car rental agencies in Calgary are Avis (800/879-2847), Budget (800/267-0505), Hertz (800/263-0600), Thrifty (800/367-2277), and Tilden (800/387-4747).

Rules of the Road

There are a few driving rules that may differ from those you're used to.
- You may make a right turn on a red light after coming to a full stop.
- You may make a left turn onto a one-way street on a red light after coming to a full stop.
- The speed limit is 30 km/h (18 mph) between 8 a.m. and 5 p.m. in school zones and between 8:30 a.m. and one hour after sunset near playground zones.
- Watch out for bus-only crossings into some communities. These vehicle traps are clearly marked with warning signs and consist of a rectangular hole in the pavement with two wheel tracks for transit buses. Smaller vehicles will get stuck between the bars, necessitating a tow and possible repairs to the underside of the vehicle.
- Yield to pedestrians at intersections. Pedestrians have the right-of-way, unless a traffic signal dictates otherwise.
- There is a stiff fine for parking in stalls designated for the handicapped.

PLUS-15 SKYWAY

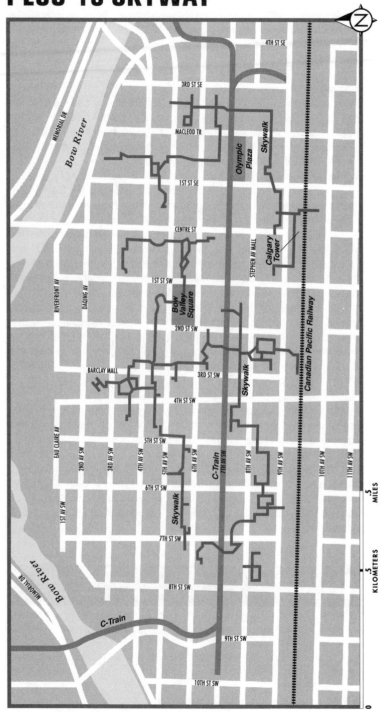

Winter Driving

Winter weather affects driving conditions and you should be prepared if you visit between October and April. Ensure that your car is equipped with all-weather radials or winter tires and reduce your speed according to road conditions.

Parking

Unlike most cities, parking in downtown Calgary is easy and relatively inexpensive. Lots offer drastically reduced rates after 4 or 6 p.m. and on weekends. With 46,000 parking spaces to choose from, there's bound to be somewhere for your vehicle to cool its jets while you spend your hard-earned money or just window-shop.

On-street parking meters are enforced Monday to Saturday, 8 a.m. to 6 p.m.; parking is free outside of those hours. But there are a few 24-hour meters, so be alert. Note the colour of the parking meter as well: red ones allow you to park for only 15 minutes. It is also important to notice any parking signs because some main traffic arteries become no-parking zones after 3:30 p.m., and your car will be towed if found in these zones. Do not attempt to park in a loading zone or within 5 meters (16 feet) of a fire hydrant, alley, driveway, or intersection. You can surely think of better fun ways to spend your money than paying a parking fine.

Besides on-street parking, there are plenty of surface lots and above-ground and underground parkades. If your vehicle is equipped with a propane tank, you will have to park above ground as they are prohibited in underground parkades. For a free copy of a downtown parking map, call the Calgary Downtown Association at 403/266-5300.

Plus-15 Skyway

Calgary's internationally acclaimed Plus-15 pedestrian walkway is the largest elevated sidewalk network in North America. Its name derives from the fact that these bridges cross downtown streets approximately 15 feet above ground. (We hadn't gone metric when the first one was built back in 1970.) Since then, 54 more Plus-15 bridges have been built, making a total of 16 kilometers (10 miles) of walkways through downtown office buildings and shopping malls. Regardless of the weather, office workers and visitors to the city no longer have to don outerwear to travel between buildings.

For 24-hour road reports, call 403/246-5853.

TOP
TOP
TOP
TOP
TOP
TOP
TOP
TOP
TOP
TOP
TOP
TOP
TOP
TOP
TOP
TOP
TOP
TOP

Top Ten Paths to Cycle
by Terry Bullick, author of *Calgary Parks and Pathways*
(Rocky Mountain Books)

1. **Bird Sanctuary to Carburn Park**. If you roughly follow the river south from the Inglewood Bird Sanctuary, you'll encounter Beaver Dam Flats, a haven for Canada's national emblem. Take a moment to perch on the escarpment and watch the activity in the train yards. Continue on to Carburn Park and enjoy the largely untouched riverbank areas and the pond to fish in.

2. **Bow River between 14th Street West and Centre Street**. This route, in the heart of downtown, is one of the busiest. Cycle the loop that surrounds Prince's Island and then lock your bike while you people-watch from the patio of the River Café.

3. **Bowness Park**. Developed in 1913, this park is as good as ever. It offers a kiddies' amusement park, picnic shelter, and canoe rentals for a spin on the lagoon. It is a great destination from downtown.

4. **Centennial Park**. Nestled in a valley, this park has its own paths that are not tied into the system but are accessible via quiet roads. A great place to escape the city, there is also a golf course at one end.

5. **Fish Creek Provincial Park**. Canada's largest urban park serves up a great diversity of land and a glimpse of wildlife. On foot it would take two or three days to explore all of the beautiful pathways and along the creek.

6. **Glenmore Pathway**. Allow two hours or more to complete this 16-kilometer (10-mile) loop that takes you through Weaselhead Flats, one of Calgary's most untouched natural reserves. Take a break at Glenmore Landing and watch the sailboats.

7. **Nose Creek**. This route starts at the zoo and winds along an enjoyable, uncrowded trail. Follow it north to Laycock Park and make a side trip west to Nose Hill, if you like.

8. **Nose Hill Park**. Calgary's second-largest park offers an incredible sense of openness with spectacular views.

9. **River Park to Stanley Park**. Following the Elbow River, this trail includes some cycling on city streets but rewards with glimpses of some of the grandest homes in Calgary.

10. **Zoo to Bird Sanctuary**. Another section of the Bow River Pathway connects the Calgary Zoo to the Inglewood Bird Sanctuary. It takes about an hour to cycle there and back but allow time to tour the sights at either end.

Major Airlines Serving Calgary

Scheduled

Air BC
Air Canada
Alaska Airlines
American Airlines
British Airways
Canadian Airlines
International

Canadian Regional
Airlines
Continental Airlines
Delta Air Lines
Horizon Air
Japan Airlines
KLM Royal Dutch
Airlines

Kelowna Flightcraft/
Greyhound Air
Lufthansa
Northwest Airlines
Swissair
United Airlines
West Jet

Charter

Air Club
International
Air Transat
Airtours
International

Asiana Airlines
Balair/CTA
Britannia Airways

Canada 3000
Royal Airlines

Cargo/Carrier

Canair Cargo
Emery Air Freight

Federal Express
FirstAir Cargo

Purolator
UPS

During 1995, a unique tourism exposition called Attractions Alberta went on display at the Calgary International Airport. This showcase of Calgary and southern Alberta is the first of its kind for airports in Canada, and maybe the world. Further expansion to the displays took place in 1996 and 1997. Visitors and residents alike enjoy these unique displays throughout the terminal, which give visitors a pre-view of the many attractions, business opportunities, and advanced education facilities that southern Alberta has to offer. View an 8-meter (26-foot) Albertasaurus chasing a smaller dinosaur atop one of the baggage carousels or enjoy the historical display that features a life-size bronze Mountie on horseback. Take a gander at the 10-meter (32-foot) colourful mural of the Calgary Exhibition and Stampede, across from the food court.

Biking on Calgary's Pathways

Calgary's popular network consists of almost 300 kilometers (180 miles) of pathway shared by joggers, cyclists, skaters, and walkers. These well-groomed paths connect the downtown core to beautiful parkland where you can explore and enjoy scenic green areas and beautiful riverbanks.

Remember to stay to the right (most pathways are now divided by a yellow line) and sound your bell or horn when passing. Cyclists and in-line skaters must yield to pedestrians, but some pathways are twinned—"Wheels and Heels"—that is, cyclists and skaters on one path, joggers and walkers on another. The speed limit on most paths is 20 km/h (12 mph).

Bike rentals for the afternoon cost about $20, and a bike trail map is $1 from the City of Calgary or cycle shops. Bikes are allowed on C-Trains during non-peak periods on weekdays (peak times are 6:30 to 9 a.m. and 3 to 6 p.m.) and at all times on weekends and statutory holidays.

Calgary International Airport

Situated just 20 minutes from downtown, Calgary International Airport was voted number one in North America for overall passenger convenience. Annually, 7 million travelers savor the modern design and friendly atmosphere of Canada's fourth-busiest airport. Calgarians and visitors enjoy non-stop scheduled flights to 36 cities within North America and overseas. Recent improvements to the airport include streamlined U.S. customs clearance, additional check-in positions, new and improved restaurant and retail services (including a true street-pricing policy), expanded facilities for group/bus travel, new terminal seating, improved commuter connection facilities, and more than 30 beautiful displays throughout the terminal. These are just a few components of the ongoing plan to keep pace with Calgary's business and tourism growth. It is also a kid-friendly airport with the addition of Kidsport, a play area on the departures level with a TV-/playroom featuring movies, Legos, bead boards, and other toys.

Canada's two largest scheduled airlines, Canadian Airlines International and Air Canada, along with their regional partner airlines, use Calgary as a major hub for their Western Canadian operations. Calgary presently has 11 commercial airlines offering scheduled passenger services, along with their code share partners, to destinations throughout North America, Europe, and Asia. Air BC and Canadian Regional Airlines provide service to smaller centres in Alberta, British Columbia, and Saskatchewan. Many major charter airlines also offer regular services from Calgary on a year-round and seasonal basis. Handling about 200,000 flights annually, the airport is a vital component of Calgary's economy, providing a vital link to the rest of the world.

Calgary International Airport

Getting to Calgary International Airport

Calgary Transit offers bus service to the airport (bus #57) from Whitehorn LRT station. Cab fare costs about $20 from most downtown locations to the airport. Many Calgary hotels offer shuttle buses free of charge for their guests. The Airporter Hotel Bus Service, 403/531-3909, a private pick-up service, has scheduled service at seven downtown hotels twice every hour between 6 a.m. and 11:30 p.m., but it will also pick up at other hotels with a reservation. Cost is $8.50 one-way or $15 return.

Train Service

Visitors can book a Rocky Mountaineer Railtour and enjoy incredible scenery in the comfort of a luxurious train coach. Two-day rail tours between Calgary and Vancouver take you through the Rockies in daylight hours only. Regular scheduled departures operate between May and October. The tour can be combined with a variety of independent package tours or customized for group travel. Call 800/665-7245.

National VIA Rail service to other Canadian destinations is available from Edmonton. Call 800/561-8630.

Bus Service

There are various affordable options for bus transportation in and around Calgary. Canada's largest motorcoach transportation company, Greyhound (403/265-9111) offers service to practically anywhere in North America, including most Alberta communities.

Red Arrow (403/531-0350) is a luxury coach line with several daily departures to Red Deer, Edmonton, and Fort McMurray. Service includes complimentary snacks and refreshments.

Express service round-trip tickets between Edmonton and Calgary aboard Greyhound or Red Arrow cost roughly $70.

Tours in the Canadian Rockies are the specialty of Brewster Transportation and Tours (403/221-8242), which offers guided bus tours to Banff, Lake Louise, Jasper, and the Columbia Icefield.

There are numerous other motorcoach sightseeing tours and charters. Check for brochures in hotel lobbies or visitor centres.

The Palliser

3
WHERE TO STAY

George Bernard Shaw once said, "The great advantage of a hotel is that it's a refuge from home life." There are 10,000 hotel rooms in Calgary, 3,000 of which are in the downtown area, but lodging is available in all quadrants of the city with knowledgeable staff to point you in the right direction for taking in the sights. The hospitality industry in Calgary aims to make your stay as pleasant as possible, and millions of visitors each year enjoy the city's warm, friendly atmosphere. Like any city its size, Calgary serves up the full spectrum of accommodation ranging from the modest to the sublime. Posh hotels with every amenity offer a pampered reprieve from daily life, while numerous motels offer convenience and moderate prices. Quaint bed and breakfasts deliver first hand knowledge of the city with breakfast. Economical hostels and RV campsites in picturesque settings round out the selection of Calgary lodgings available to visitors. If your visit spans Stampede Week in early July, reserve your accommodation well in advance, as the city is flooded with tourists at that time. Predictably, rates are usually higher then, too. Wheelchair accessibility is indicated by the ♿ symbol.

Price rating symbols:

$ Under $50
$$ $50 to $75
$$$ $75 to $125
$$$$ $125 and up

Prices throughout book indicate Canadian dollars.
(1.42 Canadian $ = 1 U.S. $ at time of printing)

DOWNTOWN CALGARY

Hotels

CALGARY MARRIOTT HOTEL
110 - 9th Ave. SW
Calgary, AB T2G 5A6
403/266-7331, 800/228-9290
$$$$ DT
You may know this hotel in its previous incarnation as the Radisson Plaza. Recently renovated, this excellent hotel offers a great location across from the Calgary Tower and attached to the Calgary Convention Centre, Glenbow Museum and Art Gallery, and Calgary Centre for Performing Arts. Fitness facilities include indoor pool, whirlpool, sauna, and exercise equipment. Parkade parking. Spacious rooms with some one-bedroom suites available. &

DELTA BOW VALLEY HOTEL
209 - 4th Ave. SE
Calgary, AB T2G 0C6
403/266-1980 or 800/268-1133
$$$$ DT
A dominant landmark in the heart of downtown, the Delta offers everything you could want. Its convenient location puts you close to Chinatown, the Zoo, Eau Claire Market, Imax Theatre, and the C-Train. One- and two-bedroom suites are available as well as four wheelchair accessible rooms. Many restaurants are nearby, but the hotel itself offers you a choice of two, one of which (the Conservatory Restaurant) won the DiRona Award for North America. Airport bus service. Valet parking. &

THE INTERNATIONAL HOTEL OF CALGARY
220 - 4th Ave. SW
Calgary, AB T2P 0H4
403/265-9600 or 800/661-8627
$$$$ DT
The International is distinctive in that it is an all-suite hotel. Some suites feature kitchens. Its central location places you close to shopping, Chinatown, Prince's Island Park. On-site fitness facilities include indoor pool, jacuzzi, and Universal gym. The hotel's restaurant and lounge offer a peaceful ambiance after a full day of business or sight-seeing. Covered parking. &

PALLISER HOTEL
133 - 9th Ave. SW
Calgary, AB T2P 2M3
403/262-1234 or 800/441-1414
$$$$ DT
The Palliser Hotel, with its regal elegance, has been a city landmark for close to a century. The Grand Dame of Calgary's hospitality industry, it is a charming and graceful presence in the city's centre. Close to the Calgary Tower, Centre for Performing Arts, Glenbow Museum, and Calgary Convention Centre, it has recently undergone extensive renovations (to the tune of $30 million) to make your stay more enjoyable. While their rates are quite high, you are treated royally. Try their famous clam chowder in the Rimrock Room, or if you're in the mood for indulgence, visit the Oak Room Lounge on Tuesday evenings for "Death by Chocolate." &

PRINCE ROYAL SUITES HOTEL
618 - 5th Ave. SW
Calgary, AB T2P 0M7
403/263-0520 or 800/661-1592
$$$-$$$$ DT
Formerly an apartment complex, this all-suite hotel features studio and one-and two-bedroom suites close to major businesses, entertainment, and shopping. Extended-stay

DOWNTOWN CALGARY

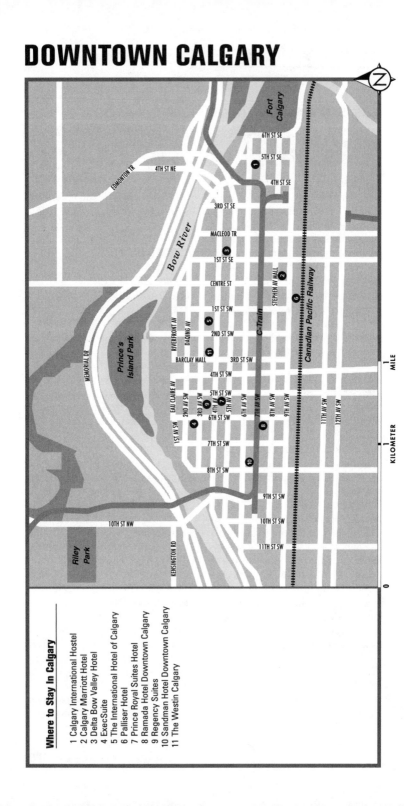

Where to Stay In Calgary

1 Calgary International Hostel
2 Calgary Marriott Hotel
3 Delta Bow Valley Hotel
4 ExecSuite
5 The International Hotel of Calgary
6 Palliser Hotel
7 Prince Royal Suites Hotel
8 Ramada Hotel Downtown Calgary
9 Regency Suites
10 Sandman Hotel Downtown Calgary
11 The Westin Calgary

History of the Palliser Hotel

The Palliser Hotel, consisting of eight floors, was built of sandstone between 1911 and 1914 by the Canadian Pacific Railway for $1 million. In 1929, three floors and a penthouse were added, making it the tallest building on the Calgary skyline for many years. Built in an E-shape to provide all rooms with natural light, it gives the appearance of three adjacent towers.

Enter the historic front doors and step back to a time of elegance and charm in lavish surroundings. Over the decades, many distinguished guests such as Queen Elizabeth and Prince Philip, Mikhail Gorbachov, Prince Albert of Monaco, Bob Hope, Neil Diamond, and Garth Brooks have stayed at the Palliser. Refurbished throughout in the 1980s, it stands today as an elegant and sophisticated Alberta landmark.

accommodations are available, depending on time of year and space. Restaurant on site. Guests may use fitness facilities. If you hate waiting for elevators, you may want to try a different hotel as the two elevators here tend to be slow. Covered parking.

RAMADA HOTEL DOWNTOWN CALGARY
708 - 8th Ave. SW
Calgary, AB T2P 1H2
403/263-7600 or 800/661-8684
$$$$ DT
Staying at this fine hotel places you within 2 blocks of Eaton Centre, T.D. Square, and Scotia Centre shopping malls with over 200 stores of all types. After a day of shopping, enjoy a swim in Ramada's heated outdoor pool or work out in their fully equipped fitness room. For extra amenities like comfortable bathrobes and daily newspaper, ask for an Executive Guestroom. Dine in Cheers Restaurant on site or relax with a drink in the lounge. For darts or pool, visit the Red Fox Pub. Valet parking. &

SANDMAN HOTEL DOWNTOWN CALGARY
888 - 7th Ave. SW

TRIVIA

In 1921, Bill Strothers (the Human Spider) scaled the exterior of the Palliser Hotel. Upon reaching the top, he rode his bicycle around the edge of the rooftop, then climbed up the flagpole and balanced on his stomach.

Calgary, AB T2P 3J3
403/237-8626 or 800/Sandman
$$$$ DT
The large indoor pool, sauna, and whirlpool will help you unwind after a day's business or sight-seeing. If you check into their corporate floor, you can expect amenities like airport service, daily newspaper, and secretarial services. A fitness facility provides weights, aerobics classes, and squash courts. Downtown location ensures proximity to shopping, entertainment, and nightlife. Underground parking.&

THE WESTIN CALGARY
320-4th Ave SW
Calgary, AB T2P 2S6
403/266-1611 or 800/937-8461
$$$$ DT
The Westin serves up first-class accommodations in the heart of downtown. The city's largest hotel attracts business travelers and tourists alike as it is close to downtown attractions and in the middle of the business district. Enjoy a refreshing dip in the indoor pool or a soothing soak in the whirlpool followed by culinary delights of the award-winning Owl's Nest Restaurant. Underground parking available. &

Extended Stay

EXECSUITE
702 - 3rd Ave. SW and 225 - 6th St. SW
Calgary, AB T2P 3B4
403/294-5800 or 888/A1Suite
$$$-$$$$ DT
A "home away from home," Execsuite offers luxury furnished apartments for relocating personnel, visiting executives and business guests, or anyone planning an extended stay in the city. At both downtown locations you have the choice of renting by the week, month, or year. These furnished apartments include fully equipped kitchens as well as voice mail, fax service, and secretarial services for the business traveler.

The Calgary White Hat

While many city officials in Calgary's early days bestowed cowboy hats as gifts on visiting dignitaries, it wasn't until after the Calgary Stampeders won the Grey Cup in 1948 that a white cowboy hat became Calgary's familiar symbol. Since then, thousands of guests have received white hats and become honorary Calgarians at White Hat Ceremonies.

Your first sighting of a white Stetson may be at the Calgary International Airport, where White Hat Volunteer Hosts conduct tours and provide smiles and helpful advice to visitors.

White hats and other souvenir merchandise are available from the Calgary Convention & Visitor's Bureau at 1300 - 6th Ave. SW.

Ask for a mountain or river valley view. Underground parking (at extra cost). Limited wheelchair access.

REGENCY SUITES
610 - 4th Ave. SW
Calgary, AB T2P 0K1
403/231-1000 or 800/468-4044
$$$ DT
Regency offers fully furnished studio and one- and two-bedroom apartment suites with kitchens at weekly or monthly rates. Business-class suites include desk, modem, and other conveniences for the business guest. Rooms have views of downtown, Eau Claire Market, or mountains. Close to pedestrian and bike trails along the river. Parking extra. &

Hostels

CALGARY INTERNATIONAL HOSTEL
520 - 7th Ave. SE
Calgary, AB T2G 0J6
403/269-8239
$ DT
This hostel offers budget accommodations for 120 people with six to eight beds per room. Some family rooms are also available. Conveniences include showers, fridge, laundry, lockers, fire pit, snack bar, member kitchen, and basic food supplies. Reservations are recommended.

SOUTHEAST CALGARY

Hotels

BEST WESTERN HOSPITALITY INN
135 Southland Dr. SE
Calgary, AB T2J 1X5
403/278-5050 or 800/528-1234
$$$ SE
The Best Western Hospitality Inn is housed in two buildings joined by an above-ground walkway. The atrium building is home to Francisco's Restaurant, a California-style establishment situated in the atrium next to the swimming pool. They put on a great Sunday brunch. The more plush Bonaventure Restaurant is situated in the Tower, along with Mingles Dance Club and the Bonaventure Lounge. Southcentre Shopping Mall is a few blocks away, as is Willow Park Village.

BLACKFOOT INN
5940 Blackfoot Tr. SE
Calgary, AB T2H 2B5
403/252-2253 or 800/661-1151
$$$$ SE
Green's Restaurant in the Blackfoot is another great place for Sunday brunch. Save up your appetite for this one. More formal dining in the Terrace Dining Room. No fitness centre, but hotel staff will bring exercise equipment to your room.

T I P

ELDERHOSTEL Canada offers some fascinating one-week educational opportunities in the province of Alberta with accommodations ranging from hostels to the deluxe Jasper Park Lodge. If you're retired or over 50 and want to find out more about ELDERHOSTEL Adventures, write to ELDERHOSTEL Canada, 308 Wellington St., Kingston, ON K7K 7A7 or phone 613/530-2222.

GREATER CALGARY

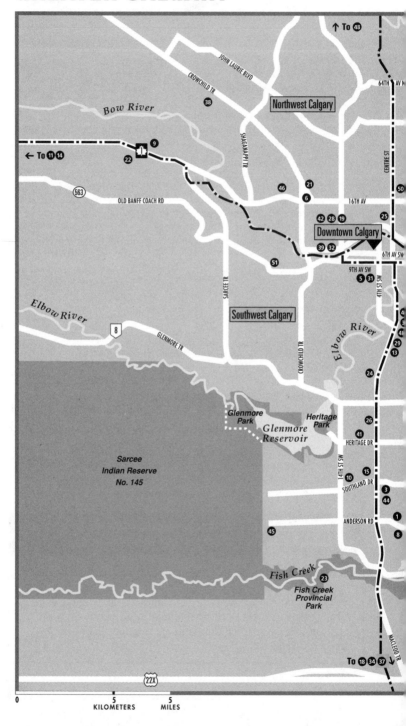

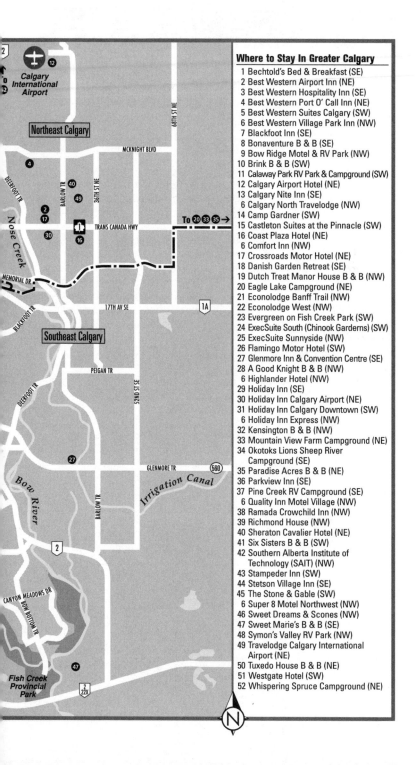

Where to Stay In Greater Calgary

1 Bechtold's Bed & Breakfast (SE)
2 Best Western Airport Inn (NE)
3 Best Western Hospitality Inn (SE)
4 Best Western Port O' Call Inn (NE)
5 Best Western Suites Calgary (SW)
6 Best Western Village Park Inn (NW)
7 Blackfoot Inn (SE)
8 Bonaventure B & B (SE)
9 Bow Ridge Motel & RV Park (NW)
10 Brink B & B (SW)
11 Calaway Park RV Park & Campground (SW)
12 Calgary Airport Hotel (NE)
13 Calgary Nite Inn (SE)
6 Calgary North Travelodge (NW)
14 Camp Gardner (SW)
15 Castleton Suites at the Pinnacle (SW)
16 Coast Plaza Hotel (NE)
6 Comfort Inn (NW)
17 Crossroads Motor Hotel (NE)
18 Danish Garden Retreat (SE)
19 Dutch Treat Manor House B & B (NW)
20 Eagle Lake Campground (NE)
21 Econolodge Banff Trail (NW)
22 Econolodge West (NW)
23 Evergreen on Fish Creek Park (SW)
24 ExecSuite South (Chinook Gardens) (SW)
25 ExecSuite Sunnyside (NW)
26 Flamingo Motor Hotel (SW)
27 Glenmore Inn & Convention Centre (SE)
28 A Good Knight B & B (NW)
6 Highlander Hotel (NW)
29 Holiday Inn (SE)
30 Holiday Inn Calgary Airport (NE)
31 Holiday Inn Calgary Downtown (SW)
6 Holiday Inn Express (NW)
32 Kensington B & B (NW)
33 Mountain View Farm Campground (NE)
34 Okotoks Lions Sheep River
    Campground (SE)
35 Paradise Acres B & B (NE)
36 Parkview Inn (SE)
37 Pine Creek RV Campground (SE)
6 Quality Inn Motel Village (NW)
38 Ramada Crowchild Inn (NW)
39 Richmond House (NW)
40 Sheraton Cavalier Hotel (NE)
41 Six Sisters B & B (SW)
42 Southern Alberta Institute of
    Technology (SAIT) (NW)
43 Stampeder Inn (SW)
44 Stetson Village Inn (SE)
45 The Stone & Gable (SW)
6 Super 8 Motel Northwest (NW)
46 Sweet Dreams & Scones (NW)
47 Sweet Marie's B & B (SE)
48 Symon's Valley RV Park (NW)
49 Travelodge Calgary International
    Airport (NE)
50 Tuxedo House B & B (NE)
51 Westgate Hotel (SW)
52 Whispering Spruce Campground (NE)

With one phone call to the Bed & Breakfast Association of Calgary (phone 403/543-3900 or fax 403/543-3901) you can find out what is available on the B & B scene, make a booking, or request a brochure with over 50 listings of local B & B's.

Quick access to downtown and the Stampede grounds. Yuk Yuk's Komedy Kabaret serves up lots of laughs while sports fans enjoy their favorite game on the big screen or play pool, darts, or VLTs in the Other Side Sports Bar. You can request a room with a mountain view. Suites also available. Ample parking. &

CALGARY NITE INN
4510 Macleod Tr. SE
Calgary, AB T2G 0A4
403/243-1700 or 888/648-3466
$$-$$$$ SE
Formerly the Howard Johnson, the Calgary Nite Inn has been recently renovated. While it has no fitness centre, guests are allowed the use of the private club next door. Children under 18 years of age stay free in their parents' room. Two restaurants and a lounge on site. Benefits of its location include proximity to Calgary's largest shoping mall and within walking distance of an LRT station. &

GLENMORE INN & CONVENTION CENTRE
2720 Glenmore Tr. SE
Calgary, AB T2C 2E6
403/279-8611 or 800/661-3163
$$$-$$$$ SE
The Glenmore Inn is in an industrial sector of the city and is easily accessible. It is close to the Calgary Soccer Centre and Race City Speedway and provides quick access to Deerfoot Trail. This full-service hotel meets the needs of both business travellers and tourists. There are 73 upgraded guest rooms plus 13,000 square feet of banquet and meeting rooms. Guest rooms feature a complimentary VCR and free movie channel. Facilities include two restaurants and a lounge (with VLTs and billiard table) as well a sauna and jacuzzi, exercise facilities, and free parking.

HOLIDAY INN
4206 Macleod Tr. SE
Calgary, AB T2G 2R7
403/287-2700 or 800/Holiday
$$$-$$$$ SE
This Holiday Inn is close to downtown, Stampede grounds, and Chinook Shopping Centre. It is within walking distance of Stanley Park and the LRT station. Take a relaxing dip in their heated indoor pool before settling down for the night in one of the 150 spacious guest rooms (including one-bedroom suites). You can even play a few Nintendo games before turning in. On-site restaurant provides a kids' menu and children under 12 eat free. &

Motels

PARKVIEW INN
3630 Macleod Tr. SE

Calgary Marriott Hotel, page 35

Calgary, AB T2H 2P9
403/243-4651
$-$$ SE
Location is a big plus to this older property since it is within walking distance of the Saddledome and the Stampede grounds. Kitchenettes available. Outdoor seasonal swimming pool. Weekly and monthly rates are available.

STETSON VILLAGE INN
10002 Macleod Tr. SE
Calgary, AB T2J 3K9
403/271-3210
$$-$$$ SE
The Stetson Village Inn offers attractive, recently renovated guest rooms at reasonable rates. This two-story facility has exterior corridors and is close to shopping (Southcentre Mall and Willow Park Village) with quick access to Spruce Meadows Equestrian Centre via Macleod Trail, one of the city's main arteries. Children under 12 stay free in their parents' room. Restaurant and saloon attached.

Bed & Breakfasts

BECHTOLD'S BED & BREAKFAST
11404 Wilson Rd. SE
Calgary, AB T2J 2E2
403/279-0544
$-$$ SE
Bechtold's offers serene but cheery accommodations. Rooms include double bed, private bath, and den with TV and pullout sofa. Hearty, low-cholesterol menu is served. Quick access to downtown, Stampede grounds, and Spruce Meadows and a short walk to upscale mall. Airport pick-up. Smoke-free and animal-free environment.

BONAVENTURE B & B
12229 Lake Erie Rd. SE
Calgary, AB T2J 2Z3
403/271-7686
e-mail: galeb@cadvision.com
$ - $$ SE
Executive-style home in private lake community offers three rooms to guests. Lounge area with fireplace, sauna, and billiard table available to guests. Full breakfast includes

coffee, tea, juice, cereal, fresh fruit, and hot item such as pancakes or french toast. Close to bus, theatres, and restaurants; 15-minute drive to downtown, Stampede grounds, or Spruce Meadows; within walking distance of Calgary's largest park. Hosts are very knowledgeable about sites and activities of the area. Families welcome. No smoking.

SWEET MARIE'S B & B
52 Mount Robson Circle SE
Calgary, AB T2Z 2B9
403/257-1516 SE

Because this home is situated on a hill, you can enjoy city and mountain views in this quiet lake community. Spacious executive home with private sitting area features fireplace and billiard table. Private entrance and private bath. Close to Deerfoot Trail, C-Train, bus, Fish Creek Park, and Spruce Meadows. Families welcome. No smoking. Continental breakfast served in bright kitchen.

DANISH GARDEN RETREAT
Box 48101
Midlake Post Office
Calgary, AB T2X 3C7
403/938-3430
$$ SE

Situated 18 km (11 mi) south of Calgary on Hwy #2. Turn left at antique railway station and follow the signs. Enjoy the Danish decor in this country setting. Two bedrooms plus family suite with private bath and entrance. Danish or vegetarian breakfast of fruit, fresh farm eggs, cheeses, salads, and homemade breads and Danish pastry. Close to U-pick saskatoon farm. If you like flowers, you're in for a real treat.

Campgrounds

OKOTOKS LIONS SHEEP RIVER CAMPGROUND
Box 387
Okotoks, AB T0L 1T0
403/938-4282
$ SE

Located alongside the Sheep River in the town of Okotoks, this beautiful tree-filled spot is across the street from a town park with cook shelter. Operating May to September, it is a 20-minute drive to Calgary, but don't forget to take in the sights of Okotoks as well (see Chapter 13, "Day Trips"). There are 62 sites, the majority of which have electricity.

PINE CREEK RV CAMPGROUND
Box 174
DeWinton, AB T0L 0X0
403/256-3002
$ SE

Just 1.4 km (1 mi) south of the city on Hwy #2, Pine Creek RV Campground has 99 fully serviced sites but few trees. Pitch & putt golf, horseshoe

---

T I P

If you're camping or otherwise cooking your own meals while visiting the Calgary area, watch for stalls or trucks selling Taber corn in August. You can't beat the taste of this sweet delight, which comes straight from the field to your table.

From November to the beginning of April, Alberta is on Mountain Standard Time. From April to October it's on Daylight Savings Time.

pits, TV-/billiard room are added attractions to this property. No tents allowed. Only a short drive to Spruce Meadows Equestrian Centre.

SOUTHWEST CALGARY

Hotels

BEST WESTERN SUITES CALGARY
1330 - 8th St. SW
Calgary, AB T2R 1B6
403/228-6900 or 800/981-2555
$$$-$$$$ SW
This hotel provides spacious, all-suite accommodations for daily, weekly, and monthly rates. Fully furnished studio and one- and two-bedroom suites available. As well as benefits of its central location, Best Western Suites offers office services, health club, sauna, and laundry facilities. Ask for mountain or skyline view.

HOLIDAY INN CALGARY
DOWNTOWN
119 - 12th Ave. SW
Calgary, AB T2R 0G8
403/266-4611 or 800/661-9378
$$$-$$$$ SW
There are benefits to the location of the newly refurbished Holiday Inn Calgary Downtown, and the fact that it's within walking distance of Stampede Park is a major one if you're planning your visit during Stampede

Week. It also offers proximity to the Glenbow Museum, Calgary Convention Centre, Saddledome, Calgary Tower, LRT station, and shopping. Facilities include a restaurant, lounge, and a year-round outdoor pool! Many guest rooms feature balconies. Children under 18 stay free in parents' room. Free guest parking. &

STAMPEDER INN
3828 Macleod Tr. SW
Calgary, AB T2G 2R2
403/243-5531 or 800/361-3422
$$-$$$ SW
Just a five-minute drive from Stampede grounds and downtown attractions, the Stampeder Inn offers moderate rates and convenience with coffee shop, dining room, and lounge on-site. It also features a fitness room, indoor pool, jacuzzi, and underground parking. The LRT line runs directly behind it, which can be viewed as a convenience or a nuisance. &

WESTGATE HOTEL
3440 Bow Tr. SW
Calgary, AB T3C 2E6
403/249-3181 or 800/661-1660
$$-$$$ SW
The Westgate is a full-service hotel with moderate rates. It features country honky tonk bar with VLTs. Minutes to Stampede grounds and downtown attractions, its location

provides easy access to the Trans-Canada Highway and Canada Olympic Park. Shopping mall and golf course next door. &

Motels

FLAMINGO MOTOR HOTEL
7505 Macleod Tr. SW
Calgary, AB T2H 0L8
403/252-4401 or 888/559-0559
$$ SW
Many kitchenettes and some family suites are available at this motel. No restaurant on-site but many close by. Large indoor swimming pool, wading pool, sauna, whirlpool, and exercise room are additional features. Weekly and monthly rates available in winter. &

Extended Stay

BEST WESTERN SUITES CALGARY
1330 - 8th St. SW
Calgary, AB T2R 1B6
403/228-6900 or 800/981-2555
$$$-$$$$ SW
This hotel provides spacious, all-suite accommodations for daily, weekly, and monthly rates. Fully furnished studio and one- and two-bedroom suites available. As well as benefits of its central location, Best Western Suites offers office services, health club, sauna, and laundry facilities. Ask for mountain or skyline view.

CASTLETON SUITES AT THE PINNACLE
9600 Southland Circle SW
Calgary, AB T2V 5A1
403/640-3900 or 888/227-8534
$$$-$$$$ SW
Castleton Suites offers upscale, apartment-style accommodations

Best Western Hospitality Inn

Best Western Hospitality Inn, page 39

for the business or leisure traveler looking for extended-stay lodgings. Furnished one- or two-bedroom suites feature balconies. Fitness facilities, sauna, jacuzzi, and weekly housekeeping are part of the package. Business services are also available. &

EXECSUITE SOUTH (CHINOOK GARDENS)
530 - 57th Ave. SW
Calgary, AB T2V 0H2
403/294-5800 or 888/A1Suite
$$$ SW
ExecSuite offers tastefully furnished one- and two-bedroom suites for those planning an extended stay. At the Chinook location you rent by the month or year. This three-story walk-up is in a residential setting, close to Chinook Shopping Centre, Calgary's largest shopping centre.

Bed & Breakfasts

BRINK B & B
79 Sinclair Cres. SW
Calgary, AB T2W 0M1
403/255-4523 or 888/274-6523
$$ SW
Split-level home decorated in country

style with a collection of teddy bears. Ten-minute walk to LRT. Full home-baked breakfast in dining room over-looking deck or in front of fireplace. One room ensuite and one with half-bath. Airport or bus pick-up available. Families welcome. Laundry facilities.

EVERGREEN ON FISH CREEK PARK
1609 Evergreen Hill SW
Calgary, AB T2Y 3A9
403/256-2237
$$-$$$ **SW**
This new executive home reflects a casual atmosphere. It features a scenic location on a park with city view and walking paths. Full break-fast. Families welcome. Three km (2 mi) to Spruce Meadows. German spoken. Airport and bus pick-up available. Laundry facilities.

SIX SISTERS B & B
48 Kentish Dr. SW
Calgary, AB T2V 2L3
403/253-3124
$$ **SW**
Cozy bungalow, with ranch-style decor, fireplace, and jacuzzi. Quiet, mature neighbourhood. Easy access to all major highways. Stampede grounds are 15 minutes away. Close to Heritage Park and two major malls. Airport and bus pick-up. Laundry fa-cilities. Continental breakfast.

THE STONE & GABLE
120 Woodborough Rd. SW
Calgary, AB T2W 4Y3
403/238-3804
$$ **SW**
Canadiana custom-designed home in quiet, residential area. Two guest rooms, tastefully decorated. Small guest lounge off kitchen, fireplace, and private dining room add to its appeal. Conveniently located with easy access to attractions. Families

welcome. Full breakfast. Laundry facilities. Airport and bus pick-up. Some French spoken. No smoking.

Campgrounds

CALAWAY PARK RV PARK & CAMPGROUND
R.R. 2, Site 25, Comp 20
Calgary, AB T2P 2G5
403/249-7372
$ **SW**
Located 10 km (6 mi) west of Calgary on Hwy #1, the advantage of this campground is its proximity to Canada's largest outdoor amusement park. (Of course, this could also be seen as a disadvantage.) Camp here and you receive a 50 percent discount off gate admission to the amusement park. Shuttle service to the Stampede grounds is available during Stampede Week. Serviced and unserviced sites.

CALGARY KOA
Box 10, Site 12, SS1
Calgary, AB T2M 4N3
403/288-0411 or 800/KOA-0842
$ **SW**
Found on the western edge of the city next to Canada Olympic Park, this campground is open mid-April to mid-October. It features an outdoor pool as well as a shuttle bus to downtown Cal-gary and other attractions. 375 sites in total, of which 120 are full-service.

CAMP GARDNER
Booking Address: 2140 Brownsea Dr. NW
Calgary, AB T2N 3G9
403/283-4993, local 226
$ **SW**
Scouts Canada operates this camp-ground close to Bragg Creek. It is set in a beautiful tree-filled area with hik-

The Westin Calgary, page 38

ing trails, playground, nature centre, and volleyball area. There are 30 RV sites (with power) and six tent sites, each with a gravel parking pad, fire pit, and picnic table. Lots of outdoor activities are possible in this natural setting that also offers the convenience of proximity to the city.

NORTHEAST CALGARY

Hotels

BEST WESTERN AIRPORT INN
Trans-Canada Hwy. & 19th St. NE
Calgary, AB T2E 7T8
403/250-5015 or 800/528-1234
$$-$$$$ **NE**
This hotel offers 24-hour limo service from Calgary International Airport, (only ten minutes away). Billing itself as your "home away from home," it offers 75 well-appointed guest rooms equipped with queen- or king-size beds, a seasonal outdoor heated pool, and sundeck. Some kitchenettes are available but they don't supply utensils. Relax in their poolside café or lounge. ♿

BEST WESTERN PORT O' CALL INN
1935 McKnight Blvd. NE
Calgary, AB T2E 6T4
403/291-4600 or 800/661-1161
$$-$$$ **NE**
Close to the airport, the Port O' Call Inn offers complimentary 24-hour shuttle service and reasonable rates. Some rooms offer mountain view. In-coming flights can be rather noisy if your patio door is open. Enjoy breakfast, lunch, or dinner any day in cozy Destiny's Restaurant. It also offers a nice brunch on Sunday with live music. Fitness facilities available and an indoor pool with whirlpool. ♿

CALGARY AIRPORT HOTEL
Calgary International Airport NE
Calgary, AB T2E 6Z8
403/291-2600 or 800/441-1414
$$$$ **NE**
The Calgary Airport Hotel (formerly the Château Airport) is conveniently attached to Calgary's International Airport. The 296 well-appointed rooms are soundproofed to muffle the noise of air traffic. The atrium in the centre of the hotel houses the in-

door swimming pool and the Atrium Terrace Restaurant. There is also a steak house in this Canadian Pacific Hotel. Covered parkade. &

COAST PLAZA HOTEL
1316 - 33rd St. NE
Calgary, AB T2A 6B6
403/248-8888 or 800/663-1144
$$$$ NE
Formerly the Marlborough Inn, the Coast Plaza has recently been refurbished with brass and marble accents. A popular hotel with the corporate crowd because of its proximity to downtown, in-room amenities include coffee makers, hair dryers, digital alarm clocks, movies, and modem jacks. Health club facilities are augmented by an indoor pool, whirlpool, and sauna. All-day restaurant, weekend nightclub, and sports lounge are convenient features. Fully equipped convention facilities for groups as large as 1,500 make it the second largest convention centre in Calgary. &

Delta Bow Valley Hotel, page 35

Rob Melnychuk/Delta Bow Valley Hotel

CROSSROADS MOTOR HOTEL
2120 - 16th Ave. NE
Calgary, AB T2E 104
403/291-4666 or 800/661-8157
$$$ NE
Check out the mountain view from Arlo's Dining Room or enjoy home-style cooking in the Crossroads Restaurant of this hotel situated on Hwy #1. Fitness club, indoor swimming pool, saunas, and whirlpool will help you relax after a busy day. There are 182 guest rooms, including seven suites (executive, family, or bridal). If you're staying the weekend, amble next door to the Crossroads Market where you'll find Western Canada's largest indoor/outdoor flea and farmer's market. Visit the Native craft centre.

HOLIDAY INN CALGARY AIRPORT
1250 McKinnon Dr. NE
Calgary, AB T2E 7T7
403/230-1999 or 800/661-5095
$$$$ NE
To drink in a view of the Calgary downtown skyline and the snow-covered peaks of the Canadian Rockies, visit the Skyline Restaurant of this Holiday Inn. Other bonuses for guests include complimentary shuttle service to the airport, heated indoor pool and saunas, king-size executive rooms, and covered parking. Did you forget your razor or shaving cream at home? They'll supply it free of charge. &

SHERATON CAVALIER HOTEL
2620 - 32nd Ave. NE
Calgary, AB T1Y 6B8
403/291-0107 or 800/325-3535
$$$$ NE
State-of-the-art health club, two waterslides, pool, sauna, jacuzzis, children's play centre, and a three-story atrium—these are all part of the

Sheraton Cavalier's $3.5 million renovation and expansion project completed in 1997. Carver's Steakhouse showcases Alberta's famous beef on its lunch and dinner menus while 154-seat Colors Café offers breakfast, lunch, and dinner daily in a family atmosphere. They pride themselves on friendliness. &

TRAVELODGE CALGARY INTERNATIONAL AIRPORT
2750 Sunridge Blvd. NE
Calgary, AB T1Y 3C2
403/291-1260 or 800/578-7878
$$-$$$ NE
Another newly renovated property, Travelodge provides easy access to downtown, shopping malls, and the airport. This moderately priced hotel features an indoor pool and whirlpool. Dine at Ryley's Restaurant and Lounge or visit one of the nearby restaurants. &

Bed & Breakfasts

PARADISE ACRES B & B
Box 20, Site 2, R.R. 6
Calgary, AB T2M 4L5
$$ NE
Located on Paradise Road, minutes from Calgary International Airport, Paradise Acres offers lake, city, and mountain views. Luxurious country setting is a 20-minute drive from city centre. Families welcome. Airport pick-up. Full breakfast. No smoking.

TUXEDO HOUSE B & B
121 - 21 Ave. NE
Calgary, AB T2E 1S3
$$ NE
This B & B is a lovely home with garden, patio, deck, and fireplace. Jacuzzi, TV room and sitting room,

and laundry facilities are available to guests. Close to downtown, airport, Stampede grounds, buses, and restaurants. Families welcome. Full breakfast.

Campgrounds

EAGLE LAKE CAMPGROUND
Box 50, Site 1, R.R. 1
Strathmore, AB T1P 1J6
403/934-4283
$ NE
Family fun in a quiet, country resort. Open mid-April to mid-September, this attractive campground is located beside a lake with a beach area, 40 minutes east of Calgary. 113 sites: some serviced and some not. Free hayrides, petting zoo, mini-golf, arcade, and canoe rental add to the fun. Store, showers, laundry facilities, and some fire pits are also available. Stay for a week and get your seventh night free. Also ask about their family fun package.

MOUNTAIN VIEW FARM CAMPGROUND
Site 8, Box 6, R.R. 6
Calgary, AB T2M 4L5
403/293-6640
$ NE
Just 4 km (2.5 mi) east of Calgary on Hwy #1, Mountain View Farm Campground offers 200 sites, some of which are fully serviced. Open year-round, it features a children's playground, fishing pond, petting zoo, mini-golf, showers, store, laundry, and fire pits.

WHISPERING SPRUCE CAMPGROUND
Box 169
Balzac, AB T0M 0E0

403/226-0097
$ NE

1.5 km (1 mi) north of Calgary on Hwy #2, Whispering Spruce is handy to the airport, Nose Hill Park, and the Calgary Zoo. Services offered are grocery store, laundry facilities, showers, TV room, snack bar, playground, and fire pits. Over 100 sites—some with full hook-up, some with power and water, and some tent sites.

NORTHWEST CALGARY

Hotels

BEST WESTERN VILLAGE PARK INN
1804 Crowchild Tr. NW
Calgary, AB T2M 3Y7
403/289-0241 or 888/774-7716
$$$ NW

Located at the corner of Crowchild Trail and Trans-Canada Hwy, this hotel is easily accessed. Relax in the atrium with its appealing tropical decor. Spacious guest rooms. Free underground parking, indoor pool, hot tub, restaurant, and lounge are additional features.

HIGHLANDER HOTEL
1818 - 16th Ave. NW
Calgary, AB T2M 0L8
403/289-1961
$$$ NW

Enjoy a bit o' Scotland at the Highlander Hotel with its Wall of Tartans in the main floor hallway and names like Glengarry Room, Brig o' Doon Lounge, and Black Angus Dining Room. If you'd like a private balcony, ask for a room facing south. Small, heated outdoor pool. Convenient location close to large shopping mall, SAIT, McMahon, and Burns Stadiums, and the University. &

HOLIDAY INN EXPRESS
2227 Banff Tr. NW
Calgary, AB T2M 4L2
403/289-6600 or 800/Holiday
$$$-$$$$ NW

While this Holiday Inn doesn't have a restaurant, a complimentary continental breakfast is provided. Many restaurants are nearby for other meals. Close to the University, stadiums, and C-Train, this hotel features a whirlpool and sauna, plus an outdoor pool shared with the Travelodge next door. &

QUALITY INN MOTEL VILLAGE
2359 Banff Tr. NW
Calgary, AB T2M 4L2
403/289-1973 or 800/661-4667
$$-$$$ NW

The Quality Inn contains over 100 large guest rooms decorated in pastels. There are six suites featuring king-size beds and whirlpool baths. You and your family will enjoy the heated indoor pool with waterslide, whirlpool, sauna, and extensive fitness centre. Enjoy the Sunday brunch at the poolside Tropical Garden Restaurant. &

RAMADA CROWCHILD INN
5353 Crowchild Tr. NW
Calgary, AB T3A 1W9

T I P

Highway #1 is also known as the Trans-Canada Highway.

403/288-7580 or 800/735-7502
$$$ **NW**

For over 20 years, the Ramada Crowchild has catered to visitors from all over the world. Their full-service restaurant offers daily buffets including a Sunday brunch. After a day of business or sight-seeing, choose between the serene Crowsnest Lounge or the more active Bugaboo Creek Pub. Free parking. &

Motels

BOW RIDGE MOTEL & RV PARK
Trans-Canada Hwy. & Bowfort Rd.
NW
Calgary, AB T3B 2V1
403/288-4441
$$-$$$$ **NW**

Across from Canada Olympic Park, this family motel offers a shuttle to the Stampede grounds. Several fast-food restaurants are nearby. There are 28 guest rooms, some with kitchenettes. Two suites available. Outdoor unheated pool.

COMFORT INN
2363 Banff Tr. NW
Calgary, AB T2M 4L2
403/289-2581 or 800/228-5150
$$-$$$ **NW**

Comfort Inn's affordable rates include a complimentary breakfast in the lobby. Some suites and kitchenettes are available. Additional features include indoor pool, jacuzzi, and sauna. Free Superchannel. Near shopping malls, the University, Foothills Hospital, and LRT station. Ask about special event rates.

DAYS INN
2369 Banff Tr. NW
Calgary, AB T2M 4L2
403/289-5571

The Palliser

The Palliser, page 35

$$-$$$ **NW**

What a deal—free continental breakfast and free movies! Sauna and whirlpool available but no swimming pool. Some kitchenettes. Close to restaurants, University, stadiums, and shopping centres.

ECONOLODGE BANFF TRAIL
2231 Banff Tr. NW
Calgary, AB T2M 4L2
403/289-1921 or 800/917-7779
$$-$$$ **NW**

This family motel features an open courtyard and playground, heated outdoor pool, and kitchen units. Family suites available in one-, two-, and three-bedroom plans. Laundromat and free movies.

ECONOLODGE WEST
101 St. and 16th Ave. NW
(Trans-Canada Hwy. W)
Calgary, AB T2M 4N3
403/288-4436
$-$$$ **NW**

Near Canada Olympic Park, EconoLodge West provides easy access to Trans-Canada Hwy, which takes you to Calaway Park, Banff, and Lake Louise. It features a courtyard, heated outdoor pool, sauna, and whirlpool. Kitchen units and some two-bedroom suites are available. All rooms have balconies.

SUPER 8 MOTEL NORTHWEST
1904 Crowchild Tr. NW
Calgary, AB T2M 3Y7
403/289-9211 or 800/800-8000
$$-$$$ NW
Complimentary continental breakfast and free movies are part of the package when you book accommodations at this motel. Domino's Pizza is attached, and several other restaurants are nearby. Small, heated outdoor pool. Attractive guest rooms, some kitchen units, and two-bedroom suites. &

CALGARY NORTH TRAVELODGE
2304 - 16th Ave. NW
Calgary, AB T2M 0M5
403/289-0211 or 800/578-7878
$$-$$$ NW
A well-maintained property, the Travelodge North doesn't have its own restaurant, but it is close to Phil's, Red Lobster, and McDonald's. It features an outdoor heated pool. Its central location places you right on Hwy #1.

Extended Stay

EXECSUITE SUNNYSIDE
727 - 1st Ave. NW
Calgary, AB T2N 0A2
403/294-5800 or 888/A1Suite
$$$ NW
ExecSuite Sunnyside offers one-bedroom suites at monthly rates for those planning an extended stay. Furnished apartments feature fully equipped kitchens. This four-story walk-up is located in the residential community of Sunnyside, close to downtown.

Bed & Breakfasts

A GOOD KNIGHT B & B
1728 - 7th Ave. NW
Calgary, AB T2N 0Z4
403/270-7628 or 800/261-4954
$$ - $$$ NW
New home on charming, quiet street. Private and ensuite baths. TVs in rooms. Huge, romantic suite. Decor includes pine and willow, crafts, collectibles, and over 50 teapots. Wonderful breakfasts. Central location. No smoking.

DUTCH TREAT MANOR HOUSE B & B
309 - 13th St. NW
Calgary, AB T2N 1Z3
403/283-3889
$$ NW
Centrally located heritage home on quiet street. Close to numerous trendy bistros, boutiques, shops, and galleries. Short walk to downtown or C-Train to the zoo or Stampede grounds. Dutch, German, and some French spoken. No smoking. Full breakfast.

KENSINGTON B & B
1412 Gladstone Rd. NW
Calgary, AB T2N 3G4
403/283-8949
$$ NW
Restored 1911 home in popular Kensington with quality restaurants, boutiques, and cappuccino bars. Across the Bow River from downtown. Close to C-Train. Gourmet breakfasts. Families welcome. No smoking.

RICHMOND HOUSE
303 13th St., NW
Calgary, AB
403/283-4262
$$–$$$ NW
Large, two-story home built in 1911. Spacious, refurbished interior.

Large garden with two decks. Near Kensington shopping area, restaurants, bars, and bookshops. Walking distance to downtown. Families welcome. No smoking. Full or continental breakfast.

SWEET DREAMS & SCONES
2443 Uxbridge Dr. NW
Calgary, AB T2N 3Z8
403/289-7004
$$–$$$ **NW**
Swim in a heated pool in a private yard. Luxurious rooms. Two-room family suite. Full breakfast. Families welcome. Bus pick-up. No smoking.

Hostels

SOUTHERN ALBERTA
INSTITUTE OF TECHNOLOGY
(SAIT)
1301 - 16th Ave. NW
Calgary, AB T2M 0L4
403/284-8013
$ **NW**
Economical accommodation is available in Owasina Hall, a 22-story highrise on a park-like campus while regular classes are finished for the summer (mid-May through mid-

August). SAIT offers two- and four-bedroom apartment-style suites with beds, bedding, towels, bathroom, living/dining area, and kitchen facilities. No TV, phone, or cooking and eating utensils. No living room furniture. Laundry and pay phones available. Pay parking adjacent to building. There are various food outlets on campus.

Campgrounds

SYMON'S VALLEY RV PARK
R.R. 4
Calgary, AB T2M 4L4
403/274-4574
$ **NW**
Symon's Valley RV Park's location at the corner of Simon's Valley Road and 144th Avenue NW provides easy access to the city centre, just 20 minutes away. It's a family-owned and -operated park open from April to October. Facilities include laundry, showers, store, and full-service restaurant. Full hook-ups at 36 sites while 107 sites have power and water. An added bonus is shuttle bus service during Stampede Week.

Calgary CVB/John Salus

4

WHERE TO EAT

Dining out in Calgary can be comfortably casual or fine dining at its most elegant. Whatever your preference, Calgary's busy restaurant scene offers excellent food to suit every taste and budget. With approximately 2,000 dining establishments in Calgary and environs, the only concern is deciding which to sample first.

An influx of immigrants to Canada, a business community increasingly attuned to the international scene, and fast-paced growth have all contributed to a proliferation of divergent eateries in Calgary. Many serve tasty fare that reflects Canada's multicultural heritage and the city's growing diversity.

Restaurants serve traditional Canadian food, American, French, German, Spanish, Italian, Chinese (Cantonese, Szechwan, and Peking), African, Mexican, Latin American, Japanese, Thai, Korean, Lebanese, Russian, East Indian, Greek, Latin American, Vietnamese, Indonesian, Moroccan, Turkish, and more.

In the heart of cattle country, Calgary steakhouses serve premium Alberta beef, world-renowned for its quality. Visitors can also sample local "cowboy cuisine" for a taste of the Wild West.

The city's fine dining establishments are second to none, with world-class chefs calling Calgary home. Wheelchair accessibility is indicated by the ♿ symbol. Dollar sign symbols indicate how much you can expect to spend per person for a meal (one entrée and one dessert).

Price rating symbols:
$ Under $10/person
$$ $11 to $20
$$$ $21 and up

All restaurants listed accept credit cards unless otherwise noted.
Prices throughout book indicate Canadian dollars.
(1.42 Canadian $ = 1 U.S. $ at time of printing)

American/Contemporary
The Cheesecake Café & Bakery (NW) p. 78
Earl's Tin Palace (SW) p. 71
Francisco's Restaurant p. 66
Hard Rock Café (DT) p. 61
Humpty's Family Restaurants (NE) p. 77
Kelsey's (DT) p. 61
The Old Spaghetti Factory (DT) p. 62
Savoir Fare (SW) p. 76
Skyline Restaurant (NE) p. 68

Asian
Kyoto 17 Restaurant (SW) p. 72
The Mongolie Grill (SW) p. 73
Oriental Phoenix Restaurant (SE) p. 67
Restaurant Indonesia (SW) p. 75

Best Breakfasts
1886 Buffalo Café (DT) p. 60
Wainwright Hotel (SW) p. 76

Caribbean
Island Experience (NW) p. 78

Chinese
Calgary Court Restaurant (DT) p. 59
Ginger Beef Peking House Restaurant (NW) p. 78
Grand Isle Seafood Restaurant (DT) p. 60
Oriental Palace Restaurant (NW) p. 79
Treasures of China (SE) p. 68
Wo Fat Chinese Restaurant (SE) p. 68

Continental
Divino Bistro Wine Bar (DT) p. 60
Kensington Berliner (NW) p. 78
Koliba Moravian Restaurant (SW) p. 72

Delis/Sandwiches
Café Metro (SE) p. 66
The Great Canadian Soup Co. (DT) p. 61

The Lazy Loaf & Kettle (NW) p. 78
Stephen Avenue Soup Co. (SW) p. 76

Diners
Bert's Mountain Mecca Café (NW) p. 77
Blackfoot Truck Stop Restaurant (SE) p. 66

East Indian
Maurya Fine East Indian Cuisine (NW) p. 79
Rajdoot Restaurant (SW) p. 74
Taj Mahal Restaurant (SE) p. 68

Fine Dining
The Conservatory (DT) p. 59
Drinkwaters Grill (DT) p. 60
Owl's Nest Dining Room (DT) p. 62
Panorama Revolving Restaurant (DT) p. 62
River Café (DT) p. 63
Teatro (DT) p. 63

French
La Caille on the Bow (DT) p. 62
La Chaumière Restaurant (SW) p. 73
La Flammery (DT) p. 62

Greek
Santorini Greek Taverna (NE) p. 77

Italian
Chianti Café & Restaurant (SW) p. 70
Ciao Baby's Restaurant (SE) p. 70
Ercole Ristorante Italiano (NE) p. 77
San Domenico Ristorante (SW) p. 75
San Remo Ristorante (SW) p. 75

Latin American
Blue House Café (NW) p. 77
El Inca Restaurant (SE) p. 66

Mexican
The Baja Bistro (SE) p. 63

Middle Eastern
Byblos Kitchen (SW) p. 69

Panorama Room, Calgary Tower, page 62

The Cedars Deli & Restaurant
(DT) p.70
Olive Grove Restaurant (SE) p. 67
Sultan's Tent (SW) p. 76

Pizza

Pizza Spot (NW) p. 79
Tom's House of Pizza (SE) p. 68

Pubs

Big Rock Grill (SE) p. 66
Mission Bridge Brewing
Company (SW) p. 73
Rose & Crown Pub (SW) p. 75
The Unicorn Pub & Restaurant
(DT) p. 63

Seafood/Fish and Chips

Cannery Row (SW) p. 69
Joey's Only (NE) p. 77

Southwestern

4th Street Rose Restaurant (SW) p. 72
Coyote Grill (SW) p. 71
Mescalero Restaurant
(SW) p. 73
Santa Fe Grill (SE) p. 67

Spanish

Don Quijote Spanish Restaurant
(DT) p. 60

La Paella Spanish Restaurant
(DT) p. 62

Steakhouses

Caesar's (DT) p. 57
Hy's Steak House (DT) p. 61
The Keg Steakhouse & Bar (SE) p. 67
M.T. Tucker's (SW) p. 73
Smuggler's Inn (SE) p. 68

Tea Rooms

Birika Tea Room (SW) p. 69
The Earl Grey Gift & Tea Room
(SE) p. 66

Thai

The King & I Thai Cuisine (SW) p. 72
Thai Sa-On Restaurant (SW) p. 76

Vegetarian

100% Natural (SW) p. 73
Community Natural Foods
(SW) p. 71
Good Earth Cafés Ltd. (SW) p. 72

Western

Buzzards Cowboy Cuisine (SW) p. 69
Ranchman's (SW) p. 74

DOWNTOWN CALGARY

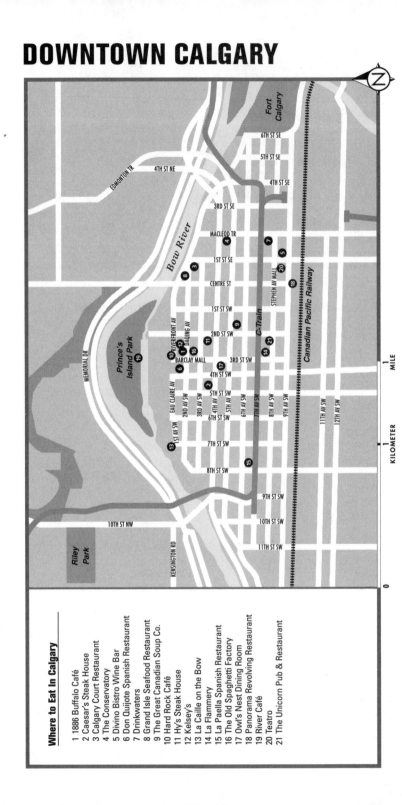

DOWNTOWN CALGARY

CAESAR'S STEAK HOUSE
512 - 4th Ave. SW, Calgary
403/264-1222
$$$ **DT**
Steaks are the specialty at Caesar's Steak House, as is the outstanding service. This traditional steak house is a great place for visitors to try Alberta beef, with the menu featuring items such as ribeye filet. The menu also includes seafood, ribs, lamb, and chicken. Main courses are accompanied by soup, salad, garlic toast, potatoes, or rice. Reservations recommended. Closed Sunday. ♿

CALGARY COURT RESTAURANT LTD.
119 - 2nd Ave. SE, Calgary
403/264-7890
$ **DT**
No matter what time of day or night, it's always busy at casual Calgary Court Restaurant. And no wonder. The Cantonese/Hong Kong–style food is tasty and fresh, portions are generous, service is fast, and what a bargain! Fill up on a variety of hot soups, noodle dishes, and more. No reservations. Breakfast, lunch, dinner, late-night service.

THE CONSERVATORY
Delta Bow Valley Hotel
209 - 4th Ave., SE
403/266-1980
$$$ **DT**
International cuisine and service par excellence is the offering at this award-winning, elegant, high-end dining room. The diverse menu includes such items as steak, seafood, bison, and rack of lamb—one of the house specials. The dining room is small and romantic, with paintings on the walls by Canadian artists. Reservations recommended. Lunch and dinner weekdays, dinner Sat. Closed Sun. ♿

Burns Building

The Burns Building, located directly across from City Hall, is recognized as a provincial historic site and currently houses Drinkwaters Grill. Built between 1911 and 1912, it was the main office for Calgary's own cattle baron, Pat Burns.

Burns moved west from Ontario in 1878 and started up a small slaughterhouse in Calgary. Soon Burns packing plants sprang up across the country, the northern states, and even Great Britain, making Burns the largest ranch operator in Canada. When Burns sold the building in 1923, it subsequently was home to Imperial Oil, Canada Safeway, Calgary Power, and Canada Cement, among others. The elegant glass canopy above the first floor, the creamy terra-cotta facade, and the lion heads and ornamental tile moldings reflect a bygone era.

DIVINO BISTRO WINE BAR
817 - 1st St. SW, Calgary
403/263-5869
$$–$$$ **DT**
Divino's menu of Californian/Italian cuisine changes weekly but always complements the extensive wine list. Highly popular is the black pepper linguini with chicken in a tomato cream sauce. There's also a varied collection of creative pastas and pizzas, and a selection of antipasto perfect for sharing. Non-smoking. Lunch and dinner daily except Sunday. &

DON QUIJOTE SPANISH RESTAURANT
309 - 2nd Ave. SW, Calgary
403/205-4244
$$–$$$ **DT**
Sample snacks at the tapas bar, sway to the rhythms of a Latin dance band at this Spanish restaurant in downtown Calgary. The tapas bar features a wide range of items, such as the lightly breaded calamari rings. The more people to share the meal, the merrier, because that means better variety. Paella, the house specialty, is a blend of chicken, seafood, and saffron rice. Reservations recommended. Lunch, dinner.

DRINKWATERS GRILL
237 - 8th Ave. SE, Calgary
403/264-9494
$$$ **DT**
Enjoy the art of casual dining at Drinkwaters, located beside the Calgary Centre for the Performing Arts in the historic Burns Building. Choose from a diverse menu that's upscale yet affordable, with Alberta beef and lamb taking centre stage. Tantalizing desserts such as Fallen Chocolate Almond Soufflé are popular with theatre goers. Lunch and dinner Mon–Sat; dinner only Sunday. Reservations recommended.

1886 BUFFALO CAFÉ
187 Barclay Parade SW, Calgary
403/269-9255
$ **DT**
Located in a rustic building dating back to 1886, the 1886 Buffalo Café specializes in breakfasts in a pioneer setting. Omelets are accompanied by a large variety of ingredients of your choice, including bacon, ham, sausage, hot peppers, cheese, pineapple, and peaches. Eggs are served any style. Other items include vegetarian chili and a breakfast sundae of yogurt, granola, fruit, and toast. No reservations.

GRAND ISLE SEAFOOD RESTAURANT
200, 128 - 2nd Ave. SE, Calgary
403/269-7783

TRIVIA

Alberta boasts six of the world's best beef processing plants, measured by quality and quantity of output. Additionally, Alberta ranchers produce more than 40 percent of Canada's total beef. Alberta beef is second to none and most Calgary restaurants serve it in one form or another. If tucking into a thick, juicy steak is on your list of things to do while you're in town, check out one of the popular steak houses.

The public is welcome to buy economical lunches in the cafeteria of the Queen's Bench Courthouse at 611 - 4th Street SW.

$$ **DT**

Overlooking the Bow River in Chinatown, Grand Isle encompasses traditional and contemporary Chinese cuisine. Dim sum is included in the daily lunch buffet. Grand Isle's menu offers more than 200 items including ginger beef, lemon chicken, Peking duck, war wonton, and oyster beef. Seafood includes lobster, crab, shrimp, scallop, soft-baked seafood, and squid. Reservations recommended. Lunch, dinner. &

THE GREAT CANADIAN SOUP CO.
2nd floor Bow Valley Square
235, 255 - 5th Ave. SW, Calgary
403/265-1164
$ **DT**

Soups are the specialty at The Great Canadian Soup Co., which offers up to 14 different kinds of soups daily. This cafeteria-style restaurant also serves sandwiches and salads as well as hot specials such as quiche and pizza. They make their own cheese bread here. Credit cards not accepted; no reservations. Lunch. Closed weekends.

HARD ROCK CAFÉ
Eau Claire Market
200 Barclay Parade SW, Calgary
403/263-7625
$$ **DT**

Action is fast and furious at the Hard Rock Café, which boasts Canada's largest collection of rock 'n' roll memorabilia, such as John Lennon's white suit, Buddy Holly's jacket, and lots of guitars—including the rooftop Gibson with neon strings that's 24 meters high (80 feet). Entertainment and atmosphere are a big part of Hard Rock Café's appeal. The diner-style food includes burgers, steak, chicken, and ribs. No reservations. &

HY'S STEAK HOUSE
316 - 4th Ave. SW, Calgary
403/263-2222
$$$ **DT**

One of Calgary's premier steak houses, Hy's has been a favorite since opening in 1955. The menu is extensive in this traditional steak house, a meeting place for the business crowd. Specialties include ribeye sandwiches and New York steak—Hy's signature steak, served with special sauce. Other choices include fresh Atlantic salmon, chicken dishes, and salad entrées. Reservations recommended. &

KELSEY'S
135 Eau Claire Market, Calgary
403/269-5599
$–$$ **DT**

Kelsey's, "your neighborhood bar and grill," offers something for everyone. The menu includes steak, ribs, pizza, seafood, burgers, pasta, Southwestern dishes, chicken, sandwiches, salads, soups, and desserts. Enjoy fresh and jumbo wings or Kelsey's Famous Pork Ribs. Lunch at Kelsey's is "fast or it's free." Lunch and dinner; children's menu. Kelsey's has a number of locations in Calgary. &

LA CAILLE ON THE BOW
100 La Caille Place
7th Street and 1st Avenue SW,
Calgary
403/262-5554
$$–$$$ DT

On its main floor, La Caille offers casual dining with beef, chicken, pastas, salads, and seafood. Upstairs it is fine dining, featuring international cuisine and wines. The varied menu includes dishes prepared at your table with a flambé cart, such as the Châteaubriand, a 16-ounce filet mignon. There is also wild game. Lunch and dinner Monday through Friday. Dinner only on weekends. Reservations recommended. &

LA FLAMMERY
TD Square, Third floor
355, 317 - 7th Ave. SW, Calgary
403/234-7555
$–$$ DT

A popular lunchtime eatery, this charming French-style bistro offers a menu featuring a pizza-like specialty called a flambée. Choose from eight savory flambées served piping hot on wooden paddles. Roll them up to eat or hold flat like a pizza—if you're not in a hurry, you can even cut them up and eat with a fork. Soups, salads, burgers, and other items are also available. Service is fast and pleasant. Reservations a must for lunch. Lunch and dinner. &

LA PAELLA SPANISH RESTAURANT
800 - 6th Ave. SW, Calgary
403/269-5911
$$ DT

La Paella serves fine Spanish and continental cuisine in a classy, traditional Spanish atmosphere. Paella, of course, is one of the most popular dishes, featuring seafood, chicken, and saffron rice. Other dishes include beef, chicken, seafood, pasta, veal, duck, and rabbit. This restaurant is popular for both business lunches and family dining. Lunch, dinner. Reservations recommended for lunch and groups of six or more. &

THE OLD SPAGHETTI FACTORY
222 - 3rd St. SW, Calgary
403/263-7223
$–$$ DT

There's pasta and more at The Old Spaghetti Factory, where the wide range of selections includes veal parmigiana and chicken breast. Entrées are accompanied by salad or soup, sourdough bread, coffee or tea, and spumoni ice cream at no extra charge. Lunch specials include a variety of hot dishes. Children's menu. Reservations for groups of six or more.

OWL'S NEST DINING ROOM
The Westin Hotel
4th Avenue and 3rd Street, SW
403/266-1611
$$$ DT

It's fine dining with elegance at the award-winning Owl's Nest Dining Room. Popular items on the varied menu include Alberta rack of lamb, beef and seafood mixed grill. French service (food prepared right at your table) evenings for groups of up to ten people. Live piano music Thur, Fri, and Sat evenings. Reservations recommended. Lunch and dinner weekdays, dinner Sat. Closed Sun. &

PANORAMA REVOLVING RESTAURANT
Calgary Tower
101 - 9th Ave. SW, Calgary
403/266-7171
$$$ DT

Rise and dine at Panorama Restaurant at the top of the Calgary Tower. The restaurant, which completes one revolution per hour, boasts sweeping views of the city, the Rockies, and prairies. And the food, beautifully presented, will not let you down. Using many local ingredients, the restaurant serves continental cuisine. A popular dinner entrée is the Tower Medley, which combines filet mignon, salmon, and tiger prawns. &

RIVER CAFÉ
Prince's Island Park, Calgary
403/261-7670
$$–$$$ DT

Northwestern woodfired Canadian cuisine is the offering at cosmopolitan River Café, in the heart of Prince's Island Park. This fine dining restaurant features such traditional Canadian delicacies as buffalo, venison, pheasant, trout, arctic char, and salmon. It has the ambiance of a rustic fishing lodge, with a patio overlooking the park. Non-smoking; reservations recommended. Lunch, dinner, weekend brunch. Closed January, February, and part of March. &

TEATRO
200 - 8th Ave. SE, Calgary
403/290-1012
$$–$$$ DT

Fine dining in a classy European setting is what you'll find at Teatro, located in a 1911 bank building beside Olympic Plaza. Serving fresh Italian-Californian cuisine, Teatro changes its menu with the seasons. Here you will find a diversity of tempting items including beef, rack of lamb, salmon, pastas, and pizzas. Reservations recommended. Lunch Mon–Fri; dinner daily. &

THE UNICORN PUB & RESTAURANT
304 - 8th Ave. SW, Calgary
403/233-2666
$$ DT

Chow down on traditional British pub grub at The Unicorn, opened in 1979 by the Irish Rovers. Enjoy the welcoming atmosphere and live entertainment at this Tudor-style pub. Popular menu items include fish and chips and meat pie. There is a variety of beers on tap. Steamed rice with chicken, beef, or vegetables are available for the health-conscious eater. Lunch, dinner. Closed Sunday. Reservations recommended. &

SOUTHEAST CALGARY

THE BAJA BISTRO
100, 225 - 28th St. SE, Calgary
403/248-3914
$$ SE

It's Mexican food with flair at Baja Bistro. Spareribs, fajitas, enchiladas, and tacos are served in a casual, relaxed environment that conjures up the warmth of Mexico. Baja Bistro prides itself on the freshness of its food. The menu has vegetarian

TRIVIA

A popular dish in many Asian restaurants, ginger beef is in fact a Calgary invention. A local Peking establishment blended strips of crispy beef soaked in a dark, sweet sauce seasoned with chiles and ginger. Its popularity prompted other Asian eateries to follow suit.

GREATER CALGARY

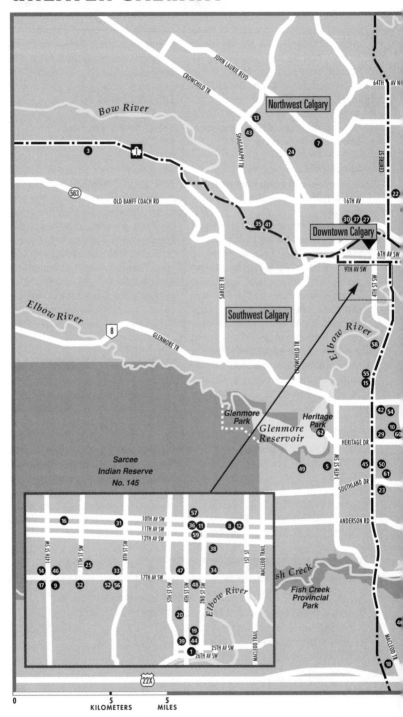

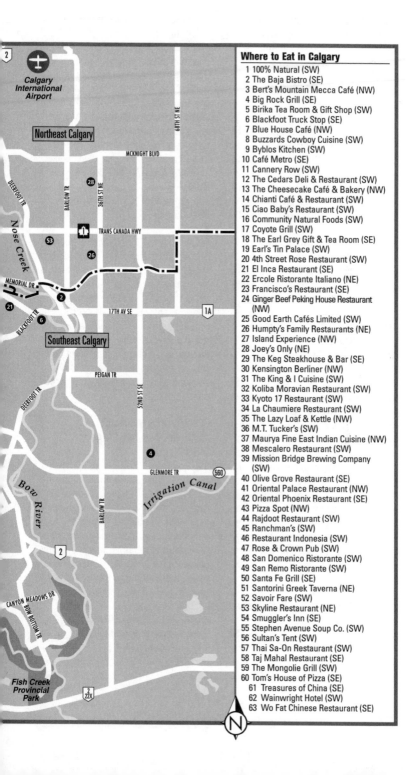

Where to Eat in Calgary

1 100% Natural (SW)
2 The Baja Bistro (SE)
3 Bert's Mountain Mecca Café (NW)
4 Big Rock Grill (SE)
5 Birika Tea Room & Gift Shop (SW)
6 Blackfoot Truck Stop (SE)
7 Blue House Café (NW)
8 Buzzards Cowboy Cuisine (SW)
9 Byblos Kitchen (SW)
10 Café Metro (SE)
11 Cannery Row (SW)
12 The Cedars Deli & Restaurant (SW)
13 The Cheesecake Café & Bakery (NW)
14 Chianti Café & Restaurant (SW)
15 Ciao Baby's Restaurant (SW)
16 Community Natural Foods (SW)
17 Coyote Grill (SW)
18 The Earl Grey Gift & Tea Room (SE)
19 Earl's Tin Palace (SW)
20 4th Street Rose Restaurant (SW)
21 El Inca Restaurant (SE)
22 Ercole Ristorante Italiano (NE)
23 Francisco's Restaurant (SE)
24 Ginger Beef Peking House Restaurant (NW)
25 Good Earth Cafés Limited (SW)
26 Humpty's Family Restaurants (NE)
27 Island Experience (NW)
28 Joey's Only (NE)
29 The Keg Steakhouse & Bar (SE)
30 Kensington Berliner (NW)
31 The King & I Cuisine (SW)
32 Koliba Moravian Restaurant (SW)
33 Kyoto 17 Restaurant (SW)
34 La Chaumiere Restaurant (SW)
35 The Lazy Loaf & Kettle (NW)
36 M.T. Tucker's (SW)
37 Maurya Fine East Indian Cuisine (NW)
38 Mescalero Restaurant (SW)
39 Mission Bridge Brewing Company (SW)
40 Olive Grove Restaurant (SE)
41 Oriental Palace Restaurant (NW)
42 Oriental Phoenix Restaurant (SE)
43 Pizza Spot (NW)
44 Rajdoot Restaurant (SW)
45 Ranchman's (SW)
46 Restaurant Indonesia (SW)
47 Rose & Crown Pub (SW)
48 San Domenico Ristorante (SW)
49 San Remo Ristorante (SW)
50 Santa Fe Grill (SE)
51 Santorini Greek Taverna (NE)
52 Savoir Fare (SW)
53 Skyline Restaurant (NE)
54 Smuggler's Inn (SE)
55 Stephen Avenue Soup Co. (SW)
56 Sultan's Tent (SW)
57 Thai Sa-On Restaurant (SW)
58 Taj Mahal Restaurant (SE)
59 The Mongolie Grill (SW)
60 Tom's House of Pizza (SE)
61 Treasures of China (SE)
62 Wainwright Hotel (SW)
63 Wo Fat Chinese Restaurant (SE)

options—almost any dish can be made without meat. Vegetarian fajitas are popular. Lunch and dinner. ♿

BIG ROCK GRILL
5555 - 76th Ave. SE, Calgary
403/236-1606
$$ **SE**
Dining is casual and relaxed at Big Rock Grill, open at the brewery site of Big Rock beer. Choose from a wide variety of grill and rotisserie entrées at this bright, spacious restaurant, where meals are made from scratch and Big Rock brews are on tap. The menu includes items such as buffalo burgers and a barbecue melt featuring marinated chicken, fresh herbs, and cheddar on a garlic baguette. Reservations recommended. Lunch and dinner. Closed weekends. ♿

BLACKFOOT TRUCK STOP RESTAURANT
1840 - 9th Ave. SE, Calgary
403/265-5964
$ **SE**
A homey feel is one of the main draws of Blackfoot Truck Stop Restaurant, which specializes in big breakfasts around the clock. Popular breakfast items are bacon and eggs, hash browns, and steak and eggs. Portions are extremely generous, prices more than reasonable. Other specialties are clubhouse sandwiches, veal cutlets, hot open-face turkey sandwiches, flapper pie, and high meringue lemon pie. Check out the train on the ceiling. Breakfast, lunch, dinner. ♿

CAFÉ METRO
17, 7400 Macleod Tr. SE, Calgary
403/255-6537
$$ **SE**
Café Metro specializes in authentic Montreal smoked meat, sliced, steamed, and served hot. Offering middle-of-the-road, casual dining and a full bar, it presents a selection of made-from-scratch pastas, California-style pizzas, desserts, and salads. Evoking the feel of an outdoor French café, Café Metro sports Montreal streetscape murals painted on the walls and clotheslines strung overhead. Lunch and dinner. Reservations for groups of eight or more. ♿

THE EARL GREY GIFT & TEA ROOM
285 Shawville Blvd. SE, Calgary
403/254-9382
$ **SE**
Fresh fruit pies, cheesecake, scones, quiche, and meat pies are among the mouthwatering concoctions at The Earl Grey Gift & Tea Room. Strawberry rhubarb pie is the bestseller in a huge selection of desserts. For those watching their waistline, there's also a full range of sandwiches and a large salad selection at this pretty Victorian tea room. Nonsmoking. Lunchtime reservations recommended. ♿

EL INCA RESTAURANT
1325 - 9th Ave. SE, Calgary
403/262-7832
$$ **SE**
Peruvian and Latin American cuisine is served at this casual, colorful little restaurant that's a delight to the eye as well as the palate. Prices are reasonable and portions generous. Pork marinated in white wine chile sauce is one typical dish. With only 35 or so seats, reservations are a must. Lunch and dinner. Closed Sunday.

FRANCISCO'S RESTAURANT
Best Western Hospitality Inn
135 Southland Dr., SE
403/278-5050
$$ **SE**

The widely varied menu at this award-winning restaurant offers something for everyone. Located in the atrium, Francisco's offers standard fare such as chicken breast, chicken fingers and burgers, as well as pastas, Californian, and Mexican cuisine. A popular dish is Swiss Roestis (like a potato pancake, with a variety of toppings). Francisco's puts on a great Sunday brunch. Reservations recommended. Breakfast, lunch, dinner, Mon through Sat. Sun brunch. &

THE KEG STEAKHOUSE & BAR
7104 Macleod Tr. SE, Calgary
403/253-2534
$$$ SE

A come-as-you-are steakhouse with bright, modern decor, The Keg specializes in steaks off the grill, slow-roasted prime rib, rock lobster tails, Alaskan king crab, and custom-made salads. The setting is casual, friendly, and upbeat. The Keg was voted favorite steakhouse by *Calgary Herald* readers. Lunch, dinner. There are a number of Keg locations in Calgary. &

OLIVE GROVE RESTAURANT & BACKGAMMON LOUNGE
Midnapore Mall
Macleod Trail and Midlake
Boulevard SE, Calgary
403/256-4610
$$ SE

Known for its excellent pizza, the Olive Grove serves authentic Middle Eastern food alongside pasta, steak, and lobster. The pizza comes with all ingredients covered by lots of cheese. Other menu items include veal, chicken, and rack of lamb. Service is fast at Olive Grove, where the decor conjures up the sun-drenched Mediterranean. Olive Grove was named one of the top 100 restaurants

in Canada. Reservations recommended. Lunch, dinner. &

ORIENTAL PHOENIX RESTAURANT
Chinook Square
15, 6708 Macleod Tr. SE, Calgary
403/253-8383
$$ SE

Flavors are varied and interesting at this Vietnamese restaurant. Menu items include stir-fried chicken in tamarind sauce, spareribs with black pepper sauce and vermicelli noodles, spring rolls, beef, chicken, and lots of satay sauce. Food is not overly spicy. Oriental Phoenix Restaurant has received favorable reviews from a variety of restaurant critics. Reservations recommended. Lunch and dinner. Closed Sunday. &

SANTA FE GRILL
9250 Macleod Tr. SE, Calgary
403/253-9096
$$ SE

Food is cooked over a mesquite grill at Santa Fe Grill, which specializes in "Texican" Southwestern cuisine. Mesquite hardwood, imported from Texas, seals in flavor and gives a

La Caille on the Bow, page 62

La Caille

smoky taste to the food. Menu items include Hickory Jack burgers, steak, and ribs. Fajitas and fresh flour tortillas are specialties. Santa Fe Grill prides itself on its fresh ingredients. Reservations for large groups only. Lunch and dinner, Sunday brunch. &

SKYLINE RESTAURANT
Holiday Inn Calgary Airport
1250 McKinnon Dr., NE
403/230-1999
$$ NE
Prompt service, good food, and a skyline view of the Rocky Mountains are what diners will find at this family restaurant. The menu features a variety of items, with a traditional and continental breakfast, lunch specials, and fine dinner meals. The lunch menu includes soup, sandwiches, and pastas. Dinner items include steak, chicken, stir-fries, salmon, lamb, ribs, baked lasagna, soups, salads, and pastas. Breakfast, lunch, and dinner.

SMUGGLER'S INN
6920 Macleod Tr. SE, Calgary
403/253-5355
$$$ SE
Prime rib portions go from 8 to 30 ounces at Smuggler's Inn, which has been catering to beef aficionados for more than 30 years. The finest grain-fed lean beef is personally selected and aged in coolers. It's worth the price, regulars say. The menu also offers pasta, seafood, chicken, vegetarian dishes, and a great salad bar. Try the steak soup. Lunch, dinner. Reservations recommended.

TAJ MAHAL RESTAURANT
4816 Macleod Tr. SE, Calgary
403/243-6362
$$ SE
At Taj Mahal Restaurant curries are cooked to taste, from mild to hot.

Popular items include lamb and chicken curry, kebabs, and tandoori dishes. A variety of vegetarian dishes is also available. Service is professional and friendly. Located at basement level, Taj Mahal Restaurant is a favorite with *Calgary Herald* readers. Lunch, dinner. Reservations suggested.

TOM'S HOUSE OF PIZZA
7730 Macleod Tr. SE, Calgary
403/252-0111
$ SE
Calgary's oldest existing pizza parlor, Tom's House of Pizza has been serving thin-crust pizza since 1963. Sausages are made at the restaurant, which boasts the hottest pepperoni in town. Tom's House of Pizza is packed with regulars—three generations of families come here to eat. There are a number of locations in Calgary. Lunch, dinner. Dinner reservations suggested. &

TREASURES OF CHINA
Macleod Plaza
Bay 45, 180 - 94th Ave. SE, Calgary
403/252-6888
$$ SE
Choose from more than 100 items at the Treasures of China epicurean buffet. Take the whole gang—there's something for everyone. Those who prefer western food will find pizza, tacos, and more. The buffet includes soup, desserts, and a Mongolian grill, where you choose the ingredients and dinner is cooked in front of you. Reservations suggested. Lunch and dinner. &

WO FAT CHINESE RESTAURANT
171, 755 Lake Bonavista Dr. SE,
Calgary
403/278-3288
$$ SE
Cantonese chow mein, Shanghai

noodles, Peking duck, ginger beef—these are some of the popular items at Wo Fat, which has garnered high praise from CBC Radio's restaurant critic. Other items on the menu at Wo Fat, which serves Cantonese and Peking cuisine, include chicken wings, ribs, dumplings, ginger chicken, and lemon chicken. There is a daily lunch buffet. Reservations recommended. Lunch, dinner. &

SOUTHWEST CALGARY

BIRIKA TEA ROOM & GIFT SHOP
Glenmore Landing
A106, 1600 - 90th Ave. SW, Calgary
403/258-3300
$$ **SW**
Warm gingerbread with lemon butter and whipped cream is just one of the dainties available at Birika Tea Room, a nice place to take your grandma. Popular main courses include tuna melt with salad; and garden salad with chicken, cashews, egg salad, and bagel and cream cheese. There are lots of loose teas, including unusual varieties such

River Café, page 63

Calgary CVB/John Salus

as mango and green tea. Reservations suggested for a table in the smoking section. Breakfast, lunch. &

BUZZARDS COWBOY CUISINE
140 - 10th Ave. SW, Calgary
403/264-6959
$$ **SW**
Alberta beef and buffalo are the specialties at Buzzards Cowboy Cuisine, rustled up in a rustic western setting. Old saddles, barn wood, open rafters—it's real cowboy decor. Here you can sample items such as buffalo steak and chuckwagon meatloaf. A big hit with visitors is Triple B-beef, beans, and biscuits, with range salad. The wine list features predominantly Canadian wines. Reservations recommended. Lunch, dinner.

BYBLOS KITCHEN
1449 - 17th Ave. SW, Calgary
403/541-1788
$ **SW**
A 30-seat Mediterranean-style eatery on busy 17th Avenue, Byblos Kitchen serves a variety of Mediterranean and Lebanese food. Approximately half the menu is vegetarian, with dishes such as falafel, hummus, tabbouleh salad, spanakopita (spinach pie), and Greek salad. Other items featured include lamb, beef, and chicken kebabs. Desserts are made at Byblos Bakery. No reservations (except for groups). Lunch, dinner. &

CANNERY ROW
317 - 10th Ave. SW, Calgary
403/269-8889
$$-$$$ **SW**
Seafood is the specialty at Cannery Row, served with style in a New Orleans atmosphere. On Bucket Night, order buckets of clams, mussels, or scallops. Sit at the oyster bar and watch your food being prepared.

Coffeehouses

Calgary offers lots of opportunity to enjoy a good cup of java in whatever flavour or presentation you prefer. Of the coffeehouse chains, there are:

- *6 locations of Good Earth Café (one in the main public library)*
- *3 locations of The Gourmet Cup*
- *10 locations of Grabbajabba*
- *5 locations of Katmandu Café*
- *3 locations of McBeans*
- *16 locations of The Second Cup*
- *8 locations of Starbucks*

The menu, which features daily specials, also includes non-seafood fare such as steak and pasta. Reservations for groups of eight or more. Lunch and dinner.

THE CEDARS DELI & RESTAURANT
1009A - 1st St. SW, Calgary
403/264-2532
$$ **SW**
Made fresh daily, the Lebanese food at The Cedars Deli & Restaurant includes a little bit of everything—beef and chicken kebabs, hummus, tabbouleh, stuffed vine leaves, falafel patties, and kivi (ground steak, bulgar wheat, and pine nuts). This small, informal restaurant offers table service after 5 p.m. The Cedars Deli has a number of locations. Lunch and dinner. Closed Sunday.

CHIANTI CAFÉ & RESTAURANT
1438 - 17th Ave. SW, Calgary
403/229-1600
$$ **SW**
You'll find reasonably priced Italian

food at this busy, casual, award-winning eatery. Chianti has a huge selection of pastas—all made fresh on site. Pasta nights Monday and Tuesday are a hit with customers. Other menu items include chicken, veal, and seafood. Half portions are available for most dishes. Reservations recommended. Lunch and dinner. &

CIAO BABY'S RESTAURANT
100, 5920 Macleod Tr. SW, Calgary
403/258-0051
$$$ **SW**
Fine Italian cuisine in a warm, comfortable atmosphere is the hallmark of Ciao Baby's. This restaurant offers an extensive menu with a variety of pasta, seafood, chicken, beef, veal, lamb, and specialty items daily. The decor is distinctive, with a domed ceiling handpainted with cherubs and a large saltwater fish tank home to a dozen tropical fish. Catch live entertainment Friday and Saturday at the piano bar and lounge. Highly recommended by CBC Radio's restaurant reviewer. Lunch, dinner. &

COMMUNITY NATURAL FOODS
1304 - 10th Ave. SW, Calgary
403/229-2383
$ SW
Who said if it's good for you, it's got to be boring? This busy health food store provides healthy and tasty food at its all-vegetarian, non-smoking cafeteria using natural and organic ingredients. Community Natural Foods makes a variety of soups, sandwiches, salads, fresh juices, and tempting baked goods. Lunch, dinner, and weekend breakfast. ⅁

COYOTE GRILL
1411 - 17th Ave. SW, Calgary

403/244-1080
$$–$$$ SW
Southern barbecue and seafood is the focus at the cozy Coyote Grill, where Western art and antiques are the backdrop for Southern cooking: smoked barbecue beef and pork ribs, barbecue chicken, seafood, fish and chips, soups, and homemade desserts. Southern and Cajun specials; daily lunch special under $5. Reservations suggested for larger groups. Lunch, dinner, Sunday brunch. ⅁

EARL'S TIN PALACE
2401 - 4th St. SW, Calgary
403/228-4141

Top Ten Asian and Middle Eastern Restaurants
by Kathy Richardier, restaurant reviewer for the *Calgary Herald* and editor of *City Palate*

1. **The King & I/You're So Sweet Noodle & Dessert House** (Thai), 820 - 11th Ave. SW, 403/264-7241 or 403/269-5366; SW.

2. **Korean Restaurant Ga-Ya** (Korean barbecue), 4640 Macleod Tr., 403/287-2622; SW.

3. **Kyoto 17 Restaurant** (Japanese), Basement 908 - 17th Ave. SW, 403/245-3188; SW.

4. **Leo Fu's Szechwan & Mandarin Restaurant** (Szechwan Chinese), 511 - 70th Ave. SW, 403/255-2528; SW.

5. **Oriental Phoenix Restaurant** (Vietnamese), 6708 Macleod Tr. SE, 403/253-8383; SE.

6. **Puspa Restaurant** (East Indian), 1051 - 40th Ave. NW, 403/282-6444; NW.

7. **Rajdoot** (East Indian), 2424 - 4th St. SW, 403/245-0181; SW.

8. **Royal Seoul Restaurant** (Korean), 1324 - 10th Ave. SW, 403/228-1120; SW.

9. **Saigon** (Vietnamese), 1221 - 12th Ave. SW, 403/228-4200; SW.

10. **Thai Sa-On Restaurant** (Thai), 351 - 10th Ave. SW, 403/264-3526; SW.

$$ SW

Ever-popular Earl's offers an eclectic menu ranging from Southwestern and Mexican to Pacific Rim and Italian. With an emphasis on freshness, the menu includes thin-crust pizzas, roast chicken dishes, ribs, and steak. A popular dish is the Grilato pasta with fettucini, sundried and fresh tomato, peppercorn, cream, brandy, grilled chicken breast, and garlic. Earl's has several locations in Calgary. Reservations suggested for lunch and groups of nine or more. &

4TH STREET ROSE RESTAURANT & BAR
2116 - 4th St. SW, Calgary
403/228-5377
$$ SW

Dining out is fun and healthy at this bright, casual, colorful café. For those watching their fat and calorie intake, plenty of delicious menu items are available including pasta, salads, low-fat vegetarian dishes, sandwiches, stir-fries, and sushi. Pizzas and burgers are also popular at this café that's filled with paintings and plants. Reservations for groups of six or more. Lunch, dinner, late night dining, and Sunday brunch.

GOOD EARTH CAFÉS LTD.
1502 - 11th St. SW, Calgary
403/228-9543
$ SW

Along with a cuppa java, this casual and popular coffeehouse specializes in good-for-you food made from scratch. The daily menu includes vegetarian dishes, with vegetarian soups, hot meals such as lasagna and ratatouille, salads, scones, muffins, and desserts. Good Earth serves specialty espresso drinks among a variety of others. Non-smoking. No reservations. Locally owned,

Good Earth Cafés has several outlets throughout Calgary. &

THE KING & I THAI CUISINE
820 - 11th Ave. SW, Calgary
403/264-7241
$$ SW

Being listed among the 100 best restaurants in Canada is one of many accolades garnered by The King & I. This highly popular eatery serves a variety of Thai favorites, including all kinds of curry and stir-fry. Typical items are chicken tenderloin with peanut sauce and spinach, and tiger prawn curry. Lunch and dinner.

KOLIBA MORAVIAN RESTAURANT
1112 - 17th Ave. SW, Calgary
403/245-2827
$$–$$$ SW

Excellent Czech and continental cuisine in pleasant surroundings is offered at Koliba, ranked among the top restaurants in Calgary by CBC Radio. Koliba features a variety of dishes, including homemade sausages, rack of lamb, roast goose in winter, roast duck in summer, roast rabbit, schnitzels, and baked scallops. Desserts include homemade strudels and crêpes filled with black currants. Call ahead for vegetarian platters. Lunch, dinner.

KYOTO 17 RESTAURANT
Basement 908 - 17th Ave. SW, Calgary
403/245-3188
$$ SW

Authentic Japanese cuisine in a contemporary atmosphere and efficient, unobtrusive service is what you'll find at Kyoto 17. For sushi fans, the "Love Boat" for two offers all kinds of sushi and sashimi, including tuna, salmon, mackerel, and scallops, beautifully presented in a little wooden boat and accompanied by soup and salad. Other dishes include chicken, beef, and noodles. Lunch, dinner. Reservations recommended.

LA CHAUMIÈRE RESTAURANT
139 - 17th Ave. SW, Calgary
403/228-5690
$$$ **SW**

For more than 20 years, La Chaumière has served fine continental cuisine in an upscale setting while racking up major awards. The menu features items such as breast of duck with orange and ginger sauce, rack of lamb, pheasant, and ostrich. La Chaumière has one of the largest wine selections in Western Canada with more than 500 labels. Reservations recommended. Lunch and dinner. Closed Sunday. &

M.T. TUCKER'S
345 - 10th Ave. SW, Calgary
403/262-5541
$$–$$$ **SW**

Good food at reasonable cost is offered at this western-style family restaurant, where prime rib is the house specialty. Or tuck into steak, seafood, chicken, or the 60-item salad bar. Tucker's has won a number of awards for food and service. Children's menu; lots of highchairs available, plus crayons to entertain youngsters. Reservations recommended. Lunch, dinner.

MESCALERO RESTAURANT
1315 - 1st St. SW, Calgary
403/266-3339
$$–$$$ **SW**

Inspired by Latin and native cultures, Mescalero's food runs the gamut from casual nachos to venison medallions. The dinner menu is a daily creation at Mescalero, which uses local, organic ingredi-

ents when possible. Plates of tapas items are a highlight. The decor is Southwestern native, with antique and native artifacts. There's a beautiful brick patio to dine on in summer. Lunch and dinner. Reservations recommended. &

MISSION BRIDGE BREWING COMPANY
2417 - 4th St. SW, Calgary
403/228-0100
$$–$$$ **SW**

New world cuisine cooked in a wood oven and unfiltered ales and lagers are the offerings at Mission Bridge Brewing Company. This is an energetic Seattle market-style brewery with a dining room serving such varied items as thin-crust pizzas, smoked salmon with purple potatoes, chicken, pork, pasta, salads, and soups. Reservations recommended. Lunch and dinner. &

THE MONGOLIE GRILL
100, 1108 - 4th St. SW, Calgary
403/262-7773
$$ **SW**

Diners create their own stir-fry at The Mongolie Grill, choosing from 30 fresh items at a self-serve bar. Food is cooked to your taste on the Mongolian grill while you watch. Ingredients include beef, pork, chicken, seafood, vegetables, and 18 specialty sauces. The meal includes soup and rice. Customers pay by weight of food; 20 percent discount for vegetarians. Reservations recommended. Lunch and dinner. &

100% NATURAL
2500 - 4th St. SW, Calgary
403/209-3100
$–$$ **SW**

Health buffs will find organic, gluten-free, wheat-free, and dairy-free food at 100% Natural. On the menu are salads, stir-fries, soups, sandwiches, and baked goods. The restaurant, which provides table service, also serves omelets and herb quiche made from free-range eggs. Meat eaters can sample free-range chicken as well as fish. Non-smoking; there are tables outside for smokers, weather permitting. Lunch, dinner. &

RAJDOOT RESTAURANT
2424 - 4th St. SW, Calgary
403/245-0181
$$ **SW**
Whether you're a vegetarian, meat-eater, or somewhere in between, there's plenty of delicious food to enjoy at the multiple award–winning Rajdoot, ambassador of fine East In-dian cuisine. Rajdoot specializes in healthy and low-fat food. The daily lunch buffet offers a wide variety of hot and cold items. Vegetarian buffet Tuesday evenings. Reservations strongly suggested. Lunch and dinner. &

RANCHMAN'S
9615 Macleod Tr. SW, Calgary
403/253-1100
$$ **SW**
For a honky-tonk two-steppin', band playin', good eatin' kind of time, saunter down to the Ranchman's where live country bands play nightly. The menu offers traditional cowboy fare and Texas-style smoked barbecue specialties. There's steak, chicken, and more; specials include all-you-can-eat ribs.

Olive Grove Restaurant, page 67

Lunch and dinner. Closed Sunday. Reservations only for large groups. ♿

RESTAURANT INDONESIA
1604 - 14th St. SW, Calgary
403/244-0645
$$ **SW**

There's plenty of curry on the menu at Restaurant Indonesia. But not to worry if spicy isn't your thing—it's mostly quite mild. People craving food that's really hot must ask for it. The menu includes items such as fried rice, beef, and shish kebab. The lunch menu offers 12 items including meat, vegetables, rice, and soup. Restaurant Indonesia has received excellent reviews. Weekend reservations suggested. Lunch and dinner. Closed Monday.

ROSE & CROWN PUB
1503 - 4th St. SW, Calgary
403/244-7757
$$ **SW**

A British-style pub, the Rose & Crown dishes up generous portions of food from its extensive, moderately priced menu. A traditional favorite is halibut

and chips. There's a wide range of other items such as ribs, jambalaya, Royal Thai chicken stir-fry, bruschetta, and baguettes. More than 30 draft beers are on tap at this completely renovated pub, where you'll find wood-burning stoves and a library. Lunch and dinner. ♿

SAN DOMENICO RISTORANTE
1800 - 4th St. SW, Calgary
403/228-1126
$$ **SW**

Pasta combinations are a favorite at San Domenico, which serves western and international cuisine with an Italian flair. Guests create their own pastas by adding items such as chicken, Italian sausage, smoked salmon, and vegetables. This is a classy, comfortable, casual restaurant with lots of windows and a great patio. San Domenico has received excellent restaurant reviews. Reservations for large groups. Lunch, dinner. Closed Sunday. ♿

SAN REMO RISTORANTE
Oak Bay Plaza

107, 2515 - 90th Ave. SW, Calgary
403/281-2482
$$ SW

San Remo serves Northern Italian cuisine with flair and elegance. The food is strongly influenced by southern French cooking—lots of cream, herbs, butter, and wine sauces. Fresh seafood is the house specialty. The veal and lobster medallions in a sherry cream garlic sauce are one of the more popular menu items. At San Remo, diners can choose four courses since portions are smaller. Non-smoking. Reservations recommended.

SAVOIR FARE
907 - 17th Ave. SW, Calgary
403/245-6040
$$$ SW

Fresh salmon burgers seasoned with capers and tarragon; marinated roasted chicken; daily fresh sheet desserts—this and more is what you'll find at Savoir Fare's intimate dining room. Dishes here feature a creative blending of spices, flavors, and ingredients. Savoir Fare, which has received numerous accolades, also offers some vegetarian selections. Non-smoking. Reservations a must. Lunch, dinner, weekend brunch. &

STEPHEN AVENUE SOUP CO.
Food Court, Chinook Centre
6455 Macleod Tr. SW, Calgary
403/252-4429
$ SW

One of the most popular items at Stephen Avenue Soup Co. is the homemade Stephen Avenue vegetable soup, chock full of a variety of vegetables and pasta, with a tomato soup base. Besides soups, Stephen Avenue also serves sandwiches and salads. Lunch and dinner. Credit cards not accepted; no reservations. &

SULTAN'S TENT
909 - 17th Ave. SW, Calgary
403/244-2333
$$$ SW

Dining at the Sultan's Tent is a culinary adventure and a feast for all the senses. Sit on cushions and eat subtly spiced Moroccan cuisine with your fingers (cutlery is provided if you insist). Wall hangings and the strains of North African music add to the exotic atmosphere. Popular items include tajines (Moroccan stew), lamb, chicken, beef, and couscous. Reservations recommended. Dinner. Closed Sunday.

THAI SA-ON RESTAURANT
351 - 10th Ave. SW, Calgary
403/264-3526
$$ SW

Authentic Thai cuisine is on the menu of the family-owned and -operated Thai Sa-On Restaurant. The wide selection of curries, from mild to spicy, is always popular. The menu offers a separate vegetarian section. Wash it down with authentic Thai beer. Reservations recommended. Lunch, dinner. Closed Sunday.

WAINWRIGHT HOTEL
Heritage Park Historical Village
1900 Heritage Dr. SW, Calgary
403/259-1900
$ SW

Experience Calgary's pioneer days with brunch at the Wainwright Hotel. The Sunday buffet brunch starts the Sunday after Canadian Thanksgiving weekend in October, continuing through the Sunday before Victoria Day in May. At the redecorated hotel, which dates back to 1910, the only modern things you'll see are place settings and tablecloths. Brunch includes sausages, bacon, eggs, pancakes, hash browns, and croissants. Non-smoking. No reservations. &

NORTHEAST CALGARY

ERCOLE RISTORANTE ITALIANO
202 - 16th Ave. NE, Calgary
403/230-4447
$$ **NE**

It doesn't matter whether you're wearing jeans or a tux, this is a place you'll feel comfortable. Ercole's look is elegant and warm, with checkered tablecloths, award-winning Italian food, and excellent choice of Italian wines. The bread is homemade, as is some of the pasta. The menu includes veal, chicken, steak, and seafood. Reservations recommended. Lunch and dinner. &

HUMPTY'S FAMILY RESTAURANTS
102, 920 - 36th St. NE, Calgary
403/273-6063
$ **NE**

Humpty's menu has earned a "Best in Family Dining" accolade from the Alberta Restaurant and Food Services Association. While this full-service family restaurant boasts a unique and varied breakfast menu, it also offers lunch and dinner. Food is fresh, tasty, and plentiful—good value for your money. Service is quick and pleasant. Several of the Humpty's restaurants located throughout Calgary are open 24 hours a day.

JOEY'S ONLY
350, 3545 - 32nd Ave. NE, Calgary
403/291-5595
$–$$ **NE**

Known for fish and chips, this casual family restaurant serves a broad selection of fresh seafood at affordable prices. There's everything from shrimp, salmon, trout, and mussels to crab legs and calamari. While primarily a seafood eatery, Joey's Only also offers chicken and steak dishes, soup, and salad. No reservations. Lunch and dinner. There are several Joey's Only restaurants in Calgary. &

SANTORINI GREEK TAVERNA
1502 Centre St. NE, Calgary
403/276-8363
$$ **NE**

This is a popular Greek restaurant conjuring up the warmth and conviviality of the sun-drenched Greek islands. Roast lamb is the house specialty. Menu items include souvlaki, shish kebabs (with beef, chicken, prawns, or scallops), and moussaka. There's lively Mediterranean entertainment Friday and Saturday evenings featuring belly dancing. Reservations recommended. Lunch and dinner.

NORTHWEST CALGARY

BERT'S MOUNTAIN MECCA CAFÉ
10231 West Valley Rd. NW, Calgary
Trans-Canada Highway West
403/286-4891
$ **NW**

Inexpensive mountains of good food are what you'll find at this diner located south of the highway. Bert's popular traditional breakfast is available throughout the day. The lunch menu includes burgers and diner-style sandwiches. Rotating specials are offered for dinner, including full roast beef dinners, stir-fries, and a number of vegetarian items. Breakfast, lunch, dinner.

BLUE HOUSE CAFÉ
2, 3843 - 19th St. NW, Calgary
403/284-9111
$$–$$$ **NW**

Seafood is the specialty at Blue House Café, which offers fine Latin American cuisine as well as steak, chicken, and pasta. A popular dish is the Blue House Delight: scallops and prawns cooked in a creamy wine sauce with herbs. Diners enjoy live Latin American guitar music several nights a week. Reservations recommended. Dinner. Closed Monday.

THE CHEESECAKE CAFÉ & BAKERY
5615 Northland Dr. NW, Calgary
403/247-2407
$$ NW

Steaks, stir-fries, and of course cheesecakes are popular at this casual family restaurant, which serves 210 items. One unique menu item is the clam chowder soup and mushrooms in a bread bowl. The Cheesecake Café, which boasts 20 kinds of cheesecakes, has won the Calgary Herald Readers' Choice best dessert award for several years. Children's menu. Lunch, dinner. No reservations. &

GINGER BEEF PEKING HOUSE RESTAURANT
Brentwood Village Mall
3802 Brentwood Rd. NW, Calgary
403/282-5090
$$ NW

Ginger beef is hot stuff at Ginger Beef Peking House Restaurant—hot spicy and hot with customers. It has won a number of Calgary Herald Readers' Choice awards. The menu includes items such as sliced chicken with satay sauce on a hot plate, pork and sparerib dishes, and grilled beef dumplings. Specials include Peking duck in a three-course meal. Reservations for larger groups only. Lunch, dinner. There is also a southeast location. &

ISLAND EXPERIENCE
314A - 10th St. NW, Calgary

403/270-4550
$$ NW

Visit Island Experience in Calgary's popular Kensington district for a taste of Caribbean cuisine. On the menu is roti (flatbread) filled with curried beef, chicken, lamb, shrimp, or goat. Also offered is a variety of vegetarian rotis, pies, and more. Island Experience emphasizes ingredients without preservatives or additives. This is a casual little restaurant with a bright and cheerful decor. Non-smoking. (Smoking permitted on patio only.)

KENSINGTON BERLINER
1414 Kensington Rd. NW, Calgary
283-0771
$$ NW

Kensington Berliner specializes in northern German cuisine and prides itself on warm, friendly service along with excellent food. It's known for specials such as the tender rouladen of beef and breaded pork schnitzels. Desserts are made in-house and include apple strudel. The setting is cozy, homey, with classical music playing in the background. Lunch and dinner; closed Monday. &

THE LAZY LOAF & KETTLE
8 Parkdale Circle NW, Calgary
403/270-7810
$ NW

The delectable scent of cinnamon buns and coffee wafts out the doors of The Lazy Loaf & Kettle, a bustling little cappuccino bar and bakery. In addition to the tempting breads and desserts, it's known for soups, sandwiches, and salads. Sandwiches are stacked high with The Lazy Loaf's thickly sliced bread. There's an outdoor patio. Non-smoking. Breakfast, lunch, dinner. No reservations. Also located in Glenbow Museum.

MAURYA FINE EAST INDIAN CUISINE
1204 Kensington Rd. NW, Calgary
403/270-3133
$$ **NW**

This small, elegant restaurant is always busy and no wonder. Maurya serves delicious food seasoned with spices and sauces ranging from subtle to spicy hot, with a wide variety of meat and vegetarian dishes. The lunch buffet offers a large assortment of hot dishes and light, delicately flavored fresh-from-the-oven bread. Non-smoking. Reservations recommended. Lunch and dinner. &

ORIENTAL PALACE RESTAURANT
9 Parkdale Circle NW, Calgary
403/283-5564
$–$$ **NW**

The food is fresh and delicious, the service fast and friendly. Oriental Palace serves Chinese cuisine in an unpretentious restaurant that's always filled with customers. Dishes encompass a wide range of Chinese cooking with beef, pork, spareribs, chicken, seafood, hot plate, and hot pot dishes. Customers who want special dishes can preorder. Lunch, dinner. &

PIZZA SPOT
4600 Crowchild Tr. NW, main floor, Calgary
403/247-6333
$$ **NW**

This busy little restaurant is known for its great pizza. A couple of examples are the Pizza Spot Pride and house special. Pizza Spot Pride consists of bacon, pepperoni, tomato, mushrooms, onion, green peppers, black olives, pineapple, and feta cheese. The house special comes with ham, shrimp, pepperoni, green pepper, tomato, and black olives. No reservations. Lunch, dinner.

Calgary CVB/Gerald Vander Pyl

5

SIGHTS AND ATTRACTIONS

Every year, Calgary attracts millions of visitors of all ages. Whether you're look-ing for culture, history, or just plain fun, it's served year-round in Cowtown. You can catch a concert at the Centre for Performing Arts, take a wild ride on one of the thrilling screamers at Calaway Park, or travel to distant planets at the Calgary Science Centre. Visit in early July and you'll find the whole city caught up in Stampede fever. Following are some of the most popular attractions Cal-gary has to offer. There's something for everyone, so select one or two to hit each day and join the fun!

DOWNTOWN CALGARY

CALGARY CENTRE FOR PERFORMING ARTS
205 - 8th Ave. SE, Calgary
403/294-7455   **DT**

Situated in the heart of downtown, the Calgary Centre for Performing Arts fills an entire city block. This beautiful $100-million facility houses five performance venues including the Jack Singer Concert Hall (2,000 seats), Max Bell Theatre (750 seats), Martha Cohen Theatre (450 seats), Engineered Air Theatre (185 seats), and the Big Secret Theatre (180 seats). The magnificent Carthy Organ,

the largest concert hall organ in Western Canada, awes visitors to the Jack Singer Concert Hall. Tours are available for $2. (See also Chapter 11, "Performing Arts," p. 169.)

CALGARY CHINESE CULTURAL CENTRE
197 - 1st St. SW, Calgary
403/262-5071   **DT**

The impressive Calgary Chinese Cul-tural Centre dominates the view east from Eau Claire Market. The blue tur-ret of the six-story Great Cultural Hall is a prominent feature of this magnifi-cent architectural achievement. The Great Cultural Hall is modeled after the Temple of Heaven in Beijing; it took Chinese artisans more than 100,000 work-hours to create the beautiful tilework inside. The inner dome sports 561 dragons and 40 phoenix. The centre includes a large authentic Chinese restaurant, a cultural museum displaying priceless artifacts and ceramic arts, an art gallery, an acupuncture centre, and a gift shop. It also features ongoing exhibitions, festivals, and special events throughout the year. Call ahead to arrange a guided tour. Hours: Museum daily 11–5; building daily 9–9. Museum admission: $2 adults, $1 students and seniors. (See also Chapter 7, "Museums and Galleries," p. 111.)

CALGARY POLICE INTERPRETIVE CENTRE
316 - 7th Ave. SE, 2nd level, Calgary
403/268-4566 DT
One of Calgary's newest attractions, the Calgary Police Interpretive Centre demonstrates how fascinating real-life crime can be. This unique hands-on facility uses interactive exhibits to show you how to solve a crime while you explore the issues of criminal activity and its consequences. It offers visitors the opportunity to safely investigate the underground elements of life in the city. You can learn about the history of the Calgary Police Service, match wits with the computer/video exhibits, or put on a set of headphones and drive a virtual police cruiser. Not

for the squeamish, the centre delivers disturbingly realistic scenes of street violence, prostitution, guns, drugs, and domestic violence. Admission: $2 adults, free for seniors and youths. Not suitable for young children.

CALGARY SCIENCE CENTRE
701 - 11th St. SW, Calgary
403/221-3700 DT
The Science Centre brings science to life with hands-on exhibits and dazzling demonstrations. Bring along the whole family and introduce them to the fun side of science with interactive displays that feature exhibits from around the world. Take a trip to the stars or travel to distant planets and constellations. The wonders of nature and mysteries of the universe unfold while you relax in comfort in the newly renovated multimedia Discovery Dome, which features computer graphics and a superb sound system. Before you leave the centre, pop into Gizmos, a gift shop offering unique toys, books, and games with a science theme. Also on-site is the Pleiades Theatre presenting live mystery productions (see Chapter 6, "Kids' Stuff," p. 99, and Chapter 11, "Performing Arts," p. 159, for more information). Hours: Vary by season. Admission: $15 families, $4.50 adults and youth, $4 seniors and children 12 and under.

CALGARY TOWER
101 - 9th Ave. SW, Calgary

TRIVIA

Peregrine falcons, an endangered species, have nested in Calgary since the mid-1980s. Up to three pairs have taken up residence in the city. Pairs have nested among the highrises downtown, on a tower at the University of Calgary, and in Fish Creek Provincial Park in south Calgary.

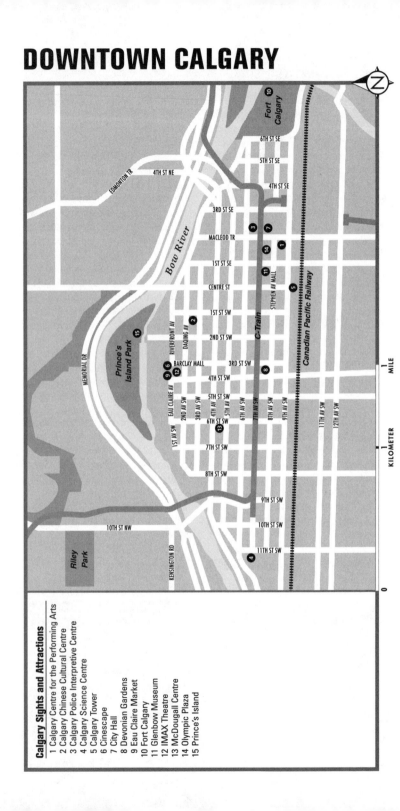

DOWNTOWN CALGARY

Calgary Sights and Attractions

1 Calgary Centre for the Performing Arts
2 Calgary Chinese Cultural Centre
3 Calgary Police Interpretive Centre
4 Calgary Science Centre
5 Calgary Tower
6 Cinescape
7 City Hall
8 Devonian Gardens
9 Eau Claire Market
10 Fort Calgary
11 Glenbow Museum
12 IMAX Theatre
13 McDougall Centre
14 Olympic Plaza
15 Prince's Island

403/266-7171　　　　　　　　　　**DT**

A city landmark for 30 years, the Calgary Tower stands 190 meters (623 feet) high and features two high-speed elevators that whisk visitors to the top in 62 seconds. The Panorama Room offers a unique dining experience with a 360-degree, panoramic view of the city skyline and mountains beyond. The elegant revolving restaurant makes one complete revolution each hour.

One level above the Panorama Room is the Observation Terrace, open daily for sightseeing. It features a snack bar and souvenir shop as well as state-of-the-art telescopes and specially tinted glass to facilitate picture-taking. There is also an interactive video display featuring 16 venues describing Calgary and its sights. Tops Bar and Grill is located at the highest level, offering light meals and late-night snacks in a casual, intimate setting. Hours: Daily 8 a.m. to 10 p.m. Admission: $5.50 adults, $3.75 youths 13–18, $2.50 children 3–12.

CINESCAPE
Eau Claire Market, 2nd floor
3rd Street and 1st Avenue SW,
Calgary
403/265-4511　　　　　　　　　　**DT**

Cinescape is an 18,000-square-foot interactive entertainment centre for the whole family. Challenge your friends and family to interactive sports, driving, or shooting simulation games. Virtual reality games are also available. Internet access, online PC games, and a restaurant will satisfy the needs of any cyber-nut. The lounge has five pool tables. You can avoid the line at the cinema next door by ordering movie tickets from your server. Hours: 11:30 a.m.–midnight Mon–Thur, 11:30 a.m.–1 a.m. Fri and Sat, 11:30 a.m.–10 p.m. Sun.

CITY HALL
Macleod Trail and 7th Avenue SE,
Calgary
403/268-2111　　　　　　　　　　**DT**

Just after the turn of the century, Calgary decided to replace the wood frame and clapboard City Hall, which also served as police station, school, library, and fire hall. The design for the new building was a mixture of styles with an emphasis on texture, grandeur, and formality. It was

Calgary Chinese Cultural Centre, page 80

Calgary CVB/Mike Ridewood

officially opened on June 26, 1911. This sandstone beauty has recently undergone extensive renovations to the tune of more than $10 million. The architects used the spirit and design of the 1911 building to guide the reconstruction while assuring it is a fully functioning office building meeting today's building and safety codes. The original four-faced clock, which tolls every hour and every half-hour, is wound once a week.

CITY TOURS
Brewster Transportation & Tours
808 Centre St. SE, Calgary
403/221-8250 DT
From May 15 to October 15, Brewster offers tours of Calgary city sights. Tours, lasting 3½ to four hours, introduce visitors to some of the historical and modern highlights of the Gateway to the Canadian Rockies. The 55-passenger motorcoach tours you around to some of the facilities constructed for the 1988 Winter Olympic Games; the fare includes admission to Canada Olympic Park and a ride up the Olympic Ski Jump tower for a great view of the city from the enclosed observation level. The tour also visits Fort Calgary, the location of the original Mounted Police post and now an historic and interpretive centre. Daily departures leave from a number of downtown hotels. Fare: $42 adults, $21 children 6–15, free for children 5 and under if sharing a seat with an adult. Brewster also offers tours to Banff, Jasper, Lake Louise, and the Columbia Icefield.

In December, Brewster traditionally runs 2½-hour **Christmas Light Tours** that take in the spectacular light displays of Confederation Park, Lake Bonavista, Lake Midnapore, Lake Sundance, Olympic Plaza, and McDougall Centre. Fare: $10 adults, $8 seniors and children.

DEVONIAN GARDENS
TD Square, 4th level
8th Avenue and 3rd Street SW, Calgary
403/268-5207 DT
Take a break from the downtown hustle and bustle and cool your heels in the relaxing atmosphere of this indoor garden on the top level of TD Square. Hours: 9–9. Admission: Free. See Chapter 8, "Parks and Gardens," p. 124, for more information.

Ten Birds Commonly Seen Around Calgary
by Mairi Babey of Inglewood Bird Sanctuary #63

Five Common Winter Birds:
- *Black-billed magpie*
- *Black-capped chickadee*
- *Blue jay*
- *Bohemian waxwing*
- *Mallard*

Five Common Summer Birds:
- *American robin*
- *Baltimore oriole*
- *Canada goose*
- *Swainson's hawk*
- *Yellow warbler*

Old city hall and the new municipal building, page 83

EAU CLAIRE MARKET
Barclay Mall
2nd Avenue and 3rd Street SW,
Calgary
403/264-6450   DT

This area includes a market, water park, and the beautiful Eau Claire YMCA (exercise equipment, pool, health club, and aerobic and fitness classes). The huge and colorful market has been compared to Granville Island in Vancouver, but it has its own distinctive flavor. It encompasses retail and restaurant establishments, cinemas, and the IMAX Theatre. The food market offers fresh pies, bagels, fruit and vegetables, seafood, meats, fudge, deli, wine, flowers, and exotic imports. Unique locally owned specialty stores offer unusual gift items, original fashions, and works of art. Some very popular restaurants (Barley Mill and Hard Rock Café) feature outdoor patios that offer great people-watching vantage points in good weather.

FORT CALGARY
750 - 9th Ave. SE, Calgary

403/290-1875   DT

In 1875 the North West Mounted Police built Fort Calgary at the confluence of the Bow and Elbow Rivers. Could any of them have foreseen that their efforts would develop into a city of 750,000 in just over a century? Along with the 1875 fort reconstruction, the site of Fort Calgary offers interactive interpretation and hands-on family activities. Costumed interpreters regale visitors with tales of the site and its people. The site is set on 16 hectares (40 acres) of riverside park and includes an Interpretive Centre. The Deane House Historic Site and Restaurant is worth a visit, open 11–2 Wed–Sun. It was built in 1906 and was moved across the frozen Elbow River, a remarkable feat in 1929. The Hunt House, behind the Deane House, is thought to be the oldest structure in Calgary on its original site. Hours: Daily 9–5 May–Oct. Rates: $3 adults, $1.50 youth, $2.50 seniors, free for children.

GLENBOW MUSEUM
130 - 9th Ave. SE, Calgary

403/268-4100 DT

Visit the Glenbow Museum for a journey into Western Canadian heritage, celebrating pioneer life and that of the First Nations peoples. Then take an exciting voyage into other lands and cultures from around the globe. Displays encompass more than 240,000 permanent items, augmented by temporary exhibitions.

Don't miss the Glenbow's art collection featuring work by contemporary Alberta artists and some of Canada's noted early artists. Special exhibitions introduce paintings, sculpture, and photography from international collections.

In the Alberta Children's Museum on the fourth floor you'll find hands-on activities, games, quizzes, and handouts that appeal to the younger crowd. (See also Chapter 6, "Kids' Stuff," p. 102.)

Hours: Daily 9–5 May–Aug; closed Mon Sept–April. Admission: $8 adults, $6 students and seniors, free for children under 7, $25 families.

IMAX THEATRE
Eau Claire Market
2nd Avenue and 3rd Street SW,
Calgary
403/974-4629 DT

Journey to the brink of a volcano; dive into icy water in the Antarctic with penguins; migrate with a vast herd of wildebeests in the Serengeti; perch atop the green canopy of a rain forest. These are some of the breathtaking images you can experience on a 5½-story screen enhanced by a superb digital sound system. The IMAX Theatre takes you to remote locations in a powerful and involving film experience. Centrally located in the Eau Claire Market, the IMAX presents matinées every day and double features every evening. Admission: Matinées $7.50 adults, $5.50 children; double features $11.50 adults, $9.50 children.

MCDOUGALL CENTRE
455 - 6th St. SW, Calgary
403/297-8687 DT

Built in 1906, this beautiful sandstone building was originally built as a school, becoming an historic site in 1982. Today it is the southern headquarters and conference centre for the provincial government. Its beautifully landscaped grounds are a popular location for outdoor concerts. Tours are free. Hours: 8:30–4:30 weekdays.

OLYMPIC PLAZA
Corner of Macleod Trail and 7th
Avenue SW, Calgary
403/268-5207 DT

Across from City Hall, this downtown park was built for the medal

TIP

Don't try driving downtown on the morning of the Stampede parade, as much of the downtown core is sealed off. If you're planning on watching the parade, ride the city transit or park on the fringes of downtown and walk.

History of the Calgary Exhibition and Stampede

While the Calgary Exhibition & Stampede is now a huge event filling ten days, it can trace its roots back to a small agricultural fair held on October 9, 1886. This was the first of its kind held in the city, organized under the auspices of the Calgary Agricultural Society, and drew crowds of about 500 to see the livestock, flower, and vegetable exhibits. Many years and several name changes later, the Calgary Industrial Exhibition had become a national, annual event, but by 1912 it was losing steam and needed a new spark of life.

That spark was provided by Guy Weadick, a trick roper who played Wild West shows, vaudeville, and traveling rodeos. Long on ideas but short on money, his dream of staging "the biggest frontier days the world has ever seen" met with interest from E. L. Richardson, the general manager of the Calgary Industrial Exhibition. Unfortunately, the $100,000 bank roll necessary to stage such an event scared Richardson off, but four prominent Calgarians (George Lane, A. E. Cross, A. J. MacLean, and Patrick Burns) came to the rescue. Known as the "Big Four," these men agreed to back the project, and the first "Stampede" was held in September of that year. Opening performances were attended by more than 14,000 enthusiastic Calgarians, but a number of unforeseen expenses prevented the Stampede's financial success.

World War I diverted Weadick's attention away from the Stampede, but in the spring of 1919 he returned to try again. The Big Four again played a prominent role in financing the Stampede, which thereafter became an annual event. In 1922, Richardson suggested merging the Exhibition with the Stampede on a trial basis. At this point Weadick added chuckwagon racing to the lineup of events, and the rest is history.

As general manager of the Calgary Exhibition and Stampede, Weadick encouraged everyone to don western garb and businesses to decorate their store fronts. This is still a part of Stampede spirit today.

Each year the Stampede gets bigger and better, and in 1976 it passed the 1 million mark for visitors.

ceremonies of the 1988 Winter Olympics. The Legacy Wall features plaques on each pillar commemorating medal winners. The plaza is a summer refuge in the core of the city with free noon-hour concerts. In winter, tie on your skates and go for a spin around the rink.

PRINCE'S ISLAND
4th Street and 1st Avenue SW, Calgary
403/268-3888 DT
Prince's Island encompasses 20 hectares (50 acres) of natural beauty situated in the centre of downtown. See Chapter 8, "Parks and Gardens," p. 122, for more information.

STAMPEDE PARADE
403/289-0049 or 403/289-6642 DT
For free Stampede fun, take in the Stampede Parade on the first Friday in July. It's the kick-off to the entire ten-day event and guaranteed to get you in the spirit. Whether you come to watch the marching bands, Scottish pipe bands, floats, clowns, Mounties on horseback, or First Nations representatives in colorful garb, you'll enjoy the parade's wide appeal. The two-hour parade begins at 9 a.m., but people start staking out their spots along the route at about 7:30. Lawn chairs and cowboy attire are de rigeur. You can also secure a spot in the bleachers for $13 by calling one of the above numbers, or you can book a seat on parade day by hailing one of the people in bright yellow hats. The parade route begins at 2nd Street and 6th Avenue SE and travels west along 6th to 10th Street SW, where it turns south. Then it covers three blocks before heading east along 9th Avenue SW to end at the corner of 2nd Street and 9th Avenue SE.

SOUTHEAST CALGARY

BOW VALLEY RANCH
Fish Creek Provincial Park
First right turn after entering the park at the south end of Bow Bottom Trail, Calgary
403/297-5293 SE
In 1896, an aristocratic rancher named William Roper Hull built the impressive sandstone Ranch House in what is now Fish Creek Provincial Park. Bought by Senator Patrick Burns in 1902, it remained in the possession of the Burns family until it was purchased by the provincial government in 1973. Empty and abandoned since 1978, the Ranch House has fallen into disrepair but a move is afoot to restore it to its turn-of-the-century grandeur with outdoor gardens, courtyard, pavilion, and patio. Dining rooms and archival displays also figure in the plans. The adjacent interpretive centre exhibits displays about wildlife and the history of the area.

CALGARY EXHIBITION AND STAMPEDE
Stampede Park
Corner of Macleod Trail and 25th Avenue SE, Calgary
403/261-0101 or 800/661-1260 SE
For ten days starting the first Friday in July, Calgarians and visitors don their jeans, boots, and cowboy hats and try out their best "Yaaa-hoo!" Stampede spirit invades Calgary, and the normally friendly city becomes even friendlier. North America's largest rodeo, Calgary's annual gathering of cowboys and cowgirls celebrating Alberta's farming and ranching history is the Greatest Outdoor Show on Earth. Pause on a corner with a map in your hand and someone is bound to ask if you need help. This city-wide celebration includes free pancake

breakfasts galore, country western music, and dance lessons at many of the bars in town.

The main Stampede action is at the Stampede grounds in Victoria Park district. It features top professional cowboys competing in rodeo events, world-famous chuckwagon races, evening stage shows, an authentic Indian village, midway rides, and an agricultural fair. Arrive early in the day to avoid the longest lines and stay late for the fireworks if you have the stamina. General admission: $8 adults, $4 minors and seniors. Tickets to infield events and midway rides are purchased separately. You'd be wise to book your tickets before arriving in the city.

CANADIAN AIRLINES SADDLEDOME
555 Saddledome Rise SE, Calgary
403/777-2177 **SE**

This facility is used as a venue when large crowds are expected. Home of the NHL Calgary Flames Hockey Club and the WHL's Calgary Hitmen, it also hosts circuses, concerts, ice shows, and motor sports events. Each of the 20,000 seats offers a good view of the action because of the unique pillarless construction. Tours are available May through September if prearranged.

INGLEWOOD BIRD SANCTUARY
3020 Sanctuary Rd. SE, Calgary
403/269-6688 **SE**

An urban oasis situated just 5 kilometers (3 miles) from downtown Calgary, the Inglewood Bird Sanctuary provides visitors with a quiet refuge from bustling city life. This 38-hectare (94-acre) park offers some 2½ kilometers (1½ miles) of level trails for people to experience riverine forest, wetlands, and grassland habitats. More than 270 species of birds, 300 species of plants, and several kinds of mammals have been spotted in the area. Most of the bird species are observed during spring and fall migrations (especially May and August) while others are year-round residents or summer or winter visitors. The public is welcome to visit the sanctuary during daylight hours.

Olympic Plaza, page 86

Calgary CVB/John Sharpe

Chinatown

Since 1910, this colourful neighborhood has drawn Chinese businesses and customers to its corner of downtown. Bordered by the Bow River and 4th Avenue SE, it encompasses food stores, bakeries, and import stores. On a warm day you may find street vendors selling fresh Oriental vegetables. The district also offers numerous Chinese and Vietnamese restaurants, most of which serve daily dim sum. Dragon City Mall, Canada's largest Chinese mall, offers a variety of merchandise including clothing, jewelry, gifts, and herbs, as well as housing the huge Regency Palace restaurant, which seats 750.

Visitor centre hours: Weekdays 9–4; weekends 10–3:30. Admission: Free.

LAKE SIKOME
Fish Creek Provincial Park, Calgary
403/297-5293 SE
This man-made lake at the southern edge of Fish Creek Park is hugely popular on hot summer days. Surrounded by sandy beaches, it is open to the public for swimming in summer and skating in winter. Playgrounds, picnic tables, and biking and walking trails are available, and concession, washrooms, showers, and change rooms open on a seasonal basis. To reach the lake, follow Bow Bottom Trail SE to its most southern end and continue south into the park until you see signs to Lake Sikome.

RAINBOW BALLOONS
7136 Fisher St. SE, Calgary
403/259-3154 SE
For a unique perspective, float over Calgary's skyline in a hot air balloon and enjoy a bird's-eye view of the majestic Rockies, rolling foothills, and the lush river valley. Rainbow Balloons takes you aloft in a colorful, seven-story balloon for a memorable flight among the gods. Included in the package is a light champagne brunch at the end of your airborne adventure. Flight duration is approximately 1½ hours. These tours are weather-dependent. Large groups can be accommodated if booked in advance. Fares: $150 one passenger; $145 each if two passengers; $140 each if four or more.

SAM LIVINGSTON FISH HATCHERY
1440 - 17A St. SE, Calgary
403/297-6561 SE
Located in Pearce Estate City Park, the Sam Livingston Fish Hatchery rears rainbow trout, brook trout, brown trout, and cutthroat trout to stock approximately 300 lakes in Alberta. Fish stocking plays an important role in conserving and enhancing fish populations that would otherwise be depleted by increased resource use, habitat loss, and degradation of natural waters by logging, mining, agriculture, and other land use practices.

To see the hatchery in action, you can take a self-guided tour or book a guided group tour. Interactive displays include an explanation of fish biology, a description of each of the trout species and how to distinguish them from each other, and fish population distribution maps. You can look down on storage tanks of smaller fry and check out larger fish up close in aquariums. Video also available for viewing. Hours: Mon–Fri 10–4 year-round, plus weekends and holidays 1–5 (April–Sept only). Admission: Free.

SOUTHWEST CALGARY

BRAGG CREEK TOURS & TRAVEL
P.O. Box 980, Bragg Creek
403/949-3400   SW
Located 30 minutes southwest of Calgary at the foot of the Rocky Mountains, Bragg Creek is a lively artisans' community. Bragg Creek Tours & Travel organizes year-round day tours for groups or individuals in and around the area at the gateway to the

Calgary Tower, page 81

Calgary CVB/Calgary Tower

Elbow River Valley section of Kananaskis Country. View a powwow or taste Native cuisine at the Steak Pit. Catch sight of wildlife and birds on a Soft Adventure or Ecotourism package. Try rafting, canoeing, trail rides, mountain biking, hiking with llamas, or golfing in summer. Experience dogsledding, cross-country and downhill skiing, or ski touring in winter. Bragg Creek Tours offers pick-up service from some Calgary hotels.

CALAWAY PARK
10 km (6 mi) west of the city on
Trans-Canada Highway, Calgary
403/240-3824   SW
Twenty-four exciting rides and 20 eateries are found on the grounds of Calaway Park, Western Canada's largest outdoor family amusement park. Other fun includes daily live musical shows put on by Calaway's resident entertainment troupe, an 18,000-square-foot maze, ball crawl, and western miniature golf. Calaway also offers an RV park and campground for travelers. Hours: Weekends only 10–8 mid-May–mid-June, daily 10–8 mid-June–early Sept, and weekends only 11–6 Sept–mid-Oct. Admission: $50 family, $12 children 3–6, $17.50 adults and children 7+. General gate admission (which excludes rides) is $8.

CANADA OLYMPIC PARK (COP)
88 Canada Olympic Rd. SW,
Calgary
403/247-5452   SW
At the former site of freestyle skiing, bobsleigh, luge, and ski jumping events during the 1988 Olympic Winter Games, you can ride a chairlift to the top of the 90-meter ski jump tower (the highest point in Calgary) for a panoramic view of the city and mountains or speed down the bobsleigh

GREATER CALGARY

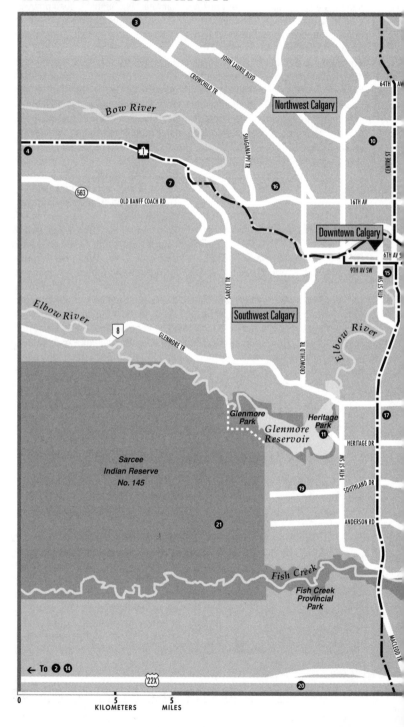

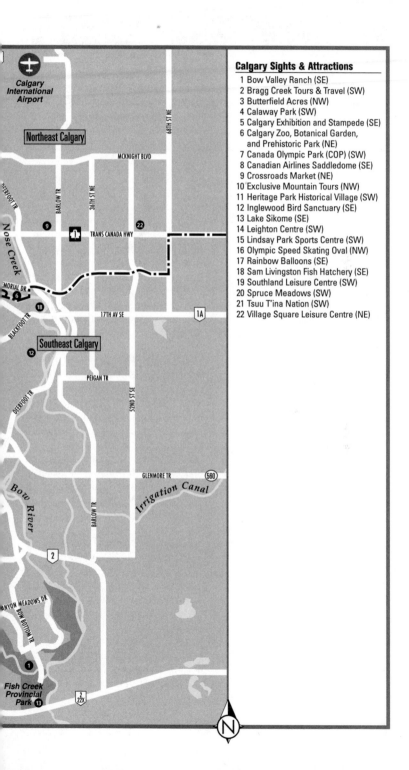

Calgary Sights & Attractions

1 Bow Valley Ranch (SE)
2 Bragg Creek Tours & Travel (SW)
3 Butterfield Acres (NW)
4 Calaway Park (SW)
5 Calgary Exhibition and Stampede (SE)
6 Calgary Zoo, Botanical Garden, and Prehistoric Park (NE)
7 Canada Olympic Park (COP) (SW)
8 Canadian Airlines Saddledome (SE)
9 Crossroads Market (NE)
10 Exclusive Mountain Tours (NW)
11 Heritage Park Historical Village (SW)
12 Inglewood Bird Sanctuary (SE)
13 Lake Sikome (SE)
14 Leighton Centre (SW)
15 Lindsay Park Sports Centre (SW)
16 Olympic Speed Skating Oval (NW)
17 Rainbow Balloons (SE)
18 Sam Livingston Fish Hatchery (SE)
19 Southland Leisure Centre (SW)
20 Spruce Meadows (SW)
21 Tsuu T'ina Nation (SW)
22 Village Square Leisure Centre (NE)

run on the Bobsleigh Bullet. Thrill-seekers can experience the speed and excitement of luging winter or summer on an iced track. For $13, sliders take off from the bottom third of the track, reaching speeds of 40 km/h (25 mph). Tours of the tower and guided bus tours of the park are available. The Naturbahn Teahouse is open from Monday to Saturday for lunch and afternoon tea as well as Sunday brunch. Also on-site is the Olympic Hall of Fame & Museum. See Chapter 7, "Museums and Galleries," p. 111, for more information.

HERITAGE PARK HISTORICAL VILLAGE
Corner of 14th Street and Heritage Drive SW, Calgary
403/259-1900   SW
Travel back in time as you stroll down turn-of-the-century Main Street at Canada's largest living historical village. On your visit to this 27-hectare (66-acre) park, you can ride the rails behind a thundering steam locomotive, sometimes accompanied by the strains of a barbershop quartet. Board the S. S. *Moyie* for a cruise around the Glenmore reservoir on a picturesque sternwheeler. Share in the spirit that developed the Canadian West when you visit the early settlers' homes, post office, bakery, blacksmith shop, and other reminders of the past. The antique amusement park offers thrills

for the whole family while the penny candy shop and ice cream parlor entice those with a sweet tooth. You can savor some down-home cooking in the Wainwright Hotel, which offers brunch on Sundays. Hours: Daily mid-May–early Sept, then weekends only through Oct. Special events planned some weekends in Nov and Dec. General admission: $10 adults, $6 children. Admission including rides: $16 adults, $12 children.

LEIGHTON CENTRE
West on Highway 22X, then follow signs south on 773, Calgary
403/931-3633   SW
This is the former home of artist A. C. Leighton. It sits on 80 acres of gorgeous ranchlands property and hosts art exhibitions year-round, as well as art camps and classes. Museum and gallery hours: 10–4 Mon–Fri and some weekends. Travel SW outside Calgary's city limits to find Leighton Centre.

LINDSAY PARK SPORTS CENTRE
2225 Macleod Tr. SW, Calgary
403/233-8393   SW
Encompassing 1.2 hectares (3 acres) and standing ten stories high, the Lindsay Park Sports Centre is a multisport facility featuring an international-class pool, dive tank, running track, weight room, fitness classes, and fitness equipment for enthusiasts at every level. There is also a sports

medicine clinic and cardiac wellness clinic. Drop-in visitors are welcome and tours are available upon request. Hours: 5 a.m.–11 p.m. Mon–Fri, 6 a.m.–10 p.m. Sat, 7 a.m.–10 p.m. Sun.

SOUTHLAND LEISURE CENTRE
200 Southland Dr. SW, Calgary
403/251-3505   SW
No matter the weather, your whole family will enjoy a day at this water park. See Chapter 10, "Sports and Recreation," p. 156, for information.

SPRUCE MEADOWS
R.R. 9, west of the city on
Highway 22X, Calgary
403/974-4200   SW

A prestigious equestrian show jumping facility just south of the city, Spruce Meadows is internationally renowned and hosts the Masters (mid-September), the toniest show jumping championship in the world, offering more than $1.5 million in prize money. It also hosts the National (early June), Canada One (late June), and the North American (early July). The accompanying Country Fair and Marketplace offers artwork, entertainment, and commercial exhibits ranging from hand-painted clothing to ostriches. Excellent training and breeding facilities. Admission: $5 adults, free for children and seniors. Visitors may

---

Alberta Dinosaurs

The meat-eater Albertosaurus is the logo for the Royal Tyrrell Museum of Palaeontology in Drumheller because it was the first dinosaur discovered in that area. In 1884, Joseph B. Tyrrell discovered a large skull, the first example of Albertosaurus found anywhere in the world. While it looks like its relative Tyrannosaurus, it is a bit smaller. It has powerful hind legs, short front legs, and long, sharp teeth.

Edmontonia looked much like Ankylosaurus with bony plates in rows along its back and jutting out like spikes from its sides. At 7 meters (23 feet) long, it was slightly smaller than Ankylosaurus and had no bony club on the end of its tail.

Chasmosaurus was 5 meters (16 feet) long with a large frill and three sharp horns on its face, making it a member of the triceratops family. It ate leaves and small branches and lived in herds within the area that is now Dinosaur Provincial Park, just east of Calgary.

Alberta was also home to many duck-billed dinosaurs and is, in fact, the richest area in the world for hadrosaur remains.

Calgary Stampede Rodeo, page 88

Just minutes from downtown, it is home to more than 1,400 mammals, reptiles, amphibians, and birds including Siberian tigers, lowland gorillas, red pandas, and exotic emerald tree boas. There are picnic areas throughout the grounds and a cafeteria in the Conservatory. While you're here, be sure to visit the unique butterfly garden. Complete your day with a walk through the sculptured landscape of Prehistoric Park, observing life-sized dinosaur models. Tours are also available. Hours: Open daily at 9 a.m. Admission summer/winter: $9.50/$8 adults, $5.50 seniors 65+, $4.75/$4 children 2–7, free for children under 2. (See also Chapter 8, "Parks and Gardens," p. 125.)

walk around on non-event days also. (See also Chapter 10, "Sports and Recreation," p. 159.)

TSUU T'INA NATION
3700 Anderson Rd. SW, Calgary
403/238-2677 **SW**
Opened in 1983, this museum on Tsuu T'ina land commemorates 100 years of Native Tsuu T'ina history. A model tipi, artifacts, and headdresses dating from 1938 are on display. Evening tours are available if you call ahead. Hours: 8–4 (closed over noon hour). Admission: Donation.

NORTHEAST CALGARY

CALGARY ZOO, BOTANICAL GARDEN, AND PREHISTORIC PARK
1300 Zoo Rd. NE, Calgary
403/232-9300 **NE**
The most important role of the modern zoo is the breeding of endangered species, and Calgary Zoo, a world-renowned zoological institution, has been very successful in this regard.

CROSSROADS MARKET
2222 - 16th Ave. NE, Calgary
403/291-5208 **NE**
Perched along the edge of the Trans-Canada Highway in the northeast quadrant of the city is Western Canada's largest indoor/outdoor flea and farmers' market. With more than 9,300 square meters (100,000 square feet), it sports a public market as well as a Native craft centre.

VILLAGE SQUARE LEISURE CENTRE
2623 - 56th St. NE, Calgary
403/280-9714 **NE**
This kid-friendly facility offers an indoor wave pool and other facilities to please the whole family. See Chapter 10, "Sports and Recreation," p. 156, for information.

NORTHWEST CALGARY

BUTTERFIELD ACRES
3 km (2 mi) north of Crowchild
Trail on Rocky Ridge Road (101st

Street), Calgary
403/547-3595 **NW**
Kids of all ages love this working farm. See Chapter 6, "Kids' Stuff," p. 99, for information.

EXCLUSIVE MOUNTAIN TOURS
32 Hudson Rd. NW, Calgary
403/282-3980 **NW**
Their 2½-hour City Tour offers panoramic views of the city, a visit to the Chinese Cultural Centre, Eau Claire Market, Olympic Plaza, and Fort Calgary as well as stops at Canada Olympic Park. Year-round, Exclusive Mountain Tours' passenger van or motorcoach will take you on morning, afternoon, or evening sunset tours any day that at least four people register for the tour. Complimentary pick-up and drop-off from most accommodations. Fare: $25 per person (admissions extra). Also available are the Dinosaur/Badlands Tour, Head-Smashed-In Buffalo Jump Tour, Mountain Lakes Tour, or tours customized to your interests.

OLYMPIC SPEED SKATING OVAL
University of Calgary
2500 University Dr. NW, Calgary
403/220-7890 **NW**
This is the world's first fully enclosed 400-meter Olympic Speed Skating Oval, built to host the speed skating events of the 1988 Winter Olympics. Currently it is home to the National Speed Skating Team. Ice is open for public skating from mid-July to the end of March. Speed/hockey skate rental is available. Self-guided tours. Call 403/220-7890 for Oval hours and prices.

Calgary CVB/Pat Price

6

KIDS' STUFF

Visitors to Calgary will find a myriad of things to do with their children—active diversions and spectator events, outdoor adventures and indoor attractions. Since Calgary's population is young in comparison to most cities, there are a great many attractions and activities geared to children. As you plan your sightseeing, it's most practical to group them based on proximity to one another. However, when dealing with children you'll also want to intermingle quiet activities with active ones. For example, after a fascinating afternoon watching a movie at the IMAX Theatre, buy supper from the hot dog vendors at Eau Claire and let the kids wear off some energy in the nearby water park before heading back to your hotel. Wheelchair accessibility is indicated by the & symbol.

ANIMALS AND THE GREAT OUTDOORS

BOWNESS PARK
West of 85th Street NW at 48th Avenue, Calgary
403/268-5211   NW
Bowness Park, a popular spot in all seasons, occupies an island in the Bow River. A winter tradition for many Calgarians is skating on the frozen Bowness lagoon, which is lit at night and offers a campfire to warm up skaters. During the summer

the lagoon (complete with fountain in the middle) can be navigated by rented paddleboat or canoe. Any time of year you can roast hot dogs and marshmallows at one of the many firepits scattered throughout the park. An amusement park operates during the summer, as does a mini-railway that takes passengers for a scenic ride through the central area of the park. Picnic shelters, playgrounds, and indoor washrooms add to the convenience of a day spent at Bowness Park.

BUTTERFIELD ACRES
3 km (2 mi) north of Crowchild Trail on Rocky Ridge Road (101st Street NW)
403/547-3595   NW
This working farm is open to the public and appeals to all ages. There are many activities of real-life farm experience suitable for families. You can fill your day with hands-on activities such as visits with the farm animals, milking goats, interpretive nature hikes, hay rides, and pony rides. There are picnic facilities, toboggan hills, and a skating pond. Take boots if it has recently rained, as it is muddy in wet weather. Hours: Daily 10–4 July–Aug, weekends only during the rest of the year. Admission: $5.25 adults, $3.75 children.

CALGARY STAMPEDE
Stampede Park
Corner of Macleod Trail and 25th Avenue SE, Calgary
403/261-0101 or 800/661-1260   SE
This is North America's premier rodeo and fair attraction, where yahoos and western garb abound for ten days in early July. Take in the livestock exhibits, tipi village, grandstand show, and midway rides and games. Watch for Family Fun Day or Kids Day at the Stampede for special deals. Every afternoon you can marvel at the rugged action of saddle bronc and bareback riding, calf-roping, steer wrestling, or bull riding. Free pancake breakfasts are served up all over the city during Stampede Week. Look in the newspaper or visitor centres for details. The Stampede Parade, which sweeps through downtown on the first Friday of July, is a must-see for visitors of all ages. Call 403/261-0101 for route information. Web site: www.calgary-stampede .ab.ca (See also Chapter 5, "Sights and Attractions," p. 88.)

CALGARY ZOO, BOTANICAL GARDEN, AND PREHISTORIC PARK

Top Ten Fun Family Things to Do in Calgary
by Louise Hudson and her eight children

1. Swim at one of the wave pools.
2. Have a wiener roast in Fish Creek Provincial Park.
3. Ride bikes in Fish Creek Provincial Park.
4. Try out the rides at Calaway Park.
5. Watch basketball games.
6. Toboggan and skate at the community lake.
7. Swim at the community lake.
8. Cheer on the Calgary Flames at their home games.
9. Enjoy the fun of the Calgary Stampede.
10. See a show at the IMAX Theatre.

You'll see a lot of black squirrels in the city, but they are not native to Calgary. Originally there were only a handful of them in an exhibit at the zoo, brought from Ontario by Calgary's first zookeeper.

Unfortunately, they were not effectively confined to the zoo, and over the years they have multiplied and virtually taken over the territory of the native red squirrel.

1300 Zoo Rd. NE, Calgary
403/232-9300   NE
Kids love to watch the more than 1,400 animals from around the world that live at the zoo. Prehistoric Park lets kids explore the world of dinosaurs. Open every day at 9 a.m. Admission summer/winter: $9.50/$8 adults, $5.50 seniors 65+, $4.75/$4 children 2–17, free for children under 2. Accessible by Whitehorn C-Train. Viewing time about two hours. (See also Chapter 5, "Sights and Attractions," p. 96, and Chapter 8, "Parks and Gardens," p. 125.)

CANADA OLYMPIC PARK
88 Canada Olympic Rd. SW,
Calgary
403/247-5452   SW
Located west on the Trans-Canada Highway, Canada Olympic Park (COP) is the site of the 1988 Olympic Winter Games. Kids will enjoy the museum's film presentations, interactive video screens, and costume and medal displays recreating the Olympic spirit (Olympic Hall of Fame & Museum, 403/247-5454). Try the ski jump simulator for a chance to experience the thrill of competition without any training. For the adventurous, there are also bobsleigh and luge rides winter or summer; call 403/247-5468. (See also Chapter 7, "Museums and Galleries," p. 111.)

FISH CREEK PROVINCIAL PARK
South part of the city from west
edge to the Bow River
403/297-5293   SW/SE
This huge natural area is home to beavers, coyotes, deer, and rabbits, as well as waterfowl, songbirds, and birds of prey including a nesting pair of peregrine falcons. Exploring the extensive bike and pedestrian pathways that snake through the park is an enjoyable pastime for families, and firepits and picnic tables make it an ideal spot for wiener roasts and picnics. Kids will enjoy the interpretive displays about wildlife at the visitor centre located at the first right turn after you enter the park at the end of Bow Bottom Trail. Follow Bow Bottom Trail further south and find Lake Sikome, a popular swimming spot in summer. Rent a horse at the riding stables at Shannon Terrace. Fish Creek Park has many points of access.

INGLEWOOD BIRD SANCTUARY
3020 Sanctuary Rd. SE (off 9th
Avenue), Calgary
403/269-6688   SE
Twenty-eight hectares (70 acres) of riverine forest make this the largest urban bird sanctuary in Canada. Besides being a popular bird-watching area during migration, the Inglewood

Bird Sanctuary provides shelter and food for birds that are sick, hurt, or unable to migrate. Walk the 2 kilometers of wood-chip trails. Pack a picnic lunch and take binoculars. Open daily from dawn to dusk. (See also Chapter 5, "Sights and Attractions," p. 89.)

OLYMPIC PLAZA
Corner of Macleod Trail and 7th Avenue SW, Calgary
403/268-5207 DT

Numerous special events are held here throughout the year, such as the Children's New Year's Eve celebrations and Calgary International Children's Festival. (See also Chapter 5, "Sights and Attractions," p. 86.)

PRINCE'S ISLAND PARK
1st Avenue and 3rd Street SW, Calgary
403/268-5211 DT

Kids will enjoy the hot dog vendors, playground, water park, and buskers near the Barclay Mall entrance on 3rd Street SW. Nearby Eau Claire Market is a colorful spot to visit, and

the Eau Claire YMCA has wonderful indoor pools. (See also Chapter 8, "Parks and Gardens," p. 122.)

MUSEUMS AND LIBRARIES

CALGARY POLICE INTERPRETIVE CENTRE
316 - 7th Ave. SE, 2nd level, Calgary
403/268-4566 DT

Visit this hands-on educational crime centre to learn about the fascinating aspects of police work and investigation. Put your detective skills to the test with interactive computer and video exhibits. Allow about two hours to see it all. Not suitable for young children. Admission: $2 adults, all others free. (See also Chapter 5, "Sights and Attractions," p. 81.)

ENERGEUM
640 - 5th Ave. SW, main floor, Calgary
403/297-4293 DT

Drill for oil, outwit the Energy Hang-

Calgary International Children's Festival

The Calgary International Children's Festival runs for five days in the latter part of May and showcases high-caliber performance artists from around the world—singers, puppeteers, dance troupes, and comedians. The action takes place downtown at the Glenbow Museum, Calgary Centre for Performing Arts, and the Calgary Public Library Theatre. Take the C-Train to Olympic Plaza, where there is free entertainment in the form of buskers, clowns, and other roving festival performers. Tickets are very reasonable at less than $10. For program schedule information or for a free festival brochure, call 403/294-7414.

man, or generate your own electricity at this unusual museum. Hours: Mon–Fri 10:30–4:30 year-round, as well as Sundays and holidays June–Aug. Special events during holidays and summer months. Admission: Free. Wheelchair accessible (except theatre). Allow two hours to visit. (See also Chapter 7, "Museums," p. 109.)

FORT CALGARY
750 - 9th Ave. SE, Calgary
403/290-1875   DT
In this 16-hectare (40-acre) riverside park, local history comes to life as interpreters in authentic costumes weave stories of the past. This reconstruction of an 1875 fort offers exhibits, displays, and interactive interpretation. Watch an award-winning video presentation in the Palace Theatre. Open daily May 1 to October 13, from 9 a.m. to 5 p.m. Admission: $3 adults , $1.50 youth 7–17, free for children 6 and under, seniors 15 percent discount. Visiting time one hour. (See also Chapter 5, "Sights and Attractions," p. 85.)

GLENBOW MUSEUM
130 - 9th Ave. SE, Calgary
403/268-4100   DT
Journey into the history of the Canadian West with a visit to the Glenbow Museum. Discover the colorful characters and events that shaped this part of the country. Kids will enjoy learning about pioneer life and the rich cultures of the First Nations through a renowned collection of native artifacts, a Siksika (Blackfoot) tipi, and elegant quillwork by the Plains Cree. A special exhibit on the third floor called "Growing Up and Away: Youth in Western Canada" will appeal especially to young people. As they move through the galleries, visitors are greeted by hands-on activities, games, quizzes, and handouts. Admission: $8 adults, $6 students and seniors, free for children under 7, $25 families. Web site: www.glenbow.org (See also Chapter 7, "Museums," p. 109.)

FUN AND EDUCATIONAL

CALGARY PHILHARMONIC ORCHESTRA

Calgary Zoo, page 99

Calgary CVB/Calgary Zoo

205 - 8th Ave. SE, Calgary
403/571-0270   DT
Box office: 403/571-0849
Young people's concerts on Saturday afternoons cost $10 to $13 for children and $15 to $19 for adults. Reserve by calling TicketMaster (403/777-0000) or the box office. Convenient parking. (See also Chapter 11, "Performing Arts," p. 167.) ♿

CALGARY SCIENCE CENTRE
701 - 11th St. SW, Calgary
403/221-3700   DT
Unravel the secrets of science with hands-on exhibits. See exciting live theatre and demonstrations designed to appeal to all ages. Take in multimedia shows as well as shows about the heavens in the Planetarium and 70 mm films in the Discovery Dome Theatre. Open seven days a week, but hours vary throughout the year. Take the C-Train to the 10th Street Station and walk one block west. Free parking. (See also Chapter 5, "Sights and Attractions," p. 81.) ♿

PUPPETS AND THEATRE

CALGARY YOUNG PEOPLE'S THEATRE
213 - 19th St. NW, Suite 5, Calgary
403/270-0980   NW

This theatre troupe performs family theatre in historic Canmore Opera House, which is part of the Heritage Park Historical Village at 1900 Heritage Drive SW in Calgary. Young People's Theatre delivers four productions per year (such as *The Secret Garden* and *Charlotte's Web*), including a vaudeville show in summer. Ticket prices range from $5 to $8. Ample parking is available. But if there's just been a major snowfall, call to make sure you can drive right to the door. Allow enough time to see the rest of Heritage Park. (See also Chapter 11, "Performing Arts," p. 161.) ♿

FRONT ROW CENTRE PLAYERS
31 Millbank Cres. SW, Calgary
403/226-3966   SW
Box office: 403/263-0079
This amateur theatre group emphasizes family entertainment with two musical productions of classics per year, ten performances each. Previous productions include *Guys and Dolls, Godspell, Annie, Oliver,* and *Grease.* Evening performances and Sunday matinées all show at the Pumphouse Theatres. Admission: $8–$10.

IMAX THEATRE
Eau Claire Market

T I P

Kids enjoy the activity and colorful sights of farmers' markets as much as adults do. The Crossroads Market (2222 - 16th Avenue NE) and the Blackfoot Farmer's Market (5600 - 11th Street SE) are open Friday, Saturday, and Sunday all summer. The Millarville Market (just outside Millarville at the racetrack) is an old-fashioned rural market southwest of Calgary. It is open Saturday mornings until noon, seasonally.

Child Friendly Calgary

Being a child-friendly city is a distinction to be proud of and Calgary boasts the first child-friendly program in North America. This innovative program urges businesses to look at the world as a child sees it. A team of youth inspectors visits hotels, restaurants, family attractions, and businesses, then rates them according to their child-friendliness. Those achieving a passing grade are listed in Child Friendly Calgary's Guide to Accredited Businesses. *To obtain an updated copy of the guide, contact Child Friendly Calgary, 720, 640 - 8th Avenue SW, Calgary, AB, T2P 1G7; (403) 266-5448, fax (403) 264-0266; e-mail: friendly@cadvision.com. Child Friendly Calgary also offers program options for children accompanying parents who are attending conventions. Staff plan and supervise activities, outings, and special events suited to the needs and schedules of the parents and children.*

2nd Avenue and 3rd Street SW, Calgary
Program info: 403/974-4629
Charge-by-phone tickets: 403/974-4646 **DT**
Treat your senses to a powerful film experience with breathtaking images on a giant (more than 5½ stories high) screen accompanied by wraparound digital sound. Matinées and evening double features available. Admission: Matinées $7.50 adults, $5.50 children; double features $11.50 adults, $9.50 children. Ample parking off 2nd Avenue. (See also Chapter 5, "Sights and Attractions," p. 86.)

LOOSE MOOSE THEATRE
2003 McKnight Blvd. NE
403/250-1414 **NE**
Box office: 403/291-5682
From September to April, Loose Moose performs children's theatre at 1 p.m. and 3 p.m. on Saturdays and Sundays. Young audiences are entertained with such time-honored classics as *Snow White* and *The Elves and the Shoemaker*. Tickets are $6 and may be bought at the door or reserved ahead. Not wheelchair accessible. Ample parking.

PLEIADES THEATRE
Calgary Science Centre
701 - 11th St. SW, Calgary
403/221-3707 **DT**
Located in the Calgary Science Centre, Pleiades offers a summer science theatre series aimed at the younger crowd. Performances are 45 minutes long and fun while being educational. Admission for the children's summer theatre is $6 to $8. Reserve by calling TicketMaster (403/777-0000) or the box office. Free parking. Devote some time to seeing the displays and

hands-on activities of the Science Centre or take in a show at the Planetarium, also on-site. &

QUEST THEATRE
310, 815 - 1st St. SW, Calgary
Box office: 403/221-3707
403/264-8575   DT
Quest Theatre targets the 6- to 12-year-old set. The original Canadian plays address issues that children encounter in daily life, such as self-esteem, racism, and conflict resolution. Performances, held in the Pleiades Theatre at the Calgary Science Centre, are Saturdays and Sundays at 1 p.m. and 3 p.m. Admission: $6.50. To reserve tickets call Ticket-Master (403/777-0000) or the box office. Free parking. &

STAGE WEST FOR KIDS
727 - 42nd Ave. SE, Calgary
403/243-6642   SE
Saturday matinées geared to kids are offered here. A special kids' buffet (including kid-popular items such as pizza, chicken nuggets, hot dogs, and ice cream) precedes live theatre performances of favorites like *Ali Addin and the Lamp* and *The City Mouse and the Country Mouse*. Lunch from 11:30 to 12:45 with show starting at 1 p.m. Complimentary birthday cake if you mention the birthday when you book your tickets. Admission: $13 kids, $16 adults. Ample parking.

STORYBOOK THEATRE
Bay 3, 3530 - 11A St. NE, Calgary
403/291-2247   NE
For more than 20 years, StoryBook Theatre has dazzled Calgary audiences with high quality children's theatre. Their season, which runs September through May, consists of two series. The Children's Cabaret, interactive theatre for 3- to 7-year-olds, includes classics such as *Jack and the Beanstalk* and *The Princess and the Pea*. Weekend performances are held at 11 a.m. and 1:30 p.m. at Crescent Heights Community Centre at 1101 - 2nd Street NW. Tickets are $5. The Adventure Theatre series, geared to children 6 years and up, includes 12 musicals per year (the likes of *Oliver* and *Anne of Green Gables*)

Calaway Park, page 106

Calgary CVB/Mike Ridewood

Fort Calgary, page 102

plus two non-musicals (such as *Cinderella* and *You're a Good Man, Charlie Brown*). Performances are at the Pumphouse Theatres on Wednesday, Thursday, and Friday evenings as well as Saturday and Sunday afternoons. Admission: \$5–\$12. Ample free parking. ♿

THEME PARKS

CALAWAY PARK
10 km (6 mi) west on Trans-Canada Highway
403/240-3822   **SW**
Western Canada's largest outdoor family amusement park, Calaway offers lots of rides to thrill kids of all ages, as well as live entertainment,

mini-golf, fishing holes, cinema 180 (which involves the viewer in a wild ride via a wrap-around theatre screen), games, and special events. Buy food there or pack a picnic lunch. Open weekends from mid-May to mid-June, daily from mid-June to early September, then weekends only until mid-October. Admission: \$50 family, \$12 children 3–6, \$17.50 adults and children 7+, free for children under 2. Includes all rides, shows, special entertainment, and GST. General gate admission (excluding rides) may be purchased for \$8. Acres of parking. (See also Chapter 5, "Sights and Attractions," p. 91.)

HERITAGE PARK HISTORICAL VILLAGE
Corner of 14th Street and Heritage Drive SW, Calgary
403/259-1900   **SW**
Kids love Heritage Park Historical Village and don't even realize they're getting a history lesson because they're having too much fun. They can board a sternwheel boat for a cruise around Glenmore Reservoir or hop on the train pulled by a steam locomotive for a spin around the park. They can check out a turn-of-the-century school or visit a blacksmith shop and watch the smithy in action. No trip to Heritage Park is complete without a visit to the penny candy store and the ice-cream parlor. The park is open daily from mid-May to early September, then weekends only to mid-October. Special events in December. Admission is \$10 for adults

TRIVIA

Sharks' teeth have been found embedded in rock in parts of Alberta.

Rodeos

No summer trip to Alberta would be complete without taking in at least one rodeo. Aside from the huge Calgary Stampede that takes over the city for ten days in July, there are smaller events just outside Calgary that let you get a taste of the rural life while entertaining the kids.

- Little Britches Parade & Rodeo in High River—May
- Airdrie Chute-Out Pro Rodeo in Airdrie—June
- Bull-o-Rama Rodeo in Bragg Creek in late June
- Okotoks Pro Rodeo in late August
- Lions Rodeo in Cochrane in late August

Mutton busting is a particularly popular event with small fry.

and $6 for children. (See also Chapter 5, "Sights and Attractions," p. 94.)

SOUTHLAND LEISURE CENTRE
200 Southland Dr. SW, Calgary
403/251-3505   **SW**
The whole family will enjoy the wave pool and water slide at Southland Leisure Centre. See Chapter 10, "Sports and Recreation," p. 156, for more information.

VILLAGE SQUARE LEISURE CENTRE
2623 - 56th St. NE, Calgary
403/280-9714   **NE**
The huge indoor wave pool at this kid-friendly establishment appeals to all ages. See Chapter 10, "Sports and Recreation," p. 156, for more information.

Frances Purslow

7

MUSEUMS AND GALLERIES

Calgary's character, equal parts down-home western traditions and sophisticated international flare, is reflected in the city's museums and art galleries. The museums include displays of early settlement (replete with fur traders, Indians, and pioneer settlers) as well as the celebration of the XV Olympic Winter Games and technological advances. On the art scene, galleries exhibit the western theme in many art media as well as abstract, modern, and classical works. You can view Native art in the form of carvings, paintings, prints, beadwork, quillwork, and weavings in numerous public and commercial galleries.

ART MUSEUMS

NICKLE ARTS MUSEUM
University of Calgary Campus
434 Collegiate Blvd. NW, Calgary
403/220-7234   NW
The Nickle Collection of ancient coins is one of the most important in Canada. Coins from ancient Greece, Rome, and Byzantium along with European medals, other forms of money, and related displays are on continual exhibition in the Coin Room. The Nickle Arts Museum also houses a permanent collection of contemporary Canadian art. In addition, it is a teaching facility hosting numerous traveling exhibitions with themes ranging from science and medicine to architecture, history, and education. U of C Department of Art faculty lecture free on Thursday. The museum shop features art image collectibles, local handmade jewelry, and books and catalogues of Canadian art. Hours: Tues–Fri 10–5, Sat 1–5. Admission: $2 adults, $1 students and seniors, Tuesdays free.

HISTORY MUSEUMS

FORT CALGARY HISTORIC PARK
750 - 9th Ave. SE, Calgary
403/290-1875 DT
Visit Calgary's birthplace, where costumed interpreters and visitor volunteers reenact life during the city's early days. In 1875 the North West Mounted Police built Fort Calgary at the confluence of the Bow and Elbow Rivers, setting the stage for further development by settlers. Visit the Discovery Room in the Interpretive Centre for interactive exhibits and hands-on fun. Hours: Daily 9–5 May–Sept, weekdays only Oct–April. Admission: $3 adults, $1.50 youth, children under 6 free. (See also Chapter 5, "Sights and Attractions," p. 85.)

GLENBOW MUSEUM AND ART GALLERY
130 - 9th Ave. SW, Calgary
403/268-4100 DT
The Glenbow counts more than 240,000 objects among its collections. Permanent displays celebrate the heritage of the Canadian West as well as explore other cultures. There are also visiting international exhibitions throughout the year. Exhibition floors offer free admission and gallery tours Thursdays. The fourth floor houses the Alberta Children's Museum with interactive displays. Enjoy lunch at the Loaf and Kettle on the main floor, then leave time to peruse the games, books, and tapes in the expanded museum shop. Hours: Daily 9–5 May–Aug; closed Mondays Sept–April. Admission: $8 adults, $6 students and seniors, free for children under 7. (See also Chapter 6, "Kids' Stuff," p. 102.)

SCIENCE MUSEUMS

CALGARY SCIENCE CENTRE
701 - 11th St. SW, Calgary
403/221-3707 DT
Discover the wonders of science and technology at the Calgary Science Centre. Explore the interactive exhibits—as much for adults as for children. Local and traveling exhibitions change year-round. Science demonstrations and art displays are ongoing. Hours: Tues–Sun 10–5. Admission: $4.50 adults and youth, $4 seniors and children 12 and under, $15 families. (See also Chapter 5, "Sights and Attractions," p. 81.)

ENERGEUM
640 - 5th Ave. SW, Calgary
403/297-4293 DT
A Place to Explore Energy, the Energeum is a 325-square-meter (3,500-square-foot) science hall devoted to

---

TRIVIA

The Aurora Borealis sculpture dominating the foyer of the Glenbow Museum and Art Gallery was designed by Torontonian James Archibald Houston. The 20-meter-high (63-foot) sculpture contains 700 pieces of prismatic acrylic glass weighing about 1.8 metric tons (2 tons). The music accompanying the sculpture is from Isao Tomita's album *Snowflakes Are Dancing*, and the lighting and sound effects are computer programmed to alternate every three or four minutes each.

energy resources—oil, natural gas, oil sands, coal, and hydroelectricity. It appeals to all ages by bringing to life the story of Alberta's energy development through fiber-optics, computer games, and working models. Hours: Year-round Mon–Fri 10:30–4:30, plus Sundays and holidays June–Aug. Admission: Free.

MILITARY MUSEUMS

MUSEUM OF THE REGIMENTS
4520 Crowchild Tr. SW, Calgary
403/974-2850   SW

Exit at Flanders Avenue to see Western Canada's largest military museum. It houses regimental collections and lifelike dioramas, models, miniatures, historical artifacts, and photos that tell the story of Canada's involvement in historic battles. It also hosts temporary exhibits of a military nature such as "The Indian Army Side by Side with Canada's Sons and Daughters." Check out the military vehicles on the grounds. Hours: Daily (except Wed) 10–4. Admission: Free.

NAVAL MUSEUM OF ALBERTA
1820 - 24th St. SW, Calgary
403/242-0002   SW

Canada's second-largest naval museum houses ship models, naval

Glenbow Museum, page 109

weapons, uniforms, badges, photographs, shipbourne equipment, and other naval artifacts. See three beautifully restored RCN fighter aircraft: the Supermarine Seafire MK, XV, the Hawker Sea Fury K, II, and the McDonnell Banshee F2H-3 Jet. Hours: Tues–Fri 1–5, Sat and Sun 10–6. Admission: Free.

OTHER MUSEUMS

AEROSPACE MUSEUM
Hangar #10, 4629 McCall Way NE, Calgary

T I P

For self-guided tours of Calgary's historical buildings, pick up booklets providing maps and information from the Municipal Building (800 Macleod Trail SE). The booklets describe the Connaught-Beltline District Heritage Walking Tour, the Mission District Heritage Walking Tour, the Stephen Avenue and Area Historical Walking Tour, and the Union Cemetery Interpretive Tour.

403/250-3752   **NE**

Trace Canada's aviation history from World War I to the '60s with the museum's collection of vintage aircraft, aeronautical engines, artifacts, and aviation art. Sometimes you can see aircraft under restoration. Guided tours by appointment. Allow one hour viewing time. Hours: Weekdays 10–5, weekends and holidays 12–5. Admission: $6 adults, $3.50 students and seniors, $2 children, $15 families.

GRAIN ACADEMY
Roundup Centre
Stampede Park, at the corner of 4th Street and 14th Avenue SE, Calgary
403/263-4594   **SE**

The entire grain handling system is reproduced in miniature in this museum featuring the history of agriculture in Alberta. Through film, authentic displays, and knowledgeable tour guides, visitors discover the province's rural past. Learn how a grain elevator works by watching the scale working elevator that provides a cross-sectional look at its working parts. Smell the wholesomeness of Alberta wheat and touch the wood of an elevator sculptured by thousands of bushels of flowing grain. Hours: Mon–Fri 10–4, plus Saturday (April–Sept) 12–4. Admission: Free.

OLYMPIC HALL OF FAME
Canada Olympic Park
88 Canada Olympic Rd. SW, Calgary
403/247-5452   **SW**

The Olympic Hall of Fame at Canada Olympic Park contains three floors of exhibits and displays of Olympic achievements, past and present—medals, costume displays, and memorabilia. As well, simulators allow you to experience the thrills and chills of ski jump and bobsleigh competition without any training. Allow enough time to take in the interactive videos and equipment displays. Hours: Daily 8–9 May–Aug, 10–5 Sept–April. Admission: $3.75 adults, $3 seniors, $2.75 students and children.

GALLERIES

ARTNEST GALLERY & FRAMING INC.
Glenmore Landing
1600 - 90th Ave. SW, Calgary
403/258-0555   **SW**

Artnest focuses on original works of art by established Canadian artists. Paintings in oil, acrylics, and watercolors, art glass, collages, pastel drawings, bronze sculptures, stone carvings, and raku pottery round out their selection. Hours: Mon–Wed and Sat 10–6, Thur and Fri 10–8. Admission: Free.

BEARCLAW GALLERY
1301 - 17th Ave. SW, Calgary
403/228-6533   **SW**

Bearclaw Gallery specializes in Canadian First Nations art, featuring such names as Maxine Noel, Norval Morrisseau, Daphne Odjig, Fred MacDonald, and Nokomis as well as local artists. Original artwork and prints, West Coast carvings and jewelry, Inuit soapstone carvings and tapestries, quill baskets, and ceramics are featured here. Hours: Mon–Sat 10–5:30. Admission: Free.

CALGARY CHINESE CULTURAL CENTRE MUSEUM
197 - 1st St. SW, Calgary
403/262-5071   **DT**

Seeing the building that houses this museum is alone worth the trip.

Opened in 1993, exhibits focus on Chinese art and culture—contemporary and traditional paintings and works of local artists as well as internationally renowned artists from abroad. Five rotating exhibitions per year highlight pottery, antiques, and artifacts. Hours: Daily 11–5. Admission: $2 adults, $1 students and seniors. (See also Chapter 5, "Sights and Attractions," p. 80.)

ILLINGWORTH KERR GALLERY
Alberta College of Art and Design
1407 - 14th Ave. NW, Calgary
403/284-7632 **NW**
Established in 1958, the Illingworth Kerr Gallery features contemporary art with an emphasis on Canadian artists. There is a year-round program of exhibitions, publications, lectures, screenings, and related events. Approximately ten shows per year. Hours: Tues–Sat 10–6, summer hours vary. Admission: Free.

MICAH GALLERY
1819 - 4th St. SW, Calgary
403/245-1340 **SW**
North American Native and Western art, jewelry, artifacts, and collectibles of traditional and contemporary design are featured at the Micah Gallery. Sculptures and carvings, weavings, pottery, and handmade fashions. Hours: Mon–Wed, Fri and Sat 10–6, Thur 10–9, Sun 12–5. Admission: Free.

Memorial Park Library

The Memorial Park Library (1221 - 2nd Street SW) is one of 2,500 public library buildings in North America financed by American philanthropist Andrew Carnegie. Completed in 1911, it was the first public library in Alberta. It remained Calgary's Central Library until 1963 when the W. R. Castell Library opened on 7th Avenue. After being declared a Provincial Historic Site in 1976, massive restoration began and the Memorial Park Library was consequently reopened as a branch library and art gallery.

Baggage carousels at the Calgary International Airport, page 115

MUTTART ART GALLERY
Memorial Park Library
1221 - 2nd St. SW, Calgary
403/266-2764   **SW**

Housed in the top floor of the Memorial Park Library, the Muttart Art Gallery is a public gallery featuring contemporary works by established and emerging Western Canadian artists. Its mandate is to develop a truly visual arts centre with more flexibility and depth than a traditional art gallery. Ten to 12 shows per year with special events, sales, shows, auctions, and lectures. Hours: Mon–Wed and Fri 12–5, Thur 10–5, Sat 12–8. Admission: Free.

NEW GALLERY
516 - 9th Ave. SW, Calgary
403/233-2399   **DT**

One of Alberta's veteran artist-run galleries, New Gallery presents about ten shows per year. Emphasis is on contemporary, cutting-edge, experimental art. Hours: Tues–Sat 12–5. Admission: Free.

PRINTS CHARMING
1409 - 11th St. SW, Calgary
403/229-0220   **SW**

Prints Charming houses the largest selection of fine art prints in Southern Alberta as well as unique giftware such as musical alarm clocks shaped like animals, candleholders, glassware, and replicas of old-fashioned tin toys. Hours: Weekdays 10–6, Thur to 7, Sat 10–5:30, Sun 12–4. Admission: Free.

T I P

If local arts and crafts are what you crave, make a trip to Bragg Creek, Canmore, or Banff for a wide assortment of Canadiana including the wares of local painters, sculptors, and other artisans.

Ten Recommended Books about Calgary and Environs
books by local authors

1. *A Bird Finding Guide to the Calgary Region* by the Calgary Field Naturalist Society
2. *Calgary Cavalcade: From Fort to Fortune* by Grant MacEwan
3. *The Calgary Gardener* by the Calgary Horticultural Society
4. *Calgary Parks and Pathways* by Terry Bullick
5. *Day-trips from Calgary* by Bill Corbett
6. *Inglewood Bird Sanctuary—A Place for All Seasons* by Dave Elphinstone
7. *A Look at Calgary's Public Art* by Barbara Kwasy and Elaine Peake
8. *Rocky Mountain Retreats: Recommended Accommodations in the Canadian Rockies* by Ken Schmaltz
9. *Calgary: Backcountry Biking in the Canadian Rockies* by Gerhardt Lepp and Doug Eastcott
10. *The Story of Calgary* by Fred Stenson

ROCKY MOUNTAIN ART GALLERY
821 - 14th St. NW, Calgary
403/283-9432 NW
For limited edition prints, originals, artisan pieces, and custom framing, visit the Rocky Mountain Art Gallery near the Alberta College of Art and Design. Robert Bateman paintings are featured alongside pencil art by Henri DeGruut, prints by Ed Tussey, and watercolors by Peter Mortimore. Local artwork by sculptor and painter Vilem Zach depicts Natives, cowboys, women, and children. Hours: Mon–Thur 10–6, Fri 10–8, Sat 10–5:30. Admission: Free.

TRIANGLE GALLERY OF VISUAL ARTS
800 Macleod Trail SE, Calgary
403/262-1737 DT
Opened in 1988, Triangle Gallery is a public gallery offering eight exhibitions per year. Focus is on local and regional artists such as John Kenneth Esler, Harry Kiyooka, and Katie Ohe, but national and international exhibitions are also hosted. Take in exhibit lectures at 11 a.m. on day of exhibition opening. Hours: Tues–Fri 10–4, Sat 12–4. Admission: Free.

WEBSTER GALLERIES
812 - 11th Ave. SW, Calgary
403/263-6500 or 888/874-5519 SW
One of the largest commercial galleries in Western Canada, Webster Galleries has an impressive selection of Inuit art. Also featured are watercolors, oils, hand-pulled

prints, bronzes, and ceramics by Canadian artists. Hours: Mon–Sat 10–6, Sun 1–4. Admission: Free.

PUBLIC ART

ATTRACTIONS ALBERTA
Calgary International Airport
The baggage carousels on the arrivals level at Calgary International Airport have been transformed into dramatic life-sized displays of attractions in Alberta. They showcase the province's colorful history, pageantry, cultures, and peoples as depicted by local museums, forts, parks, and tourist attractions. Local artist Ken Dewar created the Calgary Exhibition and Stampede Mural, which graces a feature wall near the food court. Another mural entitled "The Downtown Adventure," by Glen Semple, is a colorful collection of items sure to draw observers. After its term at the airport, the mural will become part of the civic art collection. Not only walls but ceilings, too, are sites for more displays. Three brightly colored hot air balloons are part of the Calgary Hot Air Balloon Club display, and a shiny red Stits Sky Coupe from the Reynolds-Alberta

Calgary CVB/Calgary Science Center

Calgary Science Centre, page 109

Museum in Wetaskiwin is suspended from the ceiling overlooking international arrivals.

BOW VALLEY SQUARE
At the entrance to Bow Valley Square on the corner of 2nd Avenue and 6th Street SW, there are two colorful sculptures created by Sorel Etrog. Named *Sadko* and *Kabuki*, the two massive sculptures were unveiled in 1975 and are symbolic of the close relationship between hand and tool. *Sadko* (the red one) was inspired by

TRIVIA

In front of the Calgary Board of Education building (515 Macleod Trail SE) is a grouping of very large, elongated figures sculpted by Mario Armengol. These arrived in Calgary in 1967 after their stint at the British Pavilion at Expo at Montreal. However, they remained crated for some time while controversy swirled around them. A headline in the *Calgary Herald* on December 12 of that year posed the question, "Is Calgary Ready for Nudes?" Apparently it was, because on July 8, 1968, the Duke of Kent unveiled the *Brotherhood of Mankind* (a.k.a. *Family of Man*), and the sculptures still cavort today amongst downtown office workers.

a dancer from the Japanese Sadko ballet. It is 4 meters (13 feet) high and weighs 1.8 metric tons (2 tons). *Kabuki* (yellow), which was inspired by a Japanese Kabuki dancer, is 4.3 meters (14 feet) high and weighs 2 metric tons (4,500 pounds).

CONVERSATION

Just outside the Bay on the corner of Stephen Avenue Mall and 1st Street SW is a life-sized statue of two men in conversation. The artist is William McElcheran.

PRINCE'S ISLAND PARK

Enjoy the Art in the Park on the Bow River Pathway just west of Eau Claire Market. Many sculptures have been added for the enjoyment of joggers, cyclists, and those out for a leisurely stroll. Three metal sculptures by Enzo Di Palma depict various facets of prairie life: the first is *Buffalo Grass and Tumbleweed*, which depicts buffalo grass dominating but enmeshed with the tumbleweed; the second is *Prairie Collage*, made from authentic tools and artifacts used by settlers in the early 1900s; and *Ducks* shows two ducks taking flight.

ROBERT THE BRUCE

Near the entrance to the Southern Alberta Jubilee Auditorium is an impressive 8-meter-tall (27-foot) statue of Robert the Bruce, King of the Scots from 1306 to 1329. Eric Harvie, a local philanthropist, commissioned two castings of the statue, which were presented at approximately the same time; one was unveiled in Scotland by Queen Elizabeth II while the second was unveiled in Calgary in 1967.

ROULEAUVILLE SQUARE

Rouleauville Square on 17th Avenue near 1st Street SW is now part of the Mission District, but it was originally part of a dirt trail known as Notre Dame Road, which ran through a French community called Rouleauville. The lives of early French settlers are recorded on plaques around the green space of Rouleauville Square, where stone etchings depict scenes of Calgary's past.

17TH AVENUE MURALS

When strolling along Uptown 17 (17th Avenue SW between 2nd and 14th Streets), watch for murals on the sides of buildings. Each is an original art piece by an Alberta artist in this outdoor art gallery. Since 1988, the Arts 17 Society has sponsored an annual mural competition and commissioned artists to paint the murals on buildings along 17th Avenue. The murals measure 3.5 meters by 9 meters (12 x 30 feet); plaques beneath the murals tell the name of the artwork and the artist.

City of Calgary

8

PARKS AND GARDENS

While the erratic weather patterns make gardening in Calgary a challenge, the city nonetheless is blessed with an abundance of green areas. These range from the Devonian Gardens, a 1.25-hectare (2.5-acre) indoor oasis in the heart of downtown, to Fish Creek Provincial Park spanning the southern end of the city with 1,153 hectares (2,850 acres) of lush riverine habitat rich with wildlife and natural vegetation. In total, there are 5,923 hectares (14,636 acres) of park and recreational land within the city limits. Calgary offers more than ten groomed and maintained athletic parks featuring ball diamonds, soccer and football fields, tennis courts, pools, and ice for skating.

Also noteworthy are the results of Calgarians' efforts to beautify their own properties with plantings of annuals, perennials, shrubs, and trees. Springtime in Calgary is punctuated with blossoming trees and bushes dressed in white and yellow and all shades of pink. While summers are short, gardeners make the most of them with showy displays of dramatic, bright blooms and cool pastels. The autumn landscape blazes with rich gold, burnished copper, and crimson foliage. Even in winter, dark green evergreens capped with snow nestle beside the colorful bark of red osier dogwood and the silver leaves of Russian olive.

You don't need big bucks to enjoy Calgary's parks and gardens. With the exception of the Zoo's Botanical Gardens, all sites listed are free. Hours for most parks within city limits are 5 a.m. to midnight.

Carburn Park has one of the largest overwintering populations of bald eagles in the Canadian prairies. Between five and ten eagles spend the winter along the Bow River in the city, feeding on nearby ducks.

PARKS

BOWNESS PARK
48th Ave. NW, west of 85th Street, Calgary   NW
Family fun abounds at this island park in the northwest part of Calgary. Ice skating in winter, paddleboating and picnicking during warm weather are Calgary traditions. See Chapter 6, "Kids' Stuff," p. 98, for more information.

CARBURN PARK
South of Glenmore Trail SE, between the Bow River and the community of Riverbend, Calgary   SE
To access Carburn Park by car, turn south from Glenmore Trail on 18th Street SE and follow the signs. This semi-natural area features a river pathway, picnic facilities, and lagoons suitable for fishing and canoeing. Although ice skating is not allowed, cross-country ski enthusiasts enjoy Carburn Park in winter.

CENTRAL MEMORIAL PARK
12th Avenue, between 2nd and 4th Streets SW, Calgary   SW
A formal public garden and war memorials grace this green space. One of the city's oldest parks, it was modeled after a Victorian garden featuring formal flower beds and geometric paths. In 1912 Central Memorial Library was added to the site, a stately sandstone building that served as the main Calgary library for for some years. Currently it is a branch library and houses the Muttart Art Gallery on the top floor.

CONFEDERATION PARK
Between 6th and 14th Streets NW, north of 21st Avenue, Calgary   NW
Developed in the 1960s, Confederation Park is a popular place in all seasons. The hilly areas attract tobogganers in winter while groomed trails appeal to cross-country skiers. During warmer weather, cyclists, inline skaters, and pedestrians take to the pathways in the park; tennis and baseball players use the courts and diamonds; and golfers flock to the adjacent Confederation Golf Course. In December the golf course is the site of a Christmas lights display along 14th Street that attracts carloads of onlookers.

EDWORTHY PARK
Between Sarcee Trail and the Bow River, north of Bow Trail SW, Calgary   SW
Tobogganing, cross-country skiing, fishing, cycling, canoeing, and picnicking are all popular activities at Edworthy Park and adjoining Lowery

TRIVIA

Calgary has more acres of green space per capita than any other city in Canada.

Gardens and Douglas Fir Trail. Covering 127 hectares (314 acres), the area was once a sandstone quarry but now encompasses many types of terrain from forest to grasslands, steep cliffs to floodplains. Children enjoy the playground equipment while families barbecue in the kitchen shelters. Fishermen cast their lines in the Bow River in quest of supper.

FISH CREEK PROVINCIAL PARK
P.O. Box 2780, Calgary
403/297-5293   **SW/SE**
More than a million visitors enjoy Fish Creek Provincial Park annually. It is the largest urban park in Canada and has numerous access points in the southeast and southwest quadrants of the city. Activities include skating on Lake Sikome in winter as well as cross-country skiing and snowshoeing. Selected trails are cleared during winter months. In summer the park is popular with picnickers, cyclists, hikers, and in-line skaters. Lake Sikome teems with swimmers and sunbathers on hot days. The Interpretive Centre at the south end of Bow Bottom Trail SE features displays covering 8,000 years of human history in the area as well as exhibits about local wildlife. Park hours: Daily from 8 a.m. until sundown. Interpretive Centre hours: Weekdays from 8:15–noon and 1–4:30 p.m. Lake hours vary seasonally.

GLENMORE PARK
5300 - 19th St. SW (Athletic Park),
Calgary   **SW**
The Glenmore Reservoir supplies the city with drinking water and is surrounded by 600 hectares (1,483

Fish Creek Provincial Park

Located at the south end of the city and extending from the Tsuu T'ina Reserve on the west to the Bow River on the east, Fish Creek Provincial Park is the largest urban park in Canada. Stretching over 1,153 hectares (2,850 acres), it protects more than 10 kilometers (6 miles) of river valley providing habitat for more than 150 species of birds, more than 15 different mammals, and an abundance of aquatic life and wildflowers. There are also 46 archaeological sites divulging secrets of human habitation in the area 8,000 years ago. Spend a day in Fish Creek Provincial Park and you can hardly believe you're within city limits. This beautiful natural area includes extensive pedestrian/bike paths that can be enjoyed any time of the year. Located off the southern end of Bow Bottom Trail, the Bow Valley Ranch Visitor Centre exhibits interesting interpretive displays about wildlife and the history of the area.

To find out which rare and interesting birds have been seen in the Calgary region lately, call the recorded Bird Alert at 403/237-8821.

acres) of parkland. Sailing, rowing, and canoeing are allowed on this body of water, but swimming and motorboats are strictly prohibited. Because this park (which actually consists of five park areas) is so vast, there is a wide diversity of terrain, facilities, and activities. Weaselhead Flats at the most westerly point of the reservoir is itself a large natural reserve, named after a Tsuu T'ina (Sarcee) chief who lived in the area. Numerous pathways wind through the mixed riverine and spruce forest. As well as being prime territory for bird-watchers, wildlife viewing is good here, too. North Glenmore provides picnic sites and high vantage points for watching the action on the reservoir. The Calgary Canoe Club is situated at the east end of this area while the

Prince's Island Park, page 122

Calgary Parks & Recreation Dept.

Glenmore Sailing School makes its home across the reservoir on the south bank. South Glenmore features hiking, cycling, and cross-country ski trails leading to East Glenmore and Heritage Park Historical Village (see Chapter 5, "Sights and Attractions," for more information about Heritage Park).

East Glenmore provides excellent views of moored sailboats and the S.S. *Moyie,* the sternwheeler that cruises Glenmore reservoir from Heritage Park. Glenmore Athletic Park, at the northeast end of the reservoir, features an indoor pool, ice arena, tennis courts, ball diamonds, soccer pitches, football fields, and a golf course.

JAMES SHORT PARK
115 - 4th Ave. SW, Calgary
403/268-3888   DT
James Short Park with its beautiful flower gardens sits atop an underground parkade in downtown Calgary. The cupola is a distinctive landmark that was originally part of James Short School before it was demolished. For years it graced Prince's Island until, in 1990, it was moved back to its present location, where the school once stood. One of the city's oldest tower clocks from the old Burns Building was restored and added by the Calgary Watch and Clock Collectors Association. The clock can be heard to chime four times each hour. A volunteer climbs a ladder and manually winds the clock once a week.

Top Ten Plants to Grow in Calgary
according to William R. Reader,
Parks Superintendent from 1913 to 1942

1. Bearded irises
2. Campanulas (bell flowers)
3. Columbines
4. Delphiniums
5. Dianthus
6. Hollyhocks
7. Peonies
8. Phlox
9. Poppies
10. Veronica

LAYCOCK PARK
West of Nose Creek between Beaver Dam Road and 64th Avenue NE, Calgary   NE
This small park at the north end of Nose Creek is named after Thomas Laycock, a well-known local cattle rancher in the late 1800s, whose farm encompassed this area. Laycock Park provides picnic areas and cycling and pedestrian pathways for a part of the city where there are few parks.

LINDSAY PARK
1st Street SE, just south of the Elbow River, Calgary   SW
When Calgarians talk about Lindsay Park, they are usually referring to the facilities at the Lindsay Park Sports Centre. There is, however, a smallish park surrounding this facility that nestles in a crook of the Elbow River.

Picnic tables and grassy areas define this area, which is just a few blocks south of downtown. (See also Chapter 5, "Sights and Attractions," p. 94.)

NOSE HILL PARK
North of John Laurie Boulevard NW between 14th Street and Shaganappi Trail, Calgary   NW
Nose Hill Park is one of the two major natural park spaces in Calgary, encompassing 1,128 hectares (2,786 acres) of uncultivated grassland area. The huge boulders on the hill are "glacial erratics" carried from the Jasper area on sheets of ice during the Ice Age and left behind as the glaciers receded. This hill is a favorite hiking and cycling area that affords a great view of the city skyline and mountains. There are many theories as to how it got its name. One is that,

The Calgary Horticultural Society information line (403/287-3469) provides details about the Garden Tour (a tour of approximately 20 private gardens that won the Annual Garden Competition) in early August, the Flower Show (exhibits of cut flowers, arrangements, perennials, floral art, roses, and indoor plants), and other gardening events throughout the city.

according to legend, the Siksika (Blackfoot) Indians, on seeing the hill from a distance, thought it resembled the nose of their chief.

OLYMPIC PLAZA
Corner of Macleod Trail and 7th Avenue SW, Calgary
403/268-5207   **DT**

This downtown park was created for the medal presentations of the 1988 Winter Olympics. Today the plaza serves as venue for outdoor ice skating in the winter as well as music

Olympic Plaza

Frances Purslow

concerts and other special events throughout the year. It is bedecked with flower baskets in summer.

PRAIRIE WINDS PARK
223 Castleridge Blvd. NE, Calgary   **NE**

Finished in 1990, Prairie Winds Park is a relatively new addition to the city. Man-made hills and a creek add interest to the otherwise flat terrain of the surrounding area and provide opportunities for tobogganing. The wading pool and water cannons are extremely popular with children on hot days. There are also playgrounds, a skating rink, a giant sandbox, baseball diamonds, tennis courts, and picnic facilities.

PRINCE'S ISLAND PARK
Between 1st Avenue SW and Memorial Drive NW at
3rd Street SW, Calgary   **DT**

Eleven hectares (28 acres) of green space and walkways within the embrace of the Bow River offer a breath of fresh air to office workers out for a stroll or jog on their lunch hour. A playground and water park (complete with water cannons) at Barclay Mall as well as ducks and geese along the riverbanks entertain the young set. Take a break on the riverbank and watch fishermen cast lines in one of the best fishing rivers in the country. Pack a picnic lunch or buy a gourmet hot dog and snow cone from vendors. This is a popular venue for some of the city's major events: Canada Day and Heritage Day festivities, Calgary Folk Festival, Calgary Jazz Festival, Calgary Winter Festival, and BBQ on the Bow. Enter via pedestrian bridges on 3rd Street SW connecting the park to downtown and Eau Claire Market to the south and to Memorial Drive to the north.

RILEY PARK
800 - 12th St. NW, Calgary   NW
One of Calgary's oldest parks, Riley Park has been the site of vigorous cricket games since 1919, when three cricket pitches were created along with a clubhouse that served tea at three o'clock on Sunday afternoons.

Cricket is the only official sport allowed in the park today, but many other activities abound. The wading pool attracts hordes of children anxious for a splash on a hot day. Strollers enjoy the flowers of Riley Park and the hilly flower and rock gardens in neighboring Senator Patrick Burns Memorial Park.

RIVER PARK
14A Street SW between 38th and 50th Avenues, Calgary   SW
Another small park along the Elbow River, this one is especially frequented by dog owners because it is a designated off-leash area. Other than walking trails and picnic tables, there are few amenities, but cross-country skiers and tobogganers enjoy the gentle slopes of the park. In the centre of the park are large, well-tended flower beds.

William R. Reader

In 1913, British landscape gardener and horticulturist William R. Reader became Calgary's first Parks Superintendent, a position he held for 30 years. During that time, he worked and lived on the site of the current Reader Rock Gardens and Union Cemetery (bordered by Macleod Trail, 25th Avenue SE, and Spiller Road SE). Reader laid out a magnificent rock garden incorporating pools, rivulets, stone paths, and terraces. It opened in 1923 and covered 1.2 hectares (3 acres) with more than 4,000 species of plant life, many previously unknown in Alberta. As part of his legacy, he left behind meticulous notes and records of the plants he grew, weather conditions, and the results of his testing of new plants for their suitability to Calgary's rigorous climate. William Reader also developed many parks in the city, including Riley Park and Central Memorial Park.

Devonian Gardens

SHOULDICE PARK
1515 Home Rd. NW, Calgary   NW
Shouldice Park is bisected by 16th Avenue NW, extending south to the Bow River. It is a pleasant combination of natural areas along the riverbanks and athletic facilities such as tennis courts, football fields, ball diamonds, soccer pitches, an indoor pool, and an arena. A playground and picnic area are located in the part of the park that lies north of 16th Avenue.

STANLEY PARK
4011 - 1A St. SW, Calgary   SW
Stanley Park is one of the most popular parks in the city. Hugging the east banks of the Elbow River, when temperatures soar it offers people the choice of cooling off by dipping in a swimming pool or wading in the river. Picnicking, tennis, and strolling the pathways are alternative summer pastimes in the park, and the outdoor skating rink and toboggan runs provide winter fun.

GARDENS

CENTURY GARDENS
8th Avenue and 8th Street SW, Calgary
403/268-3888   DT
Visit this oasis amidst towering downtown buildings. Relax to the sound of waterfalls and streams in this lush, green park designed to resemble a mountain meadow.

DEVONIAN GARDENS
TD Square, 4th level
317 - 7th Ave. SW, Calgary
403/268-5207   DT
Since 1977, the Devonian Gardens have offered downtown shoppers and office workers an indoor sanctuary filled with 16,000 tropical plants, 4,000 local plants, trees, fountains, trickling ponds filled with colorful koi, and regular art exhibitions and performing arts series. Benches are scattered along flower-banked pathways. Pack a lunch or pick one up at the food court on the 4th level of TD Square

and eat on one of the benches while enjoying a free concert. There is also a children's playground to give parents a breather. Hours: 9–9. Admission: Free. (See also Chapter 5, "Sights and Attractions," p. 84.)

READER ROCK GARDEN
Macleod Trail and 25th Avenue SE, Calgary **SE**

Access Reader Rock Gardens from 25th Avenue SE via a roadway that runs beside a pillared archway. This site was a bare, windy hillside in the early 1900s when William Reader became Superintendent of Calgary's Parks Department. He created a variety of gardens consisting of 40 beds that included rock walls with native alpine plants, a bog garden, a shade garden, an iris dell, and a quiet garden. The gardens were at their peak in 1942 just prior to Reader's retirement. Unfortunately, over the years the hillside garden has not been maintained, but a preservation and restoration project plan (which includes obtaining historical status) currently underway aims to return Reader Rock Gardens to its former glory.

ZOO BOTANICAL GARDENS
1300 Zoo Rd. NE, Calgary
403/232-9372 **NE**

Be one of the 850,000 annual zoo visitors and surround yourself with thousands of plants in the Zoo's Botanical Gardens. From May to October you can take a self-guided tour through the outdoor gardens, which display the wide array of plantlife that grows in Calgary. Year-round you can stroll through the Conservatory—a feast for the senses with lush foliage, fragrant blossoms, and fluttering butterflies. Special seniors' events during certain times of the year include admission, program, and lunch amid the blossoms and butterflies. Open every day at 9 a.m. Admission summer/winter: $9.50/$8 adults, $4.75 seniors (Tues–Thur), $4.75/$4 children. Accessible by Whitehorn C-Train. (See also Chapter 5, "Sights and Attractions," p. 96.)

9

SHOPPING

There's lots of good news for shoppers in Calgary. First, Alberta is the only province in Canada with no sales tax. Second, Calgarians maintain high expectations when it comes to shopping, so visitors will find everything imaginable from specialty boutiques to country markets to modern shopping centres.

Calgary is home to eight regional shopping centres totaling about 5 million square feet, as well as 110 neighborhood, community, strip, and power centres adding another 9 million square feet. There are approximately 2 million square feet of retail space in the downtown core with the largest centres being Bankers Hall, Calgary's Eaton Centre, Toronto Dominion (TD) Square, Scotia Centre, and Eau Claire Market.

SHOPPING AREAS

Downtown Calgary's elevated pedway system (called the Plus-15) links more than 50 office towers with some 500 shops and services (including seven indoor shopping centres and two department stores as well as the 2.5-acre indoor Devonian Gardens) and 42,000 parking stalls. Business, cinemas, shopping, and parking are all accessed without venturing outside. Unique shopping experiences await visitors also at Eau Claire Mar-

ket by Prince's Island Park and Dragon City Mall in Chinatown.

Bankers Hall

315 - 8th Ave. SW, Calgary   DT
Bankers Hall features an attractive skylit retail gallery of more than 50 international fashion and specialty stores, boutiques, restaurants, and services on the first three levels. A cinema is on the fourth floor. Stop by the concierge desk on the main floor to receive your welcome package,

The Canadian $1 and $2 bills have gone the way of the dinosaur and been replaced by coins. The $1 coin features a picture of the common loon and is referred to as a "loonie". The $2 coin is called a "twoonie."

which includes free hotel delivery, complimentary gift wrapping, preferred parking, and tax exemption forms.

GEOSTONES
Bankers Hall, on the Plus-15 level, Calgary
403/262-5008 DT
Step inside for a great selection of Alberta's iridescent gemstone, ammolite. Also showcased are fossils, soapstone carvings, sculptures, figurines, and Canadian jewelry by silversmith Roland Chiasson.

INTIMATELY YOURS
Bankers Hall, on the Plus-15 level, Calgary
403/265-5471 DT
Indulge yourself or a loved one at this elegant lingerie boutique. Oriental silks, satin, and lace items reflect attention to detail. Intimately Yours also offers specialty items for romantic occasions. Their sleepwear collection caters to both women and men.

Bow Valley Square

205 - 5th Ave. SW, Calgary DT
There are more than 50 stores and services on the two lower levels of this office tower, including banking, bookstore, flower shop, gift shops, restaurants, and travel agency. Also of note on the second level is Lunchbox Theatre, which presents

live theatre productions over the noon hour (see Chapter 11, "Performing Arts" p. 157).

CREATIVE INFLUENCE GIFTS AND GIFT SERVICES
Bow Valley Square, Calgary
403/571-4438 DT
Located on the main floor of Bow Valley Square, this shop carries creative and imaginative gifts for all occasions including gift baskets, balloons, and gourmet food baskets. You can shop in person or leave it to the experts. They also offer worldwide delivery service.

JOSEPH'S MEN'S WEAR
Bow Valley Square, Calgary
403/264-5305 DT
Nothing fits like a custom-made suit, and Joseph's Men's Wear has been expertly fitting Calgary businessmen for 33 years. Dress for success with custom men's wear sporting Canadian labels such as Samuelsohn, Cambridge, and Jack Victor. Excellent selection of accessories. Tailors on staff also provide same-day alterations.

Dragon City Mall

328 Centre St. S., Calgary DT
This attractive complex sits at the gateway to Calgary's vibrant Chinatown. Featuring Asian art on its walls and ceilings, Dragon City Mall offers everything Chinese from herbal

remedies to astrology, antiques, apparel, art, furniture, and culinary delights that are exotic yet economical. Check out the golden dragon on the ceiling of the atrium.

PRINCESS JEWELLERY
Dragon City Mall, Calgary
403/261-6979   DT
Traditional and contemporary jewelry imported from Hong Kong line the display cases in Princess Jewellery. Jade, black pearls, cultured pearls, diamonds, and 24-karat gold set as rings, earrings, bracelets, pendants, and even statuettes are all featured. Staff jewelers also design custom settings.

Eau Claire Market

2nd Avenue and 2nd Street SW,
Calgary   DT
Experience the excitement of a fresh food market combined with unique, locally owned specialty stores and services including fashion, art, jewelry, books, crafts, IMAX Theatre, and cinemas. The food court on the main floor is very busy over the noon hour weekdays. For family fun visit Cinescape, a multimedia entertainment centre. (See also Chapter 5, "Sights and Attractions," p. 86.)

BENKRIS & CO.
Eau Claire Market, #68 main floor,

Calgary
403/290-1950   DT
Calgary's premier kitchen shop cum cooking school carries kitchen tools, cookware, glassware, and dinnerware. If you're in need of a kitchen gadget, start here. Other location at Southcentre.

JAMZ ORIGINAL
Eau Claire Market, #73 main floor, Calgary
403/262-0370   DT
"Unique, fun, and functional" describes this comfortable sleepwear made in Calgary. Jamz Original offers boxers, nightshirts, night caps, pj's with feet, and eye covers in funky prints. Nightwear for the whole family.

MAPLE LEAF FUDGE
Eau Claire Market, #28 main floor, Calgary
403/264-0537   DT
You simply must try at least one of the 18 delicious flavours of fudge made daily at this outlet. They also carry maple syrup products, gourmet chocolates, and brittle. Take some Canadian culinary delights home with you.

PERFECTLY COUNTRY
Eau Claire Market, #91 upper floor, Calgary
403/262-1034   DT
Look here to outfit yourself in country clothing and your home in the best of

---

If you are a tourist, you can get a free three-day parking pass for use at on-street metered parking stalls June through September. Call the Calgary Parking Authority at 403/974-0678.

antiques, primitive folk art, dried florals, pottery, candles, and more. Perfectly Country is the largest supplier of illustrator Mary Engelbreit's products. Browse through these delightful items at your leisure.

PRIMETIME GIFTS
Eau Claire Market, #66 main floor, Calgary
403-268-2804   **DT**
Here is a fun place to visit when you're looking for a gift for that mature adult in your life. The shop features "ideal gifts for people older than you," such as gardening tools with larger handles for those with arthritis, microwave heatable seat cushions to increase hockey or football game viewing pleasure, and brag books for grandparents. Functional or frivolous—they have it all.

Penny Lane Specialty Shops

8th Avenue between 4th and 5th Streets SW, Calgary   **DT**
Penny Lane is a pretty spot to shop with quaint, turn-of-the-century architecture housing coffeeshops, full-service restaurants, fashion boutiques, and local art.

GIOS GENTLEMEN'S CLASSIC CLOTHIERS
Penny Lane Shops
513 - 8th Ave. SW, Calgary
403-262-4090   **DT**
Since 1985, this independent clothier has reflected European flair in its custom-designed suits. Designers include Inthema and Redaelli. Choose from Perry Ellis or Cutter and Buck sportswear. Accessories also available.

LA CHIC LADIES WEAR
Penny Lane Shops
513 - 8th Ave. SW, Calgary

Eau Claire Market

403/269-4775   **DT**
This shop specializes in exclusive European designer collections. Sizes range from 4 to 18. Accessories to complete your look are also available. They pride themselves on personalized service.

Scotia Centre

225 - 7th Ave. SW, Calgary   **DT**
Housing 35 shops and services including fashions, accessories, and restaurants, Scotia Centre offers you a visitor's gift and information bag when you drop by O'Shea's Market Ireland on the second level. It includes free gift wrapping, hotel delivery, currency exchange, and tax exemption forms.

O'SHEA'S MARKET IRELAND
Scotia Centre, Calgary
403/266-4334   **DT**
Where fashion and tradition meet, O'Shea's provides the largest selection of Irish garments and giftware in Calgary. Hand-knit sweaters for men and women are made with traditional Aran yarn or pima cotton. You can

even order one custom-made. They also feature Celtic and Claddagh jewelry, Belleek china, wool-cashmere capes, and tartans.

THOMAS JEFFREY MEN'S WEAR
Scotia Centre, Calgary
403/265-2081   DT
Stop in for quality men's wear bearing names such as Baumler, Strellson, Samuelsohn, Franco Tassi, Valenza, Lubiam, and Mondo. Thomas Jeffrey's second location is in Southcentre.

Stephen Avenue Mall

8th Avenue between 1st Street SE and 3rd Street SW, Calgary   DT
With sandstone buildings dating back to 1886, Stephen Avenue is one of the most historic areas of Calgary. This pedestrian mall is a popular people-watching spot, especially in summer. Food kiosks and live entertainment keep people coming back for more. While some stores are a bit tacky, others are well worth a visit, such as western wear giant Riley & McCormick.

A & B SOUND
140 - 8th Ave. SW, Calgary
403/232-1200   DT
Four levels of CDs, tapes, TVs, VCRs, and boom boxes fill this emporium. The imposing architecture of this restored Bank of Montreal building

features beautiful brass doors and high, vaulted ceilings.

RILEY & McCORMICK
209 - 8th Ave. SW, Calgary
403/262-1556   DT
Since 1901 Riley & McCormick has been a name in western wear, outfitting families in name-brand hats, boots, jeans, shirts, and accessories. Calgary's oldest western store offers a free mail order catalogue, available by calling 800/661-1585. Other locations at Scotia Centre, Market Mall, and the airport.

Inglewood

9th Avenue and 12th Street SE, Calgary   SE
The site of Calgary's original business district, Inglewood is now a shopping area defined by quaint architecture and ornate lamp standards. Most noted for its antique shops and collectibles, the area is an eclectic mix of secondhand stores, ethnic restaurants, and shops with character.

FAIR'S FAIR
Inglewood
Downstairs 1336 - 9th Ave. SE, Calgary
403/237-8156   SE
There's something for everyone at this secondhand bookstore boasting more than 150,000 volumes. They buy, sell,

and trade current fiction, classics, biographies, mysteries, westerns, Canadiana, and more. Staff are especially friendly and knowledgeable. Free parking on 13th Street SE. Other locations in Kensington and Uptown 17th.

JUNKTIQUES
Inglewood
1226 - 9th Ave. SE, Calgary
403/263-0619 **SE**
A fine selection of country antiques is housed here. Junktiques offers architectural rarities, stoneware, and custom reproductions. Owner David Kaufman sells untouched and refurbished furniture and custom-made reproductions. Furniture refinishing and restoration is done on-site. Each March and September Kaufman and his wife journey to Quebec, the Maritimes, and the northeastern United States, returning with a myriad of auction items. Upon their arrival back in Calgary, they have an open house at their northeast warehouse. If you're visiting at that time of year and would like to attend, phone the shop for exact dates.

Willowpark Village

10816 Macleod Tr. SE
Calgary **SE**
A leisurely stroll through this village setting reveals more than 60 shops and services including fashions, a bookstore, specialty gift stores, and restaurants. Take a break at Conversations Tea Room, where homemade scones will melt in your mouth, or savor the cannelloni at Chianti's. If you're hankering for Chinese, mosey into Ginger Beef.

CHECK-MATE SHOES
Willowpark Village, Calgary
403/271-1597 **SE**
Specializing in the hard-to-fit, Checkmate Shoes combines expert service and quality footwear for men and women. They offer affordable styles from fashion to walking shoes in men's sizes up to 13EEE and women's to 12EE.

LAMMLE'S WESTERN WEAR
Willowpark Village, Calgary
403/271-4910 **SE**
Official western wear supplier of the

Smithbilt Hats

Smithbilt Hats Ltd., a privately owned manufacturer of cowboy hats since 1919, produces more than 32,000 hats for Stampede Week sales. This Calgary company sells none of its products retail but supplies hats wholesale to western outfitters across Canada and in Europe.

Smithbilt's popular wool and wool-blend hats retail for $26 to $180, placing them in the mid-range, so no need to mortgage the house to buy one. You'll be in good company, too—Prime Minister Jean Chretien, former Soviet leader Mikhail Gorbachev, Paul Anka, Wayne Gretzky, and even the Pope all own Smithbilts.

Ammolite: "Opal of the Sea"

With iridescent hues of blue, green, red, and gold, ammolite is a rare gem obtained from ammonite fossils discovered in Southern Alberta. Coloration can vary from flaming pieces to tiny points, from colourful lines to large colour planes and even geometric formations. Recognized as an official gemstone in 1981, this rare, mineralized sea fossil shell has sometimes been confused with opal. But the price of ammolite is more affordable than opal and, as each piece is unique, the gem lends itself to one-of-a-kind jewelry.

Ammonite fossils are found all over the world, but because of the iron-rich shale near Lethbridge the ammonite fossils found there have been transformed into well-preserved, gem-quality ammolite. Only limited quantities of ammolite are available, thereby enhancing the value of this unique Canadian gemstone.

Calgary Stampede, Lammle's has dressed more Alberta cowboys than you can throw a rope at. They carry name-brand boots, shirts, jeans, belt buckles, and other accessories, as well as a large assortment of cowboy hats. There are eight other locations in Calgary (in major shopping malls) including their fashion clearance outlet at Chinook Centre.

4th Street

4th Street between Elbow Drive and 17th Avenue SW, Calgary   SW
*This stretch of eight blocks hosts the Lilac Festival in late May. At any time of the year it is a great place to window-shop and browse in the local shops filled with such unique merchandise as handmade crafts, interior decor items, and designer fashions. There are also myriad din-*ing establishments from full service to casual cafés and coffeehouses. Bagels to baklava, tandoori chicken to falafel, there's something delicious on every block.*

**MICAH GALLERY
1819 - 4th St. SW, Calgary
403/245-1340   SW**
Dedicated to North American Native artistic excellence, the Micah Gallery showcases Alberta's largest selection of Aboriginal arts and crafts. Hand-crafted jewelry, fashions, collectibles, and giftware are all displayed. Free parking.

**WILD BIRDS UNLIMITED
#18, 2100 - 4th St. SW, Calgary
403/245-6867   SW**
This unique shop is the haunt of bird lovers looking for the perfect house for their backyard feathered friends. If you want to attract birds to your

home or cottage, drop in for a look at their selection of wild birdseed, birdhouses, bird and squirrel feeders, binoculars, nature gifts, and birdbaths. Your Backyard Bird Feeding Specialist. Free parking out front.

Glenmore Landing

14th Street and 90th Avenue SW, Calgary   SW
At the south end of Glenmore Reservoir is a complex of elegant shops with bright blue roofs. Upscale fashions, bakery, bookstore, art gallery, and various eating establishments and services come together here.

DUCKS & COMPANY
Glenmore Landing
#A124, 1600 - 90th Ave. SW, Calgary
403/640-0043   SW
If you're searching out the unique, visit Ducks & Company for a look at their beautiful hand-knit cotton and wool-blend sweaters. Sweaters by Bianca Nygaard, Sigred Olsen, Funsport, IB Diffusion, and Northern Isles are for sale, along with elegant Susan Bristol

fashions and colour-coordinated coats, leggings, sweaters, and accessories by Linda Lundström. Check out their eye-popping jewelry. Second location at Strathcona Square.

PETITE COLLECTION
Glenmore Landing
#144a, 1600 - 90th Ave. SW, Calgary
403/640-2399   SW
These designer fashions are proportioned for women 5'4" or less. Labels include such names as Jones New York, Mr. Jax, Maggie London, Ellen Tracy, and Anne Klein.

Uptown 17th, the Avenue

17th Avenue between 2nd and 14th Streets SW, Calgary   SW
This scenic neighborhood sports an upscale shopping district, in the middle of which sits one of Calgary's most exclusive malls, Mount Royal Village. Enjoy spending a day browsing through the vast collection of the exotic, the elegant, and the eclectic merchandise offered by more than 400 shops. Keep an

Mountain Equipment Co-op, page 137

Roger Chayer/Talus Photographics

eye out for the colourful murals on the sides of buildings.

DON FORSTER MEN'S WEAR
1818 - 2nd St. SW, Calgary
403/228-5159 SW
Top-quality men's wear with brand names such as Warren K. Cook, Ballantyne, Burberry, and Aquascutum is the specialty here. The selection includes suits and blazers, sportswear, cotton shirts, accessories, and Tilley Endurables for men and women. Their tailor shop offers same-day service for travelers.

RAINING CATS AND DOGS
1022 - 17th Ave. SW, Calgary
403/244-1717 SW
For that pampered Persian or aristocratic Afghan, there are gifts galore at Raining Cats and Dogs. You'll find gourmet treats, squeaky toys, jackets for the cold, and even gifts for feline and canine owners. If you left your cat or dog in a "pet hotel" back home, return with a peace offering from your trip to Calgary.

RUBAIYAT
722 - 17th Ave. SW, Calgary
403/228-7192 SW
Not your average gift store, Rubaiyat is a purveyor of finely hand-crafted gifts and collectibles from all over the world, including artifacts and crafts from Africa and Asia, distinctive jewelry, and exquisite art glass.

A TOUCH OF ITALY
Mount Royal Village
320 - 17th Ave. SW, Calgary
403/229-1066 SW
Form and function come together in this shop featuring unique Italian gifts, pasta cookware, espresso coffees, fine olive oils and vinegars, and espresso/cappuccino machines.

Dragon City Mall, page 127

Frances Purslow

Fine Italian craftsmanship is reflected in the gourmet cookware and cutlery and artful ceramic designs. Stainless steel kitchen utensils from Rösle are also for sale.

Kensington

Kensington Road and 10th Street NW, Calgary NW
More than 140 trendy bookstores, boutiques, art shops, old and new clothing stores, delis, and restaurants line the streets of Kensington, just across the Bow River from downtown. Enjoy a relaxing shopping experience amidst the new and old buildings then cool your heels in a village-like atmosphere at one of the many excellent coffeehouses.

LIVINGSTONE & CAVELL EXTRAORDINARY TOYS
1124A Kensington Rd. NW, Calgary
403/270-4165 NW
Grandmas and Grandpas love this store. Here they find heirloom toys they always wanted and now they can indulge themselves or their

grandchildren. Distinctive and finely crafted toys from around the world include tin and clockwork toys, Meccano, Britains Miniatures, Wilesco steam engines, and more.

VICTORIAN ROSE
1130 Kensington Rd. NW, Calgary
403/283-9555   NW
Eyelet and lace abound in this elegant shop full of romantic clothing and hats by Linda Lundström, Simon Chang, and Ross Mayer; bridal gowns by Jessica McClintock; and jewelry, gifts, and collectibles such as pewter frames, china boxes, pillows, linens, and hand-knit sweaters. Victorian lamps sport lampshades that can be ordered in various colors embellished with your choice of trimmings.

OTHER NOTABLE STORES

ALBERTA BOOT CO.
614 - 10th Ave. SW, Calgary
403/263-4623   SW
A factory and retail store, Alberta Boot Co. is Alberta's only western boot manufacturer. Choose from more than 10,000 pairs or have a pair custom-made. Top-quality materials and workmanship distinguish their boots and ensure comfort, durability, and timeless style. Plenty of free parking.

BILLY'S NEWS & SMOKE SHOP
206 - 7th Ave. SW, Calgary

TRIVIA

Dragon City Mall is the largest Chinese mall in Canada.

403/262-2894   DT
If you're hungry for news of home, Billy's News, a Calgary institution since 1960, carries a wide selection of out-of-town newspapers as well as European fashion magazines.

BRITISH MARKET PLACE
Chinook Centre
Macleod Trail and Glenmore Trail SW, Calgary
403/258-3600   DT
Discover a slice of Britain in this shop specializing in products from the British Isles including fine china, Paddington bears, books, toys, collectibles, pictorial cork placemats, tea pots, tinware, confectionery, and biscuits.

CHAPTERS
202, 4600 Dalhousie Dr. NW, Calgary
403/202-4600   NW
This mega-bookstore houses one of the city's most comprehensive newsstands with newspapers and magazines from all over the world. Stop in at the on-site Starbucks coffee shop and enjoy a latté while you peruse the shelves. Chapter's second location is on Macleod Trail SW at 94th Avenue.

CHASE CATTLE CO.
TD Square, 3rd floor
7th Avenue and 2nd Street SW, Calgary
403/269-6450   DT
Retail Excellence Award winner in 1995, Chase Cattle Co. offers a wide selection of upscale western wear including vests, skirts, beaded shirts, cowboy hats, and boots. There are also home decor items, Native artifacts, sculptures, jewelry, branding irons, and hot pepper condiments. Chase Cattle Co. specializes in styles of the Old West for the new generation.

CHERRIES GIFTS
131 - 9th Ave. SW (at the base of the Calgary Tower), Calgary
403/262-1798   **DT**
This retail space is chock full of souvenirs of your trip to Calgary for yourself or loved ones back home. Canadiana, Aboriginal work, souvenir sweatshirts and T-shirts, mugs, and books are all in abundance. There's nothing tacky here.

CHOCOLATERIE BERNARD CALLEBAUT
1313 - 1st St. SE, Calgary
403/266-4300   **SE**
It's love at first bite at Bernard Callebaut's Chocolaterie. This site houses the head office and chocolate factory that produces Belgian chocolate confections for the other 27 outlets across Canada and the U.S. Weekdays, you can take a self-guided tour of the production line and sample a tasty treat at the end. Bet you can't eat just one! Other Calgary locations include Uptown 17th, Glenmore Landing, and Crowchild Square.

COOKBOOK CO.
722 - 11th Ave. SW, Calgary
403/265-6066   **SW**
Foodies will deem this a wonderful place to while away an afternoon browsing through the extensive selection of cookbooks and specialty foods. A cooking school also runs on the premises. Pick up a bottle of wine from Metro Vino at the back of the store before heading home to make your memorable meal.

CRAFTER'S MARKETPLACE
8228 Macleod Tr. SE, Calgary
403/974-1470   **SE**
Canada's largest indoor craft mall features display space for independent crafters to show their wares. More than 350 of North America's talented crafters and artisans showcase their hand-crafted items under one roof. While you browse the aisles, enjoy a free gourmet coffee at the Marketplace Country Store.

TEN THOUSAND VILLAGES
8318 Fairmount Dr. SE, Calgary
403/255-0553   **SE**
This not-for-profit retail outlet features handmade crafts from Third World artisans, thereby creating jobs with dignity in emerging nations. The store carries wooden carvings, brass bells and elephants, colourful wall hangings, and more.

FLAGWORKS INC.
602 - 12th Ave. SW, Calgary
403/265-5595   **SW**
This unique store features traditional and custom flags and banners. It is

When shopping for gifts for those back home or souvenirs of your trip to Alberta, consider a book of photographic essays of the area. A wide assortment of reasonably priced coffee table books is available in gift shops in the city as well as at Banff, Kananaskis, and other destinations.

also a manufacturer of several lines of sportswear for souvenir and team needs. Their FlagWear is a colourful line of flag-motif clothing for every member of the family.

FLAMES FAN ATTIC
7517 Flint Rd. SE, Calgary
403/571-9744   **SE**
The official store of the Calgary Flames Hockey Club has three other locations—Chinook Centre, North-land Village Shoppes, and the Sad-dledome—all of which feature exclusive and authentic Flames and NHL sportswear and souvenirs. Not just the usual jerseys and hats here, they also carry leather jackets, sleepwear, boxers, and golf shirts with embroidered logos. Smaller souvenir items include pens, mugs, and of course pucks. Ask about the Elston books of sports cartoons.

HIDDEN CREEK MERCANTILE
410 - 6th St. SW, Calgary
403/262-2100   **DT**
If you're looking for a unique gift for someone, order a personalized branding iron from Jack Foster, owner of Hidden Creek. These au-thentic, handmade branding irons in-corporate the initials of your choice and are great for branding steaks on the barbecue. All of the items in this delightful store are made by Alberta artisans. You'll find things here you won't see anywhere else. It's defi-nitely worth a look.

IRONWOOD INTERIOR FURNISHINGS
1008 - 12th Ave. SW, Calgary
403/229-2528   **SW**
To customize your home the way you've always wanted, visit Ironwood Interior Furnishings and peruse their vast selection of home furnishings

Chocolaterie Bernard Callebaut, page 136

and accessories. Slipcovers and bed-ding, custom draperies, upholstery, and wrought iron furniture are also featured for those with discerning tastes. Check out the painted and crackled imagery on custom wall tiles by Vancouver artist Sid Dickens as well as works by local artists.

MOUNTAIN EQUIPMENT CO-OP
830 - 10th Ave. SW, Calgary
403/269-2420   **SW**
This imposing building on the corner of 8th Street and 10th Avenue SW is chock full of quality clothing and equipment for self-propelled wilder-ness activities. The outdoor fun spe-cialists offer backpacks, outerwear, hiking boots, sleeping bags, tents, cycling, Nordic ski wear, and more. Ask about a membership; 125,000 Calgarians can't be wrong.

QUILTED BEAR
Franklin Mall
36th Street and 12th Avenue NE, Calgary
403/248-3770   **NE**

Goods and Services Tax Rebate

The Canadian government levies a Goods and Services Tax (GST) at the rate of 7 percent on most goods and services. Foreign visitors, however, may obtain a rebate of the GST on short-term accommodations and goods purchased in Canada and removed from the country within 60 days. Present your receipts at a participating Canadian Duty Free shop for a cash refund of up to $500 when leaving Canada or pick up a mail-in rebate application form at Duty Free Shops (excluding those at airports) or at the Calgary Tax Services Office at 140, 220 - 4th Avenue SE. Some of the major malls include tax rebate forms with their visitor packages (see individual mall listings). For further information, call 800/668-4748 or 403/221-7900.

More than 500 crafters and artisans display their beautiful hand-crafted items at booths in this retail superstore. Displays change on a regular basis so there's always something new to see.

SWEETAPPLE & COMPANY
Britannia Shopping Plaza
822 - 49th Ave. SW, Calgary
403/287-9735   **SW**
Exquisite handmade furniture, authentic folk art decoys, shaker boxes, baskets, clocks, and handcrafted chandeliers can be found at Sweetapple & Company. The whimsical and decorative mingle with the practical and functional, but all are pleasing to the eye. Check out their delightful log cabin lamps.

TALL GIRL & TALLCREST SHOES
Calgary Eaton Centre, 3rd level,
Calgary
403/263-1486   **DT**
Featuring fashionable clothing and footwear for the taller-than-average woman, Tall Girl carries sportswear, office wear, evening wear, lingerie, and accessories in tall sizes 8–20. Brand names in Tallcrest include Hush Puppies, Unisa, Glacée, and Nickels. Shoes, boots, sandals, slippers, and more come in sizes 10 and up.

MAJOR DEPARTMENT STORES

THE BAY
200 - 8th Ave. SW, Calgary
403/262-0345   **DT**
Canada's oldest retailer, the Bay has come a long way since its days as a fur-trading company over a hundred years ago. This department store features six floors of shops and services (including fur storage!) in a gracious old stone building. Other Bay locations in the city are Chinook Centre, Deerfoot Mall, Market Mall, and Southcentre.

EATON'S
510 - 8th Ave. SW, Calgary
403/298-4311 DT
Another Canadian institution, Eaton's is a department store with a wide range of merchandise from clothing to sporting goods to furniture. Other Eaton's locations include Northland Village Mall, Southcentre, and Sunridge.

SEARS
1616 - 14th Ave. NW, Calgary
403/289-7777 NW
Sears doesn't have a downtown location but operates from three regional malls. It offers mid-range merchandise and corresponding prices as well as installation service, custom draperies, automotive, and carpet cleaning. Sears also operates mail order shopping. Other Sears locations are Chinook Centre and Marlborough Towne Square.

MAJOR SHOPPING MALLS

BRENTWOOD VILLAGE MALL
3630 Brentwood Rd. NW,
Calgary NW
You can reach Brentwood Village via the Brentwood C-Train. Its major stores include Safeway, Kmart, and London Drugs. There are lots of eateries here to fuel you for more shopping.

CALGARY EATON CENTRE
8th Avenue and 4th Street SW,
Calgary DT
The Eaton Centre offers four levels of specialty and fashion shops and services. Anchor store Holt Renfrew features upscale fashions on two floors. There are lots of shopping opportunities in this bright and airy shopping mall and a food court on the top level.

CHINOOK CENTRE
Corner of Macleod Trail and
Glenmore Trail SW, Calgary SW
With more than 300 stores and services on two levels, Chinook Centre is the largest single mall in Calgary. Sears anchors the north end, and the Bay and Zellers anchor the south end. Members of the Soul Mates Walking Club get their exercise in a safe and comfortable environment by walking the corridors of the mall weekday mornings from 7 a.m. to 10 a.m. Anyone can join.

DEERFOOT MALL
901 - 64th Ave. NE, Calgary NE
Deerfoot Mall incorporates more than 100 shops and services with the Bay, Wal-Mart, Foody-Goody (Chinese buffet), and Shoppers Drug Mart as some of the larger merchants. Parking for RVs during Stampede Week is available. Access via 64th Avenue NE turnoff from Deerfoot Trail.

MARKET MALL
Corner of 32nd Avenue and
Shaganappi Trail, Calgary NW
Major stores at Market Mall are the Bay, Zellers, Sport Chek, Safeway, and Toys R Us. In all, there are more than 200 shops and services including Famous Players Theatres. There are lots of eating establishments to tempt the tastebuds, some fast-food and some full service.

NORTH HILL SHOPPING CENTRE
1632 - 14th Ave. NW, Calgary NW
This subregional shopping centre is on the Trans-Canada Highway (Highway 1) as it passes through the city. Sears and Safeway are the two main outlets.

NORTHLAND VILLAGE SHOPPES
Corner of Crowchild Trail and
Shaganappi Trail NW,

Calgary   **NW**

There are more than 100 shops and services, with Eaton's, Wal-Mart, Future Shop, and Pacific Linen being the major stores. Fashions for the whole family, furniture, records, cameras, stationery, books, restaurants, and services are all under one roof. You can also take a break from shopping and catch a movie at the Cineplex Odeon Theatres.

SOUTHCENTRE
Corner of Macleod Trail and Anderson Road SE, Calgary   **SE**

Southcentre attracts a lot of people for the shopping and the movie theatres. It offers extras like gift wrapping service, complimentary coat and parcel check, strollers and wheelchairs, newspapers and baby pacs. Courtesy van service is offered for those 65+, within a 10-kilometer (6-mile) radius. This is an upscale mall, with more than 200 stores and services on two levels.

TD SQUARE
7th Avenue and 2nd Street SW, Calgary   **DT**

There are more than 100 shops, services, and restaurants on the three levels of this attractive, spacious mall. Devonian Gardens occupies the fourth level. The mall is conveniently situated on the LRT line. Pick up your complimentary visitor welcome package from the customer service booth on the second level. It includes more than $300 in coupons as well as promotional items, a directory, and a unique souvenir from TD merchants.

10

SPORTS AND RECREATION

In 1981, Calgary was officially selected as the 1988 Olympic Winter Games site. This was the culmination of many years of dedicated effort, and Calgarians reaped the benefits, which included superior sport facilities. Canada Olympic Park with its luge runs and ski jump facilities, the Canadian Airlines Saddledome, and the Olympic Speed Skating Oval are all within city limits, while the Canmore Nordic Centre (site of the Nordic events) and the Nakiska Ski Area (Alpine ski events) are just west of Calgary. Other world-class sports venues are Lindsay Park Sports Centre with its international class pool and dive tank and Spruce Meadows, North America's premier equestrian centre.

Besides these outstanding venues, Calgary offers more than ten groomed and maintained athletic parks featuring arenas, soccer pitches, baseball diamonds, football fields, gymnasiums, pools, and racquet clubs in all parts of the city. Youth hockey programs are extremely popular, with about 25,000 boys and girls registered each year. Children as young as 5 sign up for a winter of hockey, dragging parents out of bed at 6 a.m. on weekends to get to the rink for practices. At the other end of the spectrum, old-timers' hockey grabs the late spots at the arenas. When spring arrives, every available green space is alive with active bodies playing baseball or soccer. Enthusiasts of roller-hockey, lacrosse, football, rugby, sailing, rowing, and golfing can also quench their thirst for action at facilities around town.

Professional sports franchises in the city include National Hockey League's (NHL) Calgary Flames, Canadian Football League's (CFL) Calgary Stampeders Football Club, and the AAA Calgary Cannons Baseball Club.

For recreational cyclists, joggers, and in-line skaters, there are more than 300 kilometers (190 miles) of pathways within city limits, as well as more challenging trails in the nearby mountains. If you'd rather take to the trails on horseback, there are several public riding stables nearby.

Recreational Facilities

Calgary offers the following amenities for fitness buffs and families out for a little recreation:

- *more than 300 kilometers (190 miles) of walking and cycling paths*
- *60 kilometers (37 miles) of cross-country ski trails*
- *58 fitness facilities*
- *226 tennis courts (several enclosed and winterized)*
- *120 sheets of curling ice*
- *270 racquet sport courts*
- *17 billiard halls*
- *10 bowling facilities*
- *321 ball diamonds*
- *298 soccer fields*
- *12 indoor swimming pools*
- *8 outdoor swimming pools*
- *10 wading pools*
- *47 arenas*
- *190 outdoor rinks*
- *674 playgrounds*
- *2,600 parks*

RECREATIONAL SPORTS

Biking

One of the best resources you can purchase for biking in and around the 300 kilometers of Calgary bike and pedestrian paths is the book *Calgary Parks and Pathways* by Terry Bullick. It contains detailed information about each of the pathway systems in the city and how they join together.

Mountain bikers will find more challenge in Kananaskis Country or in Banff National Park. Biking trail maps are available at their respective visitor centres.

Bobsleigh and Luge

Ride the Bobsleigh Bullet at Canada Olympic Park (COP) at speeds of 95 km/h (60 mph). The ride incorporates 14 turns and lasts just over a minute. Four ride at a time in these recreational bobsleighs, which are a little wider and a bit more padded than the real thing. You're given a helmet and some quick advice and off you go! The cost is $39 per person.

Thrill-seekers can also experience the excitement of luging winter or summer on an iced track at COP. For $13 sliders take off from the bottom third of the track and reach speeds of 40 km/h (25 mph). Call 403/247-5468 to book.

Bowling

THE BOWLING DEPOT
Deerfoot Mall
901 - 64th Ave. NE, Calgary
403/275-1260   NE
This facility offers 24 five-pin lanes with glow-in-the-dark pins. Every Friday and Saturday evening year-round (and Wednesday evenings in summer) they turn out the lights and you can bowl under blacklights with pulsing flashes and music playing. Even some of the balls glow!

MOUNTAIN VIEW BOWL
11, 3919 Richmond Rd. SW, Calgary
403/249-0858   SW
Another "glow bowl" location, this facility offers five-pin and ten-pin bowling under blacklights. Ever Friday and Saturday evening year-round (and Wednesday evenings in summer) you can try to hit the glow-in-the-dark pins with glow-in-the-dark balls. With lights flashing and music playing, this is a new generation of bowling!

TOPPLER BOWL
7640 Fairmount Dr. SE, Calgary
403/255-0101   SE
If you're planning on going bowling with young children, you might want to head down to Toppler Bowl, because they make it easy on youngsters— they put bumper pads in the gutters (if you request) so the balls stay on the alley and kids have a happier bowling experience.

Camping

Southern Alberta offers a smorgasbord of destinations for the camping enthusiast. Within an hour's drive of Calgary, you can camp in the mountains, on the prairies, or in the badlands. Camping fees in provincial parks range from $5 to $15 per night depending on the facilities and services. Reservations must be accompanied by a deposit.

Provincial Parks

BOW VALLEY
PROVINCIAL PARK
Kananaskis Country
403/673-2163

HIking near Calgary, pages 144–146

CRIMSON LAKE
PROVINCIAL PARK
Near Rocky Mountain House
403/845-2330

CYPRESS HILLS
PROVINCIAL PARK
Near Elkwater
403/893-3782

DINOSAUR PROVINCIAL
PARK
Near Brooks
403/378-3700

ELBOW VALLEY PROVINCIAL
RECREATION AREA
Kananaskis Country
403/949-3132

GHOST RESERVOIR PROVINCIAL
RECREATION AREA
West of Cochrane
403/932-6051

KINBROOK ISLAND PROVINCIAL
PARK
Near Brooks
403/362-2962

LITTLE BOW PROVINCIAL PARK
Near Champion
403/897-3933

PETER LOUGHEED PROVINCIAL
PARK

Kananaskis Country
403/591-7226

NATIONAL PARKS
Campgrounds in the national parks
are operated on a first-come, first-
served basis with a daily fee range
between $6 and $17.50. You must also
purchase a valid park entry permit,
available at park gates.

BANFF NATIONAL PARK
West of Calgary on Highway 1
403/762-3324

JASPER NATIONAL PARK
Northwest of Banff
403/852-6161

WATERTON LAKES NATIONAL
PARK
Southwest corner of the province
403/859-2224

Day Hiking

With the mountains so close to the
city, you can drive out and hike any
of the myriad hiking trails in the
Banff or Kananaskis areas and still
return to Calgary the same day. If exploring these picturesque areas on
foot is part of your plans, pick up hiking trail maps at visitor centres in
the provincial and national parks or

T I P

When hiking in the mountains, heed bear warnings and wear a bell or
other noise-maker. It's important to refrain from feeding any wildlife
you encounter as it's not good for their health and is potentially harm-
ful to yours, too.

Snopitch

The diamond is white, the ball is orange, and the players are having the time of their lives. Baseball in winter may seem like a bizarre thing to do, but don't tell that to the 180 teams who show up over two weekends in February for a tournament at the Marlborough Park Community Centre (6021 Madigan Drive NE). The snow is a great equalizer in snopitch. The quickest of runners are slowed down and the longest hitters often see their drives shortened by a snowdrift. The only home runs that happen are when the players can't find the ball. Layered by warm clothing and cushioned by snow, injuries are rare even though wipeouts abound. To catch the action, call Fred Gailus at 403/250-3293.

at one of the outdoor equipment stores in town. Alternatively, you can contact Kananaskis Country at 403/310-0000 for hiking information for that area, and Canadian Parks Service at 403/292-4401 for Banff/Lake Louise information. You can also purchase excellent books on mountain hiking trails.

While there are far too many trails to include a comprehensive list in this publication, the highlights include the following. Kananaskis Country offers a network of paved trails perfect for hiking and cycling. The Canmore Nordic Centre has 56 kilometers (35 miles) of cross-country ski trails perfect for hiking and mountain biking in summer. At Banff there is the wooded Fenland Trail, just off Norquay Road and a trail that skirts along Vermilion Lakes that rewards hikers with sightings of many birds. At Lake Louise a paved lakeshore trail takes you to the end of the lake where you may spot mountain goats on the slopes of Fairview Mountain. Follow the steep but popular trail

to the teahouse at Lake Agnes or hike to the Plain of Six Glaciers for a view of glaciated landscape.

While driving along the Icefields Parkway between Banff and Lake Louise, pull over at the turnouts for trailheads. There are lots of beautiful trails of varying lengths that are well worth exploring. One of the most popular trails in either winter or summer is an easy 20-minute walk into the depths of Johnston Canyon. For the more adventurous, there's a three-hour hike to the upper waterfalls and the Ink Pots springs.

About halfway between Banff and Lake Louise you can depart for a five-hour hike to Rockbound Lake, a beautiful spot behind Castle Mountain. On another day, you could follow Baker Creek Trail for a day of good fishing in the meadows.

BANFF MOUNT NORQUAY SIGHTSEEING LIFT
403/762-4421

In summer, visitors can hire guides to take them up or down the Lone Pine and North American ski runs or higher still from the top of the lift to the summit of Mount Norquay.

CAVE AND BASIN TOURS
403/762-1557
Take a walk along the interpretive boardwalk trails or a guided 45-minute tour featuring the history of the Banff area. Tours are free with admission to the Cave and Basin.

LAKE LOUISE SIGHTSEEING LIFT
403/522-3555
Pay for the lift and receive free guided tours on subalpine trails lasting 30 to 90 minutes.

MIRAGE ADVENTURE TOURS
403/678-4919
Mirage Adventure Tours features easy guided hikes of 8 kilometers (5 miles) in Kananaskis to low mountain passes.

PARKS CANADA
403/762-1550 (Banff) or 403/522-3833 (Lake Louise)
Parks Canada offers a number of guided interpretive hikes during the summer. At Banff, the Vermilion Lakes Stroll is an easy walk along the wetlands in the park. The Minnewanka Lakeside Walk is a two-hour excursion, and the Tunnel Mountain Hike is a three-hour gradual ascent. At Lake Louise, the Plain of Six Glaciers is a six-hour hike into the heart of the Rockies. The Eiffel Lake Hike explores the Moraine Lake area, and the Lake Louise Stroll is a two-hour walk along the lake.

WHITE MOUNTAIN ADVENTURES
403/678-4099
They'll drive you up to the picturesque

Sunshine Meadows where guided tours reveal some of the most scenic terrain in the Rockies.

Dogsledding

Alberta's crisp winter days and sunny skies lure many people outdoors. Snowy fun comes in a multitude of forms, but whipping along a crisp, crusted snow surface on a dogsled has got to be one of the best. You can snuggle as a passenger or mush your own sled under the supervision of an experienced guide. Some of the following dogsled tour companies include dinner, overnight packages, ice fishing, and igloo building.

HOWLING DOG TOURS
Banff
403/678-9588

KINGMIK EXPEDITIONS
Lake Louise
403/522-3525

MOUNTAIN MUSHERS DOG SLED TOURS
Banff
403/762-3647

SNOWTIME
Banff
403/762-0745

Fishing

The Bow River, which runs through the middle of Calgary, is one of the finest sport-fishing rivers in the world, with fly fishermen regularly catching 20-inch rainbow and brown trout in the Bow's clear waters. A valid Alberta fishing license is required before casting a line in the Bow, Elbow, or any

You can get a weekly report of local fishing conditions by calling the *Calgary Herald* TALKIES line at 403/243-7253 and selecting category 1130.

waterway in Calgary. Contact the local provincial Fish and Wildlife office at 403/297-6423 for rules and regulations (fish limits, dates permitted, etc.) within city limits. Those Calgarians who live in lake communities have the luxury of man-made lakes stocked with trout twice a year. They fish by boat or cast from the edge of the lake in summer and ice fish in winter.

Good trout fishing sites abound in the mountains, and visitor centres dispense fishing licenses and information. There are a number of fishing charters, guides, lessons, and equipment rentals available in the Banff/Lake Louise area.

BOW RIVER TROUTFITTERS
6, 2122 Crowchild Tr. NW, Calgary
403/282-8868 **NW**
Professional guides and certified casting instructors will ensure a successful fishing trip with Bow River float trips or mountain stream walk/wade trips. Equipment, transportation, and lunch are provided in your scenic fly-fishing adventure.

MR. T'S TROUT TOURS
Box 49015
Ogden RPO, Calgary
403/236-2990
From April to October, Mr. T's Trout Tours offers drift boat fly-fishing and guided canoe trips on the Bow River. Transportation, equipment, instruction, and a gourmet lunch are provided while you concentrate on casting for browns and rainbows.

RAINBOW & BROWN FLYFISHING FLOAT TRIPS
R.R. 1, DeWinton
403/256-9622 **SE**
Rainbow & Brown Flyfishing Float Trips is located just south of the city limits at DeWinton. They offer guided fly-fishing float trips on the Bow River from April to mid-October. Your package includes transportation, streamside lunch, and casting instruction.

Golf

The following six municipal golf courses are available to Calgarians and visitors alike and are booked through a central tee-time line. You can call four days in advance. Call 403/221-3510 with a touch-tone phone or 403/221-3525 with a rotary dial. Driving ranges, lessons, pull/ power carts, and pro shops are available. Cart rental rates: $13 for nine holes, $24 for 18 holes, $19 for twilight. Green fees range from $22.50 to $25 on weekends (18 holes) and $20 to $22.50 on weekdays. Twilight $8 to $15.

CONFEDERATION PARK GOLF COURSE
3204 Collingwood Dr. NW, Calgary
403/974-1800 **NW**
Nine holes, 3,221 yards, par 36.

LAKEVIEW GOLF COURSE
5840 - 19th St. SW, Calgary
403/974-1815 **SW**
Nine holes, 1,612 yards, par 30.

Kayaking, page 152

lic, although some restrict the times available for public bookings. They are all within city limits or a short drive from the city. For courses set in the most spectacular scenery, book tee-times at the Canmore or Kananaskis Golf Courses.

MAPLE RIDGE GOLF COURSE
1240 Mapleglade Dr. SE, Calgary
403/974-1825   SE
Eighteen holes; 5,832 to 6,570 yards, par: red 71, yellow 72.

MCCALL LAKE GOLF COURSE
1600 - 32nd Ave. NE, Calgary
403/974-1805   NE
Twenty-seven holes. Nine-hole course 952 yards, par 27; 18-hole course 5,568 to 6,788 yards, par 71.

RICHMOND GREEN FAMILY GOLF COURSE
2539 - 33rd Ave. SW, Calgary
403/974-1820   SW
Nine holes, 1,214 yards, par 27.

SHAGANAPPI POINT GOLF COURSE
1200 - 26th St. SW, Calgary
403/974-1810   SW
Twenty-seven holes. Nine-hole course 2,267 yards, par 31; 18-hole course 5,230 to 5,297 yards, par 69.

The following semi-private and public golf courses are also open to the pub-

BUFFALO RUN GOLF COURSE
37th Street and Anderson Road SW, Calgary
403/949-3733   SW
Nine holes.

CANMORE GOLF COURSE
West of Canmore, Alberta
403/678-4784
Eighteen holes. Public bookings three days in advance.

CARSTAIRS GOLF COURSE
North of Carstairs, Alberta
403/337-3382
Eighteen holes. Public bookings three days in advance.

COCHRANE GOLF COURSE
240 River View Dr.
Cochrane, Alberta
403/932-5103
Nine holes. Public bookings two days in advance.

COTTONWOOD GOLF COURSE
12 km (7 mi) southeast of city on Highway 2
403/938-7200
Eighteen holes. Public bookings 3½ days in advance. Restricted on weekends.

COUNTRY HILLS GOLF COURSE
9703 Centre St. N., Calgary
403/274-9100   NW
Thirty-six holes. Public bookings three days in advance.

D'ARCY RANCH GOLF COURSE

South of Calgary on Highway 2A, Calgary
403/938-4455 or 800/803-8810
Eighteen holes. Public bookings two days in advance.

DOUGLASDALE GOLF COURSE
7 Douglaswoods Dr. SE, Calgary
403/279-7913 SE
Eighteen holes. Public bookings four days in advance.

ELBOW SPRINGS GOLF COURSE
West of Calgary on Highway 8, Calgary
403/246-2800
Twenty-seven holes. Public bookings three days in advance.

ELKS GOLF COURSE
2502 - 6th St. NE, Calgary
403/276-5040 NE
Eighteen holes. Public bookings after 1 p.m. for next day.

FOX HOLLOW GOLF COURSE
1025 - 32nd Ave. NE, Calgary
403/277-4653 NE
Eighteen holes. Public bookings two days in advance.

HARVEST HILLS GOLF COURSE
10820 - 6th St. NE, Calgary
403/226-1051 NE
Nine holes. Public bookings one day in advance.

HEATHER GLEN GOLF COURSE
100th Street and Glenmore Trail SE, Calgary
403/236-4653 SE
Eighteen holes. Public bookings three days in advance.

HERITAGE POINTE GOLF COURSE
10 minutes south on Highway 2, east on Dunbow Road, Calgary
403/256-2002

Twenty-seven holes. Public bookings one week in advance.

HIGHWOOD GOLF COURSE
South of High River on Highway 2A, Calgary
403/652-2402
Twenty-seven holes. Public bookings two days in advance.

INGLEWOOD GOLF COURSE
34th Avenue and Barlow Trail SE, Calgary
403/272-4363 SE
Eighteen holes. Public bookings two days in advance.

KANANASKIS GOLF COURSE
West of Calgary on Highway 4, Calgary
403/261-4653 or 403/591-7272
Thirty-six holes of Robert Trent Jones design. Public bookings up to 60 days in advance.

LAKESIDE GREENS GOLF COURSE
Just east of the city on Highway 1A in Chestermere
403/569-9111
Eighteen holes. Public bookings five days in advance.

LINKS OF GLEN EAGLES
West of the city at Cochrane
403/932-5656
Eighteen holes.

NANTON GOLF COURSE
35 minutes south of Calgary on Highway 2
403/265-4235
Eighteen holes. Public bookings five days in advance.

MCKENZIE MEADOWS GOLF COURSE
West of McKenzie Lake Boulevard SE, Calgary
403/257-2255 SE

Eighteen holes. Public bookings three days in advance.

REDWOOD MEADOWS GOLF COURSE
On the western edge of Calgary on Highway 22
403/949-3663
Eighteen holes. Public bookings three days in advance.

RIO VISTA GOLF COURSE
2nd Street SE, High River, Alberta
403/652-1443
Nine holes. Public bookings one day in advance.

RIVER'S EDGE
GOLF COURSE
2 km west of Highway 2 on 370th Avenue, Calgary
403/938-7872
Nine holes. Public bookings two days in advance.

SHAW-NEE SLOPES GOLF COURSE
40 - 146th Ave. SW, Calgary
403/256-1444 **SW**
Eighteen holes. Public bookings four days in advance.

SPRINGBANK LINKS
4 km west of Canada Olympic Park, Calgary
403/288-3673
Eighteen holes.

STRATHMORE GOLF COURSE
East of Calgary on Highway 1
403/934-2299
Eighteen holes. Public bookings four days in advance.

TURNER VALLEY
GOLF COURSE
South of four-way stop in Black Diamond, Calgary

Calgary Flames, page 160

403/933-4721
Eighteen holes. Public bookings four days in advance.

VALLEY RIDGE GOLF COURSE
1618 Valley Ridge Park NW, Calgary
403/288-9457 **NW**
Twenty-seven holes. Public bookings one day in advance.

WINTERGREEN GOLF COURSE
West of Bragg Creek, Calgary
403/949-2407
Eighteen holes. Public bookings four days in advance.

WOODSIDE GOLF COURSE
525 Woodside Dr., Airdrie
403/948-7224
Eighteen holes. Public bookings five days in advance.

Go-Karts

KART GARDENS FAMILY FUN CENTRE

9555 Barlow Tr. NE, Calgary
403/250-9555 NE
This is Western Canada's biggest go-kart track for the young and young-at-heart. Full-size, fast, responsive karts run on a high performance track. Also on-site is an 18-hole miniature golf course, bumper boats, games room, snack bar, volleyball court, horseshoe pitch, and barbecue area. The Centre offers a variety of birthday party packages. Hours: Daily 11–10, mid-April–mid-Oct. Second location at 5202 - 1st Street SW.

Horseback Riding

HAPPY TRAILS RIDING STABLES
Fish Creek Provincial Park, Calgary
403/251-3344 SW
Trail rides are available through the trees, valleys, and across Fish Creek. Happy Trails also offers riding lessons and hay rides.

CANMORE/KANANASKIS AREA
If you're willing to drive outside the city for your riding pleasure, you'll have a greater range of choice. Numerous dude ranches such as Rafter Six Ranch Resort, 888/267-26240, offer horseback riding, carriage, and hay rides. There are also stables in the Canmore/Kananaskis area that offer trail rides from one-hour to multi-day duration. Some include river rafting in their packages.

BOUNDARY STABLES
403/591-7171

JOHNNY'S RIDING STABLES
403/678-4171

KANANASKIS GUEST RANCH
403/673-3737

BANFF/LAKE LOUISE AREA
Banff Springs Corral,
Banff
403/762-4551
BREWSTER STABLES
Lake Louise
403/522-3511

EMERALD LAKE LODGE
403/762-0745

HOLIDAY ON HORSEBACK
Banff
403/762-4551

MARTIN STABLES
Banff
403/762-4551

TIMBERLINE TOURS
Lake Louise
403/522-3743

Rafting

Head to the mountains for the excitement and adventure of river rafting. You don't have to be a dare-devil—some tours are relaxing floats on the Bow River. The Kananaskis River offers more excitement; Kootenay River is good for families; and turbulent Kicking Horse provides a truly whitewater experience. The following rafting companies offer various rafting adventures with experienced guides and equipment provided. Some include lunch, overnight trips, and surf-and-saddle combinations. Rapids in the area are rated from Class I (tame) to Class IV (turbulent).

ALPINE RAFTING
COMPANY
Banff or Lake Louise
403/762-5627 or 800/663-7080

**HYDRA RIVER
GUIDES**
Banff
403/762-4554 or 800/644-8888

**KANANASKIS RIVER
ADVENTURES**
Kananaskis Village
403/591-7773

KOOTENAY RIVER RUNNERS
Banff
403/762-5385 or 800/599-4399

**ROCKY MOUNTAIN
RAFT TOURS**
Banff
403/762-3632

**ROCKY MOUNTAIN
RAFTING CO.**
Banff or Lake Louise
800/808-7238

WILD WATER ADVENTURES
Lake Louise
888/771-9453

Sailing and Canoeing

Glenmore Reservoir is a 429-hectare (1,000-acre) reservoir lake that is home to two yacht clubs and the largest inland sailing school in North America. It also has boat stalls, racks, and mooring available for rent on a seasonal basis at two locations. Call 403/268-4718. Sailboat rentals are available weekends only throughout July and August. Telephone 403/221-3858 for reservations. The Sailing School runs adult, teen, and junior programs that can be booked by calling 403/268-3800.

The **Calgary Canoe & Rowing Club** is located on the north shore of the reservoir at 7305 - 24th Street SW. It features touring and racing lessons, training facilities and equipment, and sightseeing tours for any level of paddler. They also offer programs for kayakers and rowers. Canoes and kayaks can be rented from them by calling 403/246-5757. You can also launch your canoe in various parks around the city. They are:

Ten Ski Facilities In or Around Calgary

1. Canada Olympic Park, Calgary, 403/286-2632

2. Fernie Snow Valley, Fernie, B.C., 250/423-4655

3. Fortress Mountain, Kananaskis, 403/591-7108

4. Kimberley Ski Resort, Kimberley, B.C., 250/427-3927

5. Lake Louise Ski Area, Lake Louise, 403/256-8473

6. Nakiska, Kananaskis, 403/591-7777

7. Norquay, Banff, 403/762-4551

8. Panorama Resort, Panorama, B.C., 250/342-6941

9. Sunshine Village, Banff, 403/762-6500

10. Wintergreen, Bragg Creek, 403/949-3335

BEAVER DAM FLATS
Lynn View Road between 61st and
66th Avenues SE, Calgary   SE

BOWNESS PARK
West of 85th Street NW on 48th
Avenue, Calgary   NW

CARBURN PARK
South of Glenmore Trail and east
of Riverbend, Calgary   SE

CENTENARY PARK
St. Patrick's Island, Bow River,
Calgary   DT

SANDY BEACH
Along the Elbow River between
Glenmore Athletic Park and the
community of Riverdale Park,
Calgary   SW

Skating

Ice skating is a popular winter pastime in Calgary and one you can participate in at no cost outdoors or minimal cost indoors. **Bowness Park** in northwest Calgary offers free skating on the lagoon, a favorite spot for families. **Lake Sikome** in Fish Creek Provincial Park in southeast Calgary offers skating on the lake when it's cleared of snow. Skaters can even enjoy their sport downtown at **Olympic Plaza** at the corner of Macleod Trail and 7th Avenue SW. Most communities have outdoor rinks for public use at no cost.

Calgary Parks and Recreation has 17 arenas located throughout the city, providing ice for hockey, ringette, broomball, figure skating clubs, and recreational users. Some of these indoor arenas also offer public skating during certain hours at very reasonable rates. Most family skate and public skate hours are clustered on weekends and holidays, but they vary from rink to rink, so call 403/268-3850 for information. Indoor community rinks also offer public skating, but are too numerous to list here. Check the yellow pages in the phone book and call the number of the rink nearest you for times and rates.

Finally, the **Olympic Speed Skating Oval**, 403/220-7890, at the University of Calgary allows public skating at specific times. They also rent speed skates and hockey skates. Inside the oval are two hockey rinks and alongside is a running track.

Skiing (Cross-Country)

Cross-country ski buffs get lots of fresh air and exercise in numerous parks within city limits, or they can take a quick drive to sample the 60 kilometers (37 miles) of groomed trails of the world-class Canmore Nordic Centre, on Calgary's doorstep. Kananaskis Country offers more than 300 kilometers (190 miles) of trails in total while Banff National Park features 120 kilometers (75 miles) of groomed trails and hundreds of kilometers more for backcountry skiers. At the Lake Louise Visitor Centre and the Banff Visitor Centre, Parks Canada sells an excellent booklet for only $1 that provides ski trail details and maps.

The following companies provide guided cross-country ski tours through the Kananaskis area.

MIRAGE ADVENTURE TOURS
403/678-4919

WHITE MOUNTAIN ADVENTURES
403/678-4099

You can cross-country ski within the boundaries of these Calgary parks:

BEAVER DAM FLATS
Lynn View Road between 61st and 66th Avenues SE, Calgary   SE

CARBURN PARK
South of Glenmore Trail and east of Riverbend, Calgary   SE

CONFEDERATION PARK
5A Street west to 14th Street NW between 23rd and 30th Avenues NW, Calgary   NW

EDWORTHY PARK
South bank of the Bow River between Boothman Bridge and Crowchild Trail NW, Calgary   NW

FISH CREEK PROVINCIAL PARK
Spans the south end of the city, Calgary   SW/SE

GLENMORE PARK
North and south side of Glenmore Reservoir, Calgary   NE

NOSE CREEK
64th Avenue NE to the Bow River, Calgary

NOSE HILL
North of John Laurie Boulevard between 14th Street and Shaganappi Trail NW, Calgary NW

WEASELHEAD FLATS
West end of Glenmore Reservoir, Calgary   SW

Spruce Meadows, page 159

Calgary CVB/CMike Ridewood

Skiing (Downhill) and Snowboarding

In late fall, you can pick out the skiers and snowboarders in a crowd because they are constantly searching the sky for snowflakes that signal the beginning of their favorite season. Downhill skiing and snowboarding begin within the city limits at **Canada Olympic Park**, 403/247-5452, which was the site of the freestyle skiing, bobsleigh, ski jumping, and luge events of the 1988 Olympic Winter Games. This family ski area features rental packages, lessons, and three chair lifts.

Just west of the city, near the hamlet of Bragg Creek, is **Wintergreen Ski Area**, 403/949-3333, featuring downhill runs that are lit at night. Amenities include ski school, sundecks, cafeteria, daycare, and rental shop.

Both of these facilities offer a day of skiing at affordable rates.

One hour west of the city, in Kananaskis Country, are two first-class ski areas. **Nakiska**, 403/591-7777, was the site of the Alpine events of the XV Winter Olympics. Optimum conditions on 28 runs are maintained with state-of-the-art snow-making equipment. **Fortress Mountain**, 403/264-5825, is a great family resort with on-slope accommodations. Both locations are popular with snowboarders as well as skiers.

The Banff/Lake Louise area is a downhill skier's paradise with some of the finest slopes and scenery in the world. **Sunshine Village**, 403/762-6500, a 15-minute drive west of Banff, is known for its outstanding beauty and great natural snow conditions. The high-speed quad chair whisks you to the top in five minutes.

Banff Mount Norquay, 403/762-4421, offers world-class mogul skiing as well as excellent beginner terrain. It is only 6 kilometers (4 miles) from Banff townsite.

Lake Louise Ski Area, 403/522-3555, is 60 kilometers (37 miles) west of Banff, offering an awesome combination of mountain scenery and abundant snowfall. Encompassing 1,620 hectares (4,000 acres), it is Canada's largest ski resort.

Sleigh Rides

If you've ever imagined yourself wrapped in blankets in a horse-drawn sleigh, here's your chance to try it out. You can hire one just for yourself or go as a group. One package even includes dinner at the luxurious Chateau Lake Louise.

BREWSTER LAKE LOUISE
SLEIGH RIDES
Lake Louise
403/522-3511 ext. 1210

HOLIDAY ON HORSEBACK
Banff
403/762-4551

SLEIGH RIDE AND DINNER
Lake Louise
403/762-0745

Swimming

The three water parks below offer extra-large pools that manufacture waves at certain times of the day. It's a fun experience for the whole family. Toddlers, however, can be knocked over by the force of the waves, so it's best to keep them in the shallow area when the waves are on, or put a life jacket on them. Tubes can be rented for reasonable rates. Each of the water parks boasts an exciting water slide.

The city also sports smaller indoor and outdoor pools with public access hours. As well, Calgary offers a number of outdoor wading and spray pools for youngsters. Call **Calgary Parks and Recreation**, 403/268-3888, for a complete list of facilities.

Lake Sikome, a man-made lake at the southern point of Fish Creek Provincial Park, is a popular swimming spot for families on hot summer days. There is no charge for swimming here and facilities include indoor washrooms, showers, picnic tables, concession, and first aid station.

Woods Park, on Elbow Drive between 29th Avenue and 36th Avenue SW, is a peaceful green space where swimmers enjoy the cool waters of the Elbow River. Similarly, **Lindsay Park**, which nestles between the Elbow River and Macleod Trail, provides access to a favorite swimming location in the river that bends around the park.

FAMILY LEISURE CENTRE
11150 Bonaventure Dr. SE, Calgary
403/278-7542

SOUTHLAND LEISURE CENTRE
2000 Southland Dr. SW, Calgary
403/251-3505   SW
The whole family will enjoy the wet fun of Southland's wave pool, where you can rent a tube and ride the huge mechanically generated waves. Between wave sessions you can jump from the rope suspended above the pool, or ride the Southland Screamer, a twisting, turning water slide that makes part of its trip in the dark before shooting you through a water curtain. There are also ice arenas, wall-climbing facilities, gymnasium, and fitness classes.

VILLAGE SQUARE LEISURE CENTRE
2623 - 56th St. NE, Calgary
403/280-9714   NE
If you like to ride the swell of waves, try out the huge indoor wave pool at this kid-friendly facility. For a heart-thumping experience scoot down the Pepsi Thunder Run Waterslide, which is more than six stories tall. It will blast you through a flash-flood water curtain accompanied by sound effects, a mega drop, and hairpin turns. Other recreational opportunities here include ice skating in the arenas, dry sports in the gymnasium, fitness classes, and wall climbing.

Tobogganing

Whether you prefer riding solo on a snow-racer or crazy carpet, or with a group on an inner tube or toboggan, there's no dearth of tobogganing opportunities in Calgary. The following parks have toboggan hills that can be enjoyed every day there's enough snow cover.

CONFEDERATION PARK
5A Street west to 14th Street NW between 23rd and 30th Avenues NW, Calgary   NW

EDWORTHY PARK
South bank of the Bow River between Boothman Bridge and Crowchild Trail NW,
Calgary   NW

NOSE CREEK
64th Avenue NE to the Bow River, Calgary   NE

NOSE HILL
North of John Laurie Boulevard between 14th Street and Shaganappi Trail NW,
Calgary   NW

PRAIRIE WINDS
North of McKnight Boulevard and east of 52nd Street NE, Calgary NE

RIVER PARK
Between 38th and 50th Avenues along 14A Street SW, Calgary SW

SANDY BEACH
Along the Elbow River between Glenmore Athletic Park and the

Spruce Meadows

This $20-million equestrian show jumping facility is located at the south Calgary city limits, approximately 3 kilometers (2 miles) west of Highway 2 on Highway 22X. The venue covers 122 hectares (300 acres), about half of which are pasture, hay, and parking with the remaining encompassing the facilities. Six outdoor competition rings are used during tournaments, which attract more than 300,000 spectators annually.

The three main tournaments hosted at Spruce Meadows are the National, which features the Canadian Show Jumping Championship in June; the North American, which crowns the North American Champion in July; and the Masters in September, which attracts the world's finest athletes and offers the largest purse of any show jumping tournament. In 1996, prize money for the three Spruce Meadows tournaments totaled over $2.6 million.

As well, more than 25 televised programs originate from Spruce Meadows annually. This programming airs in some 25 countries reaching more than 100 million people.

Each year the Dutch government provides 4 metric tons of freshly cut flowers for Holland Day during the Masters equestrian show jumping tournament at Spruce Meadows.

community of Riverdale Park, Calgary   SW

Wall Climbing

MOUNTAIN MAGIC EQUIPMENT
224 Bear St., Banff
403/762-2591
In Banff experienced climbers with shoes and ropes can use a 9-meter (30-foot) indoor climbing wall and a 4.5-meter (15-foot) bouldering wall at no charge at Mountain Magic Equipment. Indoor or outdoor classes are available.

SOUTHLAND LEISURE CENTRE
2000 Southland Dr. SW, Calgary
403/251-3505   SW
Within the city limits Southland Leisure Centre provides opportunities for rock climbing, albeit indoors. You must fill out a questionnaire, sign a waiver, and demonstrate certain skills before you'll be allowed to participate in supervised climbing. The Centre provides all basic climbing equipment for registered programs and drop-in times.

Spectator Sports

CALGARY HITMEN HOCKEY CLUB
120, 1212 - 1st St. SE, Calgary
403/571-2222   SE
The Western Hockey League continues to be one of the main sources of talent for the National Hockey League. The Hitmen's inaugural season was 1995–96 when it was started up by a group of Calgary businessmen, pro hockey players (including Theoren Fleury of the Calgary Flames and Joe Sakic of the Colorado Avalanche, and pro wrestler Bret Hart. The team plays its 36 home games from September to March in the Canadian Airlines Saddledome. Call for schedule and ticket prices.

Horse Racing

STAMPEDE PARK RACE TRACK
1410 Olympic Way SE (off 12th Avenue), Calgary
403/261-0214   SE
Thoroughbred and harness racing takes off every Wednesday, Friday, Saturday, Sunday, and holidays from late July until mid-October at Stampede Park. Post times are 6:30 p.m. Wednesdays and Fridays and 1:30 p.m. on weekends and holidays. Stampede Park also simulcasts thoroughbred and harness racing from Hastings Park, Northlands, Delmar, Meadowlands, and Woodbine. General admission is $2 and clubhouse is $4.

Motor Racing

RACE CITY MOTORSPORT PARK
114th Avenue and 68th Street SE,

Calgary

403/264-6515 SE

One of the most modern and unique motor-sport facilities in North America, Race City Speedway is the venue for stock car, drag and sports car, and motorcycle racing. The facility features a ¼-mile NHRA dragstrip, a ½-mile high-banked paved oval, and 2-mile and 1½-mile roadcourses. It also hosts national events. This family entertainment runs from May to September with ticket prices in the $10 to $15 range. Seniors half-price and children 12 and under free.

Rugby

CALGARY RUGBY UNION
P.O. Box 5888, Station A, Calgary
403/255-9199 SE

Calgary's Rugby Union teams play from May through October at 9025 Shepherd Road SE. There are 15 teams in the city (including two female teams) consisting of players 15 years to over 40.

Soccer

CALGARY SOCCER CENTRE
7000 - 48th St. SE, Calgary
403/279-8453 SE

The Calgary Soccer Centre, which opened in 1992, is home to 670 indoor soccer teams and is the largest indoor soccer facility in North America. More than 600,000 people move through it during the indoor soccer season. It features two large domed indoor soccer facilities with six indoor soccer fields on state-of-the-art playing turf. In addition, there are four outdoor soccer fields. Lacrosse, field hockey, and lawn bowling devotees also use this venue for games or practices.

Show Jumping

SPRUCE MEADOWS
West of Macleod Trail on
Highway 22X, Calgary
403/974-4200 SW

If equestrian events are your passion, you've come to the right place. The world-class equestrian show jumping facilities at Spruce Meadows feature three international competitions annually, but you can tour the grounds and buildings for free any time of the year. During competitions, admission prices are the same as they were 21 years ago when the facility first opened, because owners Ron and Ann Southern believe that the power and beauty of horses are truly a sight to behold and shouldn't be reserved for those with money. Admission for events: $5 adults, free for children and seniors.

Professional Sports

CALGARY CANNONS
BASEBALL CLUB
Burns Stadium

TRIVIA

A friendly rivalry exists between Calgary and the provincial capital, especially in the area of professional sports. A popular bumper sticker seen on the streets of Calgary reads: "My two favorite hockey teams are the Calgary Flames and whoever is playing the Edmonton Oilers."

2255 Crowchild Tr. NW, Calgary
403/284-1111 NW

The Cannons are a AAA baseball club playing in the Pacific Coast League. They are the farm team for the Pittsburgh Pirates in the American Baseball League and play at Burns Stadium. Games are usually played in the evening with some Sunday afternoon games. They are cheap family entertainment with tickets ranging from $6 to $9 and many games featuring promotional giveaways like sports bags, hats, and water bottles. Fireworks Night on June 30 is always popular. The season runs April to September.

CALGARY FLAMES HOCKEY CLUB
P.O. Box 1540, Station M, Calgary
403/261-0475 SE

Calgary's love affair with professional hockey began when the Flames moved from Atlanta in 1980. Since then the club, which is a National Hockey League franchise, has shown great success, bringing home the Stanley Cup in 1989. Their home games are played to crowds of 20,000 at the Canadian Airlines Saddledome, located at 12th Avenue and 5th Street SE. With more than $37 million spent

on renovations, the Saddledome is a world-class entertainment venue featuring pillarless construction so every seat in the house has a good view. Flames' mascot Harvey the Hound's antics are worth the price of the ticket alone. The season runs from October to April. Weekday game time is 7:30 p.m.; on weekends 6 p.m. and 8:30 p.m. Ticket prices: $9.75 to $34. Reserve tickets ahead of time to avoid disappointment.

CALGARY STAMPEDERS FOOTBALL CLUB
McMahon Stadium
1817 Crowchild Tr. NW, Calgary
403/289-0258 NW

Three-time Grey Cup Champions, the Stampeders have played in the Canadian Football League since 1945. The Stamps are a formidable football force with a regular-season record of 58–14 over the last four seasons. With their own brand of hard-hitting action, they thrill more than 300,000 fans annually at McMahon Stadium from June to November. This is an outdoor stadium, so dress for the weather. Tickets range in price from $20 to $40, with 25 percent off children's tickets.

Calgary CVB/Alberta Ballet

11

PERFORMING ARTS

Calgary boasts a lively performing arts scene. Whether your taste runs to light comedies or heavy drama, enlightening satires or murder mysteries, you'll find it at one of the many venues throughout the city. Evening theatre performances abound along with a sprinkling of matinées. Avid theatre-goers can even take in a play at lunchtime during the work week.

Resident and touring dance companies in this great city range from ballet to contemporary jazz. To catch a touring Broadway production, check with the Jubilee Auditorium. For more musical enjoyment, the Calgary Opera and the Calgary Philharmonic Orchestra offer first-class entertainment. Wheelchair accessibility is indicated by the ♿ symbol.

THEATRE

ALBERTA THEATRE PROJECTS
220 - 9th Ave. SE, Calgary
Box office: 403/294-7402 or
888/388-4287
403/294-7475   DT
For more than 25 years Alberta Theatre Projects (ATP) has entertained Calgarians with thought-provoking, invigorating live theatre ranging from musicals such as *My Fair Lady* to the avant-garde *Angels in America*. This not-for-profit theatre company features Canadian actors, hired on a show-by-show basis, to perform in the Martha Cohen Theatre of the Calgary Centre for Performing Arts. Viewing time typically spans two hours. Tickets for ATP performances range from $10 to $35 and are available by calling TicketMaster or the box office. Underground parking is available. ♿

CALGARY YOUNG PEOPLE'S THEATRE
213 - 19th St. NW, Suite 5, Calgary
403/270-0980   NW
The historic Canmore Opera House is the venue for this theatre troupe,

One of Calgary's first suburban theatres, the Tivoli Theatre was constructed in 1937 featuring curves and fins inspired by Buck Rogers' vehicles.

which performs family theatre appealing to all ages. It is representative of a common setting for social activities in a turn-of-the-century mining town. Built in 1898, this log building was first used for dancing and music and later transformed into a movie house. Don't be fooled by its name—it no longer resides in Canmore but is part of the Heritage Park Historical Village at 1900 Heritage Drive SW. Calgary Young People's Theatre delivers four productions per year, including a vaudeville show in summer. Past productions include such classics as *The Secret Garden* and *Charlotte's Web*. Ticket prices range from $5 to $8. Ample

Christianne Riel and Jon Villars in a Calgary Opera presentation of La Boheme, *page 166*

Calgary Opera/Trudie Lee Photography

parking is available. But if there's just been a major snowfall, call to make sure you can drive right to the door. &

FRONT ROW CENTRE PLAYERS
31 Millbank Cres. SW, Calgary
Box office: 403/263-0079
403/226-3966   **SW**

This amateur theatre group emphasizes family entertainment with two musical productions of classics per year, ten performances each. Previous productions include *Guys and Dolls, Godspell, Annie, Oliver,* and *Grease.* Evening performances are augmented by Sunday matinées, all at the Pumphouse Theatres. Tickets are $8 to $10. &

LOOSE MOOSE THEATRE
2003 McKnight Blvd. NE
Box office: 403/291-5682
403/250-1414   **NE**

Artistic director Keith Johnstone has developed the Loose Moose Theatre Company into one of the most innovative and influential improvisation companies in the world. They serve up improvised theatre and comedy on Friday, Saturday, and Sunday evenings year-round. From September to April, Loose Moose performs children's theatre on weekend afternoons. (See Chapter 6, "Kids' Stuff," for more information.) Tickets for evening improv are $3 to $8 and may be bought at the door or reserved ahead. Not wheelchair accessible. Ample parking.

LUNCHBOX THEATRE
Bow Valley Square, 2nd level
205 - 5th Ave. SW, Calgary
Box office: 403/265-4292
403/265-4297   DT

Founded in 1975, Canada's leading noon-time theatre performs one-act plays Monday to Saturday at 12:10 p.m. from October through May. Mainly producing comedies, Lunchbox Theatre "doesn't try to solve the world's problems over the lunch hour." This professional company commissions and develops new Canadian plays with some of their original works produced nationally and internationally. Some have even become award-winning films and teleplays. Previous successes include *The Wild Guys, Parallax Garden,* and *Dads in Bondage.* Tickets are $8 and reservations are recommended. Call 403/265-4292. You can also purchase a Lunchbox Theatre Playpass, entitling you to eight flexible admissions throughout the season. Nearby parking is available in the Bow Valley Square Parkade. Lunchbox is wheelchair accessible, but they request you reserve ahead as theatre seats are removed to accommodate wheelchairs.

MAENAD THEATRE
P.O. Box 4642
Station C, Calgary
403/263-7543   DT

Maenad Theatre, Calgary's women-centred theatre collective, uses various venues throughout the city to perform new works by Canadian women. Its focus is to encourage, produce, and present works that portray strong roles and break stereotypes for women. Their season runs from September to May with most performances at 8 p.m., but some matinées are also offered. Tickets range from $12 regular admission to $8 for students, seniors, and the unwaged. They can be reserved ahead or bought at the door of the performance site.

MOUNTAIN SONG NATIVE THEATRE
Box 980, Bragg Creek
403/949-3400

Mountain Song performers are dedicated to the enhancement and understanding of Native arts and culture through high quality entertainment. On the first Thursday of every month (except January and February) at the Bragg Creek Steak Pit on White Avenue, the performers present a colorful mix of stories, song, and dance by Alberta's indigenous peoples. Admission is $22.95 plus a required meal purchase. Menu includes some Native cuisine featuring venison, buffalo, and salmon. Advance tickets are available at the Bragg Creek Shopping Centre from Bragg Creek Tour and Travel office, 403/949-3400; Bragg Creek Steak Pit, 403/949-3633; or the Micah Gallery in Calgary, 403/245-

---

T I P

If you decide to take in Lunchbox Theatre on a Saturday, park in the Bow Valley Parkade and have your parking voucher stamped at the performance for free parking all day.

1340. Doors open at 7 p.m. and show starts at 8 p.m. All proceeds go to the Awo-Taan Native Women's Shelter. Ample parking. &

ONE YELLOW RABBIT
1232 - 17th Ave. SW, 2nd floor, Calgary
403/244-9177 **SW**
This nationally acclaimed creation company performs original works in the Big Secret Theatre of the Calgary Centre for Performing Arts. Incorporating inventive choreography by company member Denise Clarke, One Yellow Rabbit entertains Tuesday to Sunday evenings from September through April with matinées on weekend afternoons. Previous performances include *Doing Leonard Cohen, Mata Hari*, and *Ilsa, Queen of the Nazi Love Camp*. In January, One Yellow Rabbit hosts the High Performance Rodeo, enticing theatre groups from all over the world. Ticket prices range from $8 to $20 with matinées often advertised as "pay what you can." Call TicketMaster or the box office to reserve. Underground parking. &

PLEIADES THEATRE
Calgary Science Centre
701 - 11 St. SW, Calgary

Top Ten Movies Filmed in Alberta

Calgary's reputation as a major film industry centre is established with such prominent projects as CBC's television series *North of 60* and *Lonesome Dove*, as well as Paramount Pictures' episodic series *Viper*. Spectacular locations include mountains, foothills, prairies, and badlands, all within an hour of Calgary's modern city skyline (Metropolis in *Superman III*). Movies featuring Alberta scenery as a backdrop to the action are:

1. *Betrayed* (Debra Winger, Tom Berenger) 1987
2. *Bookworm* (Anthony Hopkins, Alex Baldwin) 1996
3. *Buffalo Bill and the Indians*
   (Paul Newman, Robert Altman) 1975
4. *Cool Runnings* (John Candy) 1993
5. *Dead Bang* (Don Johnson) 1988
6. *Heaven and Earth* (Japan) 1989
7. *Legends of the Fall*
   (Anthony Hopkins, Brad Pitt, Aidan Quinn) 1993
8. *Little Big Man* (Dustin Hoffman) 1970
9. *River of No Return*
   (Marilyn Monroe, Robert Mitchum) 1953
10. *Unforgiven* (Clint Eastwood, Morgan Freeman) 1991

The Grand Theatre

The Grand Theatre, housed in the Lougheed Building at 604 - 1st Street SW, was said to be one of the most famous legitimate theatres on the North American continent in the early 1900s. Some of the greatest names of stage and screen played live at the Grand: Sophie Tucker, Ethyl Barrymore, the Marx Brothers, Jack Benny, George Burns and Gracie Allen, Fred Astaire, and Sarah Bernhardt.

In its day, the Grand had the largest stage in Canada and acoustics touted as the best in North America. It was the venue for plays, musicals, operas, revues, symphony concerts, minstrel shows, public lectures, political rallies, and the occasional movie or animal circus.

403/221-3707   **DT**

Calgary's mystery stage specializes in thrillers such as *Dead Serious* and Agatha Christie's *The Mousetrap* (adapted to an Alberta setting). Evening performances and matinées are given. Located in the Calgary Science Centre, Pleiades also offers a summer science theatre series for children. (See Chapter 6, "Kids' Stuff," for more information.) Admission for mystery performances ranges from $11 to $17. Reserve by calling TicketMaster or the box office. Free parking. ♿

SUN.ERGOS
2203, 700 - 9th St. SW, Calgary
403/264-4621   **DT**

For a truly unique theatre adventure, catch a performance by Sun.Ergos, a two-man company of theatre and dance. Robert Greenwood and Dana Luebke tour nationally and internationally, creating magical characters with authentic costumes and the simplest of props. With original choreography and scripts, they combine their talents

to present exciting, colourful performances that inspire. Local performances are held in the Dr. Betty Mitchell Theatre of the Jubilee Auditorium. Evening performances as well as weekend matinées are given. Tickets range from $15 for regular admission to $10 for seniors, students, unemployed, disabled, and single parents, and $5 for children 12 and under. Ample parking. ♿

THEATRE CALGARY
220 - 9th Ave. SE, Calgary
403/294-7440   **DT**

For 30 years, Theatre Calgary has thrilled audiences with large-scale musicals, popular classics, and contemporary performances. Focusing on well-established two- or three-act plays, Theatre Calgary is equally adept at celebrating the Christmas spirit in *A Christmas Carol* and at unfolding the intense drama and mystery of the life of Edith Piaf. Southern Alberta's largest professional theatre company performs in the Max Bell Theatre of the Calgary Centre for Performing Arts. Performances run evenings and weekend matinées. Tickets range from $25 to $55 with cheaper rush seats available. Reserve through TicketMaster or purchase at the box office, which opens one hour before show time. Underground parking available. &

THEATRE JUNCTION
207, 1506 Centre St. N., Calgary
403/276-1682   NE
Modern classics (by Ibsen, Shaw, Tennessee Williams, and the like) are the genre embraced by Theatre Junction. Since 1991, they have entertained audiences with four plays per year such as A *Streetcar Named Desire*, *The Philanthropist*, and *Rosencrantz and Guildenstern are Dead*. Featuring local actors, this is homegrown theatre at its best. From October through April, performances are Wednesday to Saturday evenings in the Dr. Betty Mitchell Theatre of the Jubilee Auditorium. Tickets are $10 to $18 and are available through TicketMaster or the box office. Ample parking. &

CLASSICAL MUSIC AND OPERA

CALGARY BOYS CHOIR
305 - 10th Ave. SE, Calgary
403/262-7742   DT
This world-renowned choir of 120 boys has dazzled audiences locally and internationally since 1973, performing a full range of music from classical to contemporary. For many Calgarians, it simply wouldn't be Christmas without the Calgary Boys Choir annual Christmas Concert in the Jack Singer Concert Hall of the Calgary Centre for Performing Arts. In the spring, their second major production is also held there while various smaller concerts are performed throughout the season at several churches and other venues in the city. Tickets for major concerts range from $12 to $17, and less for smaller performances. Reserve through TicketMaster or the choir office.

CALGARY GIRLS CHOIR
6620 Crowchild Tr. SW, Calgary
403/686-7444   SW
This all-girls choir is relatively new on the choral scene. It performs at the Max Bell Theatre of the Calgary Centre for Performing Arts, the University of Calgary Theatre, and several churches. Tickets are between $5 and $15 depending on venue and are available through TicketMaster or the choir office.

CALGARY OPERA
601, 237 - 8th Ave. SE, Calgary
403/2627286
Box office: 403/264-5614   DT
The pageantry and grandeur of live opera have thrilled Calgary audiences for more than 25 years. In past seasons the Calgary Opera, which produces mainstage opera in the Jubilee Auditorium, has performed such classics as *Tosca, La Bohème, La Traviata*, and popular operettas such as *The Mikado, The Merry Widow*, and *The Gondoliers*. They perform three major productions per year, offered up as evening performances as well as matinées. Tickets range from

Barbershop Music

Barbershop music is alive and well in Calgary. The Western Hospitality Singers are an all-male chorus that provides fun-filled evenings of entertainment in several venues throughout the city. The group represented Canada in 1996 at the International Barbershop Convention in Salt Lake City, Utah. To obtain tickets or information about upcoming performances, call Jim at 403/547-4138.

The Chinook Winds Chorus, composed of more than 100 female members, has won seven first place medals in regional competitions of Sweet Adelines International. Its major public performance of four-part barbershop music is usually held in the Jubilee Auditorium in November; tickets cost $15. To obtain tickets or find out about upcoming performances, call Jean at 403/277-1836.

$25 to $65 and can be reserved by calling TicketMaster or the box office. Ample parking. &

CALGARY PHILHARMONIC ORCHESTRA
205 - 8th Ave. SE, Calgary
Box office: 403/571-0849
403/571-0270 DT
The fact that Calgarians love the Calgary Philharmonic Orchestra (CPO) is reflected in its status as the best-subscribed orchestra in Canada on a per capita basis. From September to May, it serves up a wide variety of musical entertainment ranging from classical to pops, baroque to the young people's series. More than 100,000 people per year thrill to the dynamic sound of the CPO under the leadership of Music Director Hans Graf. Catch performances at the Jack Singer Concert Hall in the Calgary Centre for Performing Arts or in the Jubilee Auditorium. The CPO celebrates each

Christmas with the Calgary Philharmonic Chorus and Handel's Messiah. Ticket prices for evening performances range from $21 to $55. See Chapter 6, "Kids' Stuff," for information about young people's concerts on Saturday afternoons. Reserve by calling TicketMaster or the box office. Convenient parking. &

MOUNT ROYAL COLLEGE CHOIRS
4825 Richard Rd. SW, Calgary
403/240-6821 SW
Five choirs comprise the internationally renowned Mount Royal College Choirs. The youngest group is the Mount Royal Songsters with singers ranging in age from 6 to 9 years. Members can graduate through the Junior Children's Choir, the Children's Choir, and the Youth Choir to Kantorei, which is the adult community choir. From September through June, the choirs perform classical and folk music from all centuries.

Performances are generally in the evening with occasional afternoon concerts, and their preferred venues are various churches around the city. The Christmas Concert is held in the Jack Singer Concert Hall in the Calgary Centre for Performing Arts. Tickets range from $5 to $14.

DANCE

ALBERTA BALLET
Nat Christie Centre
141 - 18th Ave. SW, Calgary
403/245-4222   SW
Best known for the Christmas tradition of its annual presentation of *The Nutcracker,* Alberta Ballet performs new creations and celebrates works of distinction. Its 20 dancers perform two mixed programs per season at the Jubilee Auditorium, and the company regularly hosts internationally renowned guest companies including Mikhail Baryshnikov's White Oak Dance Project. For more than 30 years, this versatile company has performed contemporary dance and classical ballet as diverse as *Carmen, Equus,* Mozart's *Requiem,* and *Lifted by Love,* a piece choreographed by Peter Pucci of New York to five of k. d. lang's songs. Tickets range from $13.75 to $46.50 and can be reserved through TicketMaster. For subscription information call 403/245-4549. Ample parking. ♿

DANCERS STUDIO WEST
2007 - 10th Ave. SW, Calgary
403/244-0950   SW
Dancers Studio West is a creation company that presents and produces modern dance out of Studio Theatre II at 2007 - 10th Avenue SW. It also presents touring companies during its September to May season.

Its main event is Alberta Dance Explosions, a festival of new choreography every February. Tickets are $10 to $15. Parking available. ♿

DECIDEDLY JAZZ DANCEWORKS
1514 - 4th St. SW, Calgary
403/245-3533   SW
For over a decade, this Calgary company has wowed audiences with jazz-related dance styles such as swing, tap, funk, Latin, and African, accompanied by the syncopation and rhythm of live jazz accompaniment. Canada's only professional jazz company dedicated to jazz dance, the youthful troupe of 12 dancers presents one major show per season at the Calgary Centre for Performing Arts as well as performing in the Calgary International Jazz Festival in June. Their energetic performances are usually in the evening with occasional matinées offered. The season runs November though June and tickets range from $15 to $30 for adults. They can be reserved through TicketMaster or by calling the box office. Underground parking. ♿

SPRINGBOARD DANCE
304, 524 - 17th Ave. SW, Calgary
403/245-3242   SW
Alternative contemporary modern dance is what Springboard Dance is all about. This part-time collective of modern dancers and choreographers performs new Canadian works in the Big Secret Theatre in the Calgary Centre for Performing Arts as well as the Pumphouse Theatres, Dr. Betty Mitchell Theatre, and warehouse spaces. Past productions include *The Big Ball, Relentless, Echoes of the Flesh,* and others. Tickets are $12 to $18 (sometimes 2-for-1 Wednesdays) and can

be reserved ahead or bought at the door. Meter or off-street parking available. ♿

VENUES

CANMORE OPERA HOUSE
Heritage Park Historical Village
1900 Heritage Dr. SW, Calgary
403/259-1900   SW
In 1898, the H. W. McNeill Co. Brass Band of Canmore's original mining settlement built this log building for local band practices and performances. The Band Hall (as it was originally called) accommodated a 5-meter (16-foot) stage where the band generated an atmosphere of dancing and music. In 1915, electricity was installed and it became a movie house. Seven years later the south wall was expanded to double the seating capacity and its name was changed to the Canmore Opera House. In 1964 the Opera House was donated to Heritage Park, where it is used as a venue for performances by various groups. This historical building comfortably seats 200. The parking lots are a bit of a walk to the Opera House, but you can drive right to the building for wheelchair accessibility.

CALGARY CENTRE FOR PERFORMING ARTS
205 - 8th Ave. SE, Calgary
403/294-7455   DT
Situated in the heart of downtown, this venue stretches the length of an entire city block and comprises five performance venues and convention facilities. Open year-round, it offers guided tours on Monday and Saturday at 11 a.m. The $100-million complex opened in 1985. Just outside its doors is Olympic Plaza. Its facilities include the spectacular Jack Singer

Concert Hall, which seats 2,000 and is one of the best acoustic halls in North America. It is home to the Carthy Organ (the largest concert hall organ in Western Canada) and the Calgary Philharmonic Orchestra. The intimate Max Bell Theatre has a seating capacity of 750 and is home to Theatre Calgary. The annual play festival, playRites, is also performed here. State-of-the-art Martha Cohen Theatre is a Georgian-style, courtyard-shaped theatre seating 450. Alberta Theatre Projects uses this venue as it is ideal for intimate drama. One Yellow Rabbit performs out of the Big Secret Theatre, with a seating capacity of 180. The theatre has a balcony and main floor/lounge area. Engineered Air Theatre seats 185 and is a community-use facility for musical performances, lectures, workshops, play readings, and so on. Underground parking is available. ♿

JUBILEE AUDITORIUM SOUTHERN ALBERTA
1415 - 14th Ave. NW, Calgary

Sun.Ergos, a company of theatre and dance, page 165

© Mattiazzi

Pumphouse Theatres

This unique performing arts venue was originally a water pumping station, built in 1913 to draw water from the nearby Bow River for the city's use. Water Pumping Station No. 2 performed its duties until 1969, when it was retired and the Bearspaw Dam came on line to supply water to North Calgary. Soon after, an active member of the Calgary arts community named Joyce Doolittle noticed the abandoned brick building scheduled for demolition. She immediately perceived its potential as a unique theatre space and set to work convincing the civic government, who owned the building, that it was worthy of rescue from the wrecking ball.

In 1975, the provincial government designated the Pumphouse and its surrounding area a Registered Historic Resource Site and major renovations ensued. The end result was two fully functioning theatres: the Victor Mitchell Theatre, with seating capacity for more than 300, and the Joyce Doolittle Theatre, which seats 100. One of the original pumps is on display at the Joyce Doolittle Theatre.

403/297-8000   **NW**
The Jubilee Auditorium is the venue of choice for many large events ranging from Sharon, Lois, and Bram concerts to musicals such as *Les Misérables*. Its seating capacity of 2,700 and convenient parking make it a perfect home for the Calgary Opera and the Alberta Ballet. The more intimate Dr. Betty Mitchell Theatre (seating capacity of 230) is also housed here and is used by several theatre groups including Sun.Ergos. &

LUNCHBOX THEATRE
Bow Valley Square, 2nd level
205 - 5th Ave. SW, Calgary
403/265-4297   **DT**
The entrance to this venue is on the Plus-15 level of an office/shopping building. It seats 191 with provision for wheelchairs if reserved ahead, as seats are removed to accommodate them. Bring a bag lunch to the 50-minute performance over the lunch hour or use the Pied Pickle 2-for-1 voucher on your ticket after the show. Parking available in the Bow Valley Square Parkade. &

PUMPHOUSE THEATRES
2140 Pumphouse Ave. SW, Calgary
403/263-0079   **SW**
Situated in an open park on the banks of the Bow River, this Historical Resource Site incorporates two performance spaces: the Victor Mitchell Theatre, which seats 300, and the

Joyce Doolittle Theatre with 100-person capacity. Besides hosting the annual Festival of One Act Plays, the Pumphouse is also home to Story-Book Adventure Theatre and various other theatre groups. Free parking adjacent. &

CANADIAN AIRLINES SADDLEDOME
555 Saddledome Rise SE, Calgary
403/777-2177 **SE**
The Saddledome accommodates a wide range of events adapting from an ice rink to basketball court, concert stage to rodeo grounds. Seating 20,000, it is by far the largest venue in the city, making it perfect for large-scale rock concerts, circuses, and sporting events. Home to the National Hockey League's Calgary Flames, the unique saddle design is representative of Calgary's strong western heritage. Attractive on the outside, it is utilitarian inside. Its pillar-free interior allows everyone an unobstructed view of the action, but if you're seated in the "nosebleeds,"

binoculars are necessary to see the features of the performers.

TOMALI THEATRE
Arts and Media Club, 2nd floor
108A - 7th Ave. SW, Calgary
403/262-8422 **DT**
This unique facility is the venue for a variety of theatrical events ranging from improv groups and one-act plays to Native dancers. Besides taking in the theatre, you can also have dinner in the restaurant on the same site and then play various games such as pool, darts, shuffleboard, and pinball. You needn't be a member of the Arts and Media Club to make use of this "full fun facility." Ample parking.

BUYING TICKETS

TICKETMASTER INC.
300, 237 - 8th Ave. SE, Calgary
403/777-0000 **DT**
This entertainment ticket sales agency has ticket centres across Canada. There is a service charge

Martha Cohen Theatre of the Calgary Centre for Performing Arts, page 169

Brian Harder

Every Friday the *Calgary Herald* publishes a comprehensive list of events in their "What's Up" section to let you know what's going on around town.

added to the price of the tickets, but you can save a bit by picking up your tickets at one of the 12 Calgary outlets. For charge-by-phone service, call 403/777-0000; the Artsline (for performances at the Calgary Centre for Performing Arts) is 403/299-8888. Web site: www.ticketmaster.ca

Hard Rock Café - Calgary

12

NIGHTLIFE

Calgary's youthful exuberance is reflected in its proliferation of watering holes that pulse with music and neon lights well into the night. Entire city blocks are built around Calgary's exciting nightlife, offering all manner of after-dark amusement. You can mosey into cowboy country at one of the many popular western clubs or surround yourself with jazz, blues, rock, or pop depending on your taste or mood. Surprisingly, a cover charge is the exception rather than the rule at Calgary bars. Microbreweries are springing up in Cowtown and you can visit any of them for a tour or to sample beers brewed right on the premises.

DANCE CLUBS

CRAZY HORSE
1315 - 1st SW, Calgary
403/266-1133 **SW**
This popular dance bar is a favorite with twenty-somethings: there is usually a line by 9 most weekend evenings. The bar is set in a comfortable old boiler room below Mescalero Cantina.

HARD ROCK CAFÉ
Eau Claire Market
200 Barclay Parade SW, Calgary
403/263-7625 **DT**
A rock 'n' roll diner by day becomes a

rocking nightspot after 10 on Friday and Saturday (Thursday too, May to August). Tables are removed from the centre section of the main floor to reveal a dance floor. A DJ provides the music while a smokescreen and light show add atmosphere. Be warned: the music is loud—the staff wear earplugs. No cover charge. Hours: 11 a.m.–midnight Mon–Wed, 11 a.m.–2 a.m. Thur–Sat, 11–11 Sun.

SEÑOR FROG'S
739 - 2nd Ave. SW, Calgary
403/264-5100 **DT**
This dance club features hot Latin music and Mexican food. Dancing is

TIP

Because of Calgary's high altitude, visitors to the city often feel fatigued, and the effects of alcohol during the adjustment period are heightened.

Thursdays to Sunday nights at this multilevel seaside cantina. Dress code stipulates collared shirts for men and no sandals or cut-offs. Cover charge is $5 after 9 p.m. Hours: 5 p.m.–midnight Sun–Wed, 5 p.m.–2 a.m. Thur–Sat.

MUSIC CLUBS

Jazz

KAOS JAZZ AND BLUES BISTROS
718 - 17th Ave. SW, Calgary
403/228-9997 **SW**
This premier jazz and blues bar features live entertainment every night. One Sunday a month is Singer/Songwriter Night, providing neophytes a chance to perform their own material in this intimate venue. Cover charge ranges from $5 to $10. Hours: 3 p.m.–2 a.m. Mon–Fri, 10 a.m.–2 a.m. Sat and Sun.

Blues

KING EDWARD HOTEL
438 - 9th Ave. SE, Calgary
403/262-1680 **DT**
The King Eddy may not be an upscale nightclub, but it is one of the most popular stops for musicians on the blues circuit, treating Calgarians to some of the best blues around every night of the week. Not only does it provide a venue for top blues performers, it also nurtures up-

and-coming talent. The regular Saturday afternoon jam sessions allow local blues players to mix with the pros. Normally no cover charge but sometimes there is, depending on the band. Hours: noon–1:30 a.m. Mon–Sat, 9 p.m.–12:30 a.m. Sun.

Rock

BACKSTREET LOUNGE
Smuggler's Inn
6920 Macleod Tr. S., Calgary
403/253-5355 **SE**
Live rock bands entertain patrons seven days a week at this watering hole in south Calgary. Classic steakhouse decor includes dark wooden tables, large, upholstered chairs, and dim lighting. There are drink specials every night. No cover charge. Hours: 5 p.m.–2 a.m. Mon–Sat, 8 p.m.–2 a.m. Sun.

Country and Western

COWBOYS DANCE HALL
5th Street and 9th Avenue SW,

TRIVIA

New York City's trendy *Details* magazine rated the King Edward Hotel one of the best blues bars in North America.

two-step lessons are offered on Tuesday and Wednesday nights. Cover charge only during Stampede or when a top band is performing. Hours: 11 a.m.–2 a.m. Mon–Sat. Open some Sundays.

RANCHMAN'S
9615 Macleod Tr. S., Calgary
403/253-1100   SW

This is one of the authentic western bars in Calgary, where real rodeo cowboys wet their whistles. The official hospitality location of the Canadian Professional Rodeo Association, Ranchman's offers up cowboy fare along with band playin', two-steppin', pool shootin', and entertainment. While it's popular at any time of the year, it really jumps during Stampede. Hours: 11 a.m.–2:30 a.m. Mon–Sat. No cover charge Mon–Wed; Thur is Ladies' Night, so no charge for women but men pay $8; $8 Fri and Sat. Cover charge is $10 after 4 p.m. every night during Stampede.

Calgary
403/265-0699   DT

An immensely popular nightspot, expect a lengthy line at Cowboys Dance Hall. This downtown playground can roll 2,000 customers through on a Friday night. It appeals to the white collar "Urban Cowboy" crowd and features live country western music, although not exclusively. Wednesday is Ladies' Night so no cover charge for women. On Thursday draft beer is 25 cents a glass. Cover charge is $5 ($10 during Stampede). Hours: 6 p.m.–2 a.m. Wed–Sat. Open Mon, Tues, and Wed for special concerts.

DUSTY'S SALOON
1088 Olympic Way SE, Calgary
403/263-5343   SE

For some Calgarians it wouldn't be Stampede without a visit to Dusty's Saloon. Conveniently located a few blocks north of the Stampede grounds, Dusty's features live entertainment year-round, usually country or country rock with the occasional blues or rock band. The decor is classic western-style with a rustic log interior and high ceilings. It features a solid oak floating dance floor. Free

ROCKIN' HORSE SALOON
7400 Macleod Tr. S., Calgary
403/255-4646   SE

Live country music gets the patrons tappin' their toes every weekend evening at this country nightclub. This large facility seats up to 850 in its main bar, saddle bar, and cigar bar. It features a huge dance floor with high-tech sound, light, and video. The games room is equipped with eight pool tables and a video arcade. Cover

Want to learn the two-step? Several of the western bars in town offer free country dance lessons during the week. Bring a friend or go solo.

Microbrews

Hammerhead Red, Grasshopper, Black Pilsner, and Rutting Elk Red Ale are some of the colourful names coming out of local microbreweries. The craft beer industry is spiraling, with microbreweries and brew pubs springing up all over the province. Big Rock Brewery in Calgary, Drummond Brewing Company in Red Deer, and Bow Valley Brewing Company in Canmore are just a few of the new players producing ales, lagers, bitters, and stouts that appeal to the budget as well as the tastebuds. Some Canadian brewers have successfully expanded into the U.S.

The Mission Bridge Brewing Company (2417 - 4th Street SW) invites anyone interested in how beer is made to attend Brewer's Corner on Friday evenings from 5 to 7.

charge is $7 during Stampede and $3 the rest of the year. Hours: 5 p.m.–2 a.m. Wed–Sat; open daily at 11 a.m. during Stampede.

PUBS AND BARS

BRITISH CANADIAN SPORTS CLUB
6307B Centre St. S, Calgary
403/259-3304　　　　　　　**SW**
Located next to the Glenmore Bingo Hall, this cozy British-style pub has a rustic wood interior. Live bands play rock or country rock on Friday and Saturday nights as well as some Thursdays. Full menu is available. No cover charge. Hours: 10 a.m.–2 a.m. Mon–Sat, 11–7 Sun.

DIAMOND JACKS PUB
20 Crowchild Circle NW, Calgary
403/241-3988　　　　　　　**NW**
This pub has a cozy atmosphere with its dark wood and dim lighting. A full menu is offered inside and on the huge patio, which sports a gazebo and firepit. Live bands perform every weekend. No cover charge. Hours: 11 a.m.–3 a.m. seven days a week.

DIXON'S PUB
34, 15425 Bannister Rd. SE, Calgary
403/254-1200　　　　　　　**SE**
Sail the seas at Dixon's Pub with its unique decor of nets, lanterns, and other ship paraphernalia on two levels. Entertainment is offered in the form of live music, three pool tables, interactive games, and big screen television. No cover charge. Hours: 11 a.m.–2 a.m. seven days a week.

HOSE & HYDRANT PUB
1030 - 9th Ave. SE, Calgary
403/234-0508　　　　　　　**DT**
The Hose & Hydrant is located in a 91-year-old retired firehall in his-

toric Inglewood. It is decorated with all manner of firefighting paraphernalia. Thirteen types of draft on tap are dispensed from converted fire extinguishers. There's a popular outdoor pool table under a canopied patio. No cover charge. Hours: 11 a.m.–midnight Sun–Wed, 11 a.m.–2 a.m. Thur–Sat.

MISSION BRIDGE BREWING COMPANY
2417 - 4th St. SW, Calgary
403/228-0100 SW
Its own home brews are served at this popular English-style pub. Relax with a drink on benches, in booths, at high-top tables, or stand around the bar. Dartboards and live entertainment provide diversion. They prefer 48 hours' notice if you'd like a tour of the brewery. No cover charge. Hours: 11:30–1 a.m. Sun–Wed, 11:30–2 a.m. Thur–Sat.

ROSE & CROWN PUB
1503 - 4th St. SW, Calgary
403/244-7757 SW
An 80-year-old building sports two patios that extend the seating space of the newly renovated Rose & Crown Pub. All three interior levels offer stone fireplaces and comfortable seating in couches and wing-back chairs. Wood for the interior was imported from pubs in Ireland. Nightly live entertainment spans light jazz to rock 'n' roll. No cover charge. Hours: 11 a.m.–2 a.m. Mon–Fri, 10 a.m.–2 a.m. Sat and Sun.

Brewery Tours

If you like to talk to brewers and see brewing in action, call ahead and arrange for a tour at any of the following locations:

Banff Brewery Corp., *3833 - 29th St. NE, Calgary; 403/250-3883; NE.*

Big Rock Brewery, *5555 - 76th Ave. SE, Calgary; 403/720-3239; SE.*

Bow Valley Brewery Co., *109 Boulder Crescent, Canmore; 403/678-2739.*

Brew Brothers Co., *6025 Centre St. S., Calgary; 403/258-2739; SE.*

Brewsters, *834 - 11th Ave. SW, Calgary; 403/263-2739; SW.*

Grizzly Paw Pub and Brewing Co., *622 Main St., Canmore; 403/678-9983.*

Mission Bridge Brewing Co., *2714 - 4th St. SW, Calgary; 403/228-0100; SW.*

Wild Rose Brewery, *9, 5815 - 40th St. SE, Calgary, 403/720-2733; SE.*

THE ROXBURY
1006 - 11th Ave. SW, Calgary
403/244-2440 **SW**
This upscale, non-competitive billiards bar offers a full food menu and a whisky menu featuring more than 30 single malts. The California eclectic decor surrounds nine classic mahogany ball-and-claw tables, which are a treat to play on at $9.50 an hour. Darts and video games provide alternate entertainment. No cover charge. Hours: 11:30 a.m.–midnight Mon–Thur, 11:30 a.m.–2 a.m. Fri and Sat.

ST. LOUIS HOTEL
8th Avenue and 4th Street SE, Calgary
403/262-6341 **DT**
Book a table at the St. Louis for noon on a Friday and participate in the hour-long World-Famous Indoor Horse Races. This crazy event has been a favorite with Calgarians for years. You place your bets against other tables on imaginary horses you know nothing about. Then a racing caller gets on a platform and goes into a comedy routine, inventing pitfalls of each invisible jockey and steed. He calls the race over the sound of a real racetrack crowd and, although no one can see it, one of the horses wins. No cover charge. Hours: 10 a.m.–1 a.m.

BARS WITH RESTAURANTS

BARLEY MILL EATERY & PUB
Eau Claire Market
201 Barclay Parade SW, Calgary

Invention of the Caesar

The Caesar, the Bloody Mary's spicy cousin, was invented by Walter Shell, a bartender at the Owl's Nest of the Westin Hotel. More than 25 years ago, Walter mixed up his first Caesar without the convenience of premixed clamato juice. Back then he had to mix his own clam juice, tomato juice, and spices. After his concoction won a competition, the Caesar's popularity grew. Today, it is a common drink across Canada.

Here is a recipe for the famous Caesar:
Dip the rim of a chilled glass in celery salt, then add:

- *1 ounce of vodka*
- *9 ounces of clamato juice*
- *dash of Worcestershire sauce*
- *dash of Tabasco sauce*
- *salt and pepper to taste*

Garnish with a stalk of celery.

403/290-1500   **DT**

This popular restaurant and pub sports a large upstairs patio that doubles the seating capacity in summer. It's a great vantage point for people-watching outside busy Eau Claire Market. The comfortable atmosphere is enhanced by the stone fireplaces and rustic wood interior recycled from an old whisky distillery in central Alberta. The centerpiece of the imported 100-year-old Scottish bar is a couple of huge, shiny, copper beer vats. The Barley Mill offers 24 drafts on tap, as well as 35 imported bottled brews and 30 single malt scotches. No cover charge. Menu includes salads, pastas, and American entrées. Hours: 11 a.m.–3 a.m.

BIG ROCK GRILL
5555 - 76th Ave. SE, Calgary
403/236-1606   **SE**

English pub-style Big Rock Grill is open at the brewery site of Big Rock, the big name in Calgary beer. It features grill and rotisserie entrées (including bison burgers and venison when available), with seven of its brews on tap as well as Guinness. A river rock fireplace and antique tables and chairs add to the atmosphere. Groups of ten or more can combine a visit with a brewery tour. Reservations recommended. Lunch and dinner. ♿

BIG WALLY'S
217 - 10th St. NW, Calgary
403/283-5739   **NW**

Early Canadian junk decorates the walls and ceiling of this casual, friendly bar and family restaurant, with menu featuring burgers, sandwiches, and pub fare. Big screen television and pool tables offer recreation while you down a brew or two. No cover charge. Hours: 11 a.m.–1 a.m. Mon–Thur, 11 a.m.–2 a.m. Fri and Sat, 11 a.m.–midnight Sun.

BILLY MACINTYRE'S CATTLE COMPANY
3630 Brentwood Rd. NW, Calgary
403/282-6614   **NW**

Billy MacIntyre was a rancher in the 1800s who owned much of what is now the area around Lethbridge, extending down into the U.S. You can taste some of the recipes from his ranch, most notably the apple barbecue sauce. The bar features a dance floor with music provided by a DJ. The restaurant offers a full menu, including ribs, steak, chicken, seafood, and pasta. No cover charge. Hours: 11:30 a.m.–1 a.m. Sun–Wed, 11:30 a.m.–2 a.m. Thur–Sat.

BOTTLESCREW BILL'S
1st Street and 10th Avenue SW, Calgary
403/263-7900   **SW**

A traditional English-style pub and

Big Rock Brewery, page 179

restaurant offers steak and Guinness pie, stew, sandwiches, burgers, and salads. Bottlescrew Bill's specializes in beer (130 brands) and is home to the famous Buzzard Breath Ale house beer. Bottlescrew Bill's hosts some unusual events (see sidebar). No cover charge. Hours: 11 a.m.–2 a.m.

BREWSTERS BREWING CO. AND RESTAURANT
834 - 11th Ave. SW, Calgary
403/261-2739   SW
This bar and restaurant wraps you in comfort with its benches, booths, and solid oak tables and chairs. Choose from pastas, salads, steaks, seafood, chicken, veal, or shepherd's pie. Pool tables and VLTs offer diversion or you can request a tour of the brewing facilities. Other Brewsters locations are at 755 Lake Bonavista Drive SE and 25 Crowfoot Terrace NW. No cover charge. Hours: daily 11 a.m.–late.

COYOTE GRILL
1411 - 17th Ave. SW, Calgary
403/244-1080   SW
This is an intimate Southern barbecue restaurant and bar with seating for 50. The menu offers a wide selection of ribs as well as quesadillas, salads, seafood, etc. Decor is Southwestern with some diner-like counter seating. No cover charge. Hours: 11–11 Mon–Sat, 11–9 Sun.

T I P

For a gander at some fine Harley-Davidsons, mosey over to the Melrose Café and Bar (730 - 17th Avenue SW) on a Monday evening during spring, summer, or fall. Members of one of the city's Harley Owners' Groups meet at the Melrose and park their hogs along the curb.

DON QUIJOTE
309 - 2nd Ave. SW, Calgary
403/205-4244 DT

Latin bands provide accompaniment to a full menu of Spanish food and drinks at Don Quijote. The Mediterranean decor of sandstone, clay tiles, and arched windows compliments the menu of Spanish dishes as well as veal, pasta, and seafood. Wrap-around outdoor patio provides more seating in summer months. Cover charge is $5 after 9 p.m. Hours: 11:30 a.m.–2 a.m. seven days a week.

MOOSE MCGUIRE'S BEANERY & BAR ROOM
1941 Uxbridge Dr. NW, Calgary
403/289-9184 NW

Modeled after a Chicago-style tavern, this sports bar features a brick and dark wood interior. You can enjoy a selection from the full menu (appetizers, soups, salads, burgers, pizza, and sandwiches) and play a game or two at one of the four pool tables. Big screen televisions offer viewing of your favorite sporting events. Sixteen draft beers, 32 scotches, and countless liqueurs are available. No cover charge. Hours: 11:30 a.m.–late Mon–Fri, noon–late Sat and Sun.

SWAN'S RESTAURANT & PUBLIC HOUSE
1336 - 9th Ave. SE, Calgary
403/233-7574 SE

Stand around the horseshoe bar in this turn-of-the-century building, or relax on a couch or in a booth. There is standard pub fare available in the bar area and a full menu in the dining room. If in the mood for a British eating experience try their pie and chips, or select one of their pastas, salads, pizza, or Cajun cuisine. Good selection of draft, bottled, or imported beers and spirits. Happy hour

is 4 to 7 daily with free games at the pool tables from 2 to 4 p.m. No cover charge. Hours: 11:30 a.m.–2 a.m. Mon–Sat, 2–10 p.m. Sun.

TOPS BAR & GRILL
Calgary Tower
101 - 9th Ave. SW, Calgary
403/266-7171 DT

Tops Bar & Grill is at the top of the Calgary Tower, offering a panoramic view of the city skyline and mountains. Light meals and late night snacks are available in a casual, intimate setting. Burgers, chicken fingers, salmon filet, or stir-fries are some of the choices. No cover charge but there is an elevation charge of $5.50 to ride up to the bar and grill. Hours: Summer 11–11, winter 5–10.

THE UNICORN
304 - 8th Ave. SW, Calgary
403/233-2666 DT

Opened in 1979 by the Irish Rovers, the Unicorn has live music nightly. Traditional pub fare (Cornish pasties, bangers and mash, fish and chips, or steak and kidney pie) is served up with entertainment by professional bands on Friday and Saturday, blues jam sessions on Wednesday, and Acoustics Night on Tuesday. Mondays feature Battle of the Bands with rookie bands competing to win a free half-hour recording session. Thursday is reserved for the semi-finals of the Battle of the Bands.

COMEDY CLUBS

YUK YUK'S KOMEDY KABARET
Blackfoot Inn
5940 Blackfoot Tr. SE, Calgary
403/258-2028 SE

Part of the largest chain of comedy clubs in the world, Yuk Yuk's offers excellent professional stand-up comedy three days per week. There are three comedians per show and shows change weekly. The atmosphere is casual. Performances are at 8 p.m. Thur, 8 and 10:30 Fri, 7:30 and 10:15 Sat. Reservations are recommended. Cover charge: $5.35 Thur, $11.75 Fri, $12.85 Sat.

ENTERTAINMENT CENTRES

PURPLE TURTLE
Carriage House Inn
9030 Macleod Tr. SE, Calgary
403/640-7500 SE
Wear the latest electronic helmet and enjoy virtual reality games at the Purple Turtle. There are pool tables and shuffleboard to play as well as golf and racing simulators. The modern, angular decor is enhanced by an eye-catching fish tank. On Wednesday to Saturday nights you can dance to music spun by a DJ. Full menu is available. Normally no cover charge. Hours: noon–2 a.m. Mon–Sat.

SCHANK'S
9627 Macleod Tr. S., Calgary

403/253-7300 SW
This huge entertainment centre allows grown-ups to work up a sweat playing high-tech video games and golf simulators. There are skiing, shooting, and driving games, pool tables, VLTs, and a mini-golf range that winds through the bar. No cover charge. Hours: 11:30 a.m.–2 a.m. daily.

DINNER THEATRE

MOUNTAIN SONG NATIVE
DINNER THEATRE
Bragg Creek Steak Pit, Bragg Creek
403/949-3400
On the first Thursday of each month (except January and February), performers representing Alberta's First Nations peoples present stories, song, and dance at the Bragg Creek Steak Pit in this picturesque hamlet just west of the city. Admission is $22.95 plus a required meal purchase. Menu includes some Native cuisine such as venison, buffalo, and salmon. Doors open at 6:30 p.m. and show starts at 8. In Calgary, tickets are

Mission Bridge Brewing Company, page 177

Mission Bridge Brewing Company

available from the Micah Gallery at 403/245-1304.

MURDER MYSTERY BY PEGASUS PRODUCTIONS
115 Westminster Dr. SW, Calgary
403/246-4811　　　　　　　**SW**

Pegasus Productions uses a variety of venues for its interactive murder mystery performances. Shows are up-close and intimate, and emphasize humor with scenes happening in and around the guests' tables. Keen audience members can participate directly in the performance if they choose. One of the regular events is a fund-raiser for the Calgary Zoo with dinner amongst the gardens in the Conservatory while you transform into a sleuth in search of whodunit. Tickets cost $25 to $40 depending on venue.

MYSTERIES FROM HISTORY DINNER THEATRE
Deane House Historic Site and Restaurant
806 - 9th Ave. SE, Calgary
403/269-7747 or TicketMaster
403/777-0000　　　　　　　**DT**

Each Friday evening at the historic Deane House Restaurant, Shadow Productions performs a murder mystery dinner theatre. There is some interaction with the audience when actors ask patrons questions to help solve the mystery. Tickets are $46.50, which includes a four-course meal, GST, and gratuities. Main courses vary but examples are prime rib with Yorkshire pudding and chicken breast stuffed with feta cheese. The Deane House is a Calgary historic site, built in 1906 for Captain Richard Burton Deane of the North West Mounted Police.

STAGE WEST
727 - 42nd Ave. SE, Calgary
403/243-6642　　　　　　　**SE**

For more than 15 years, Stage West has entertained Calgary audiences with a wide range of dinner theatre including comedies, musicals, mysteries, and other crowd-pleasers. No heavy drama here. Top-notch performers such as Jamie Farr and Gale Gordon have performed at this spacious venue. A full 120-item buffet (seafood, chicken, beef, salads, etc.) is included with the price of a ticket and seating is tiered for optimum viewing. Tickets range from $27 (matinée) to $59. See Chapter 6, "Kids' Stuff," for details of Stage West's children's shows and buffet every other Saturday. This is a non-smoking facility.

Calgary CVB/Greg Fulmes

13

DAY TRIPS FROM CALGARY

Calgary is nestled at the base of the foothills that form the transition from majestic Rocky Mountains to expansive fields of grain known as the Prairies. This location encourages outdoor pursuits, and Calgarians as well as visitors take advantage of the many sights and adventures within a day's drive of the city.

DAY TRIP: Banff National Park and Banff Townsite

Distance from Calgary: 120 kilometers (75 miles) west of the city; 90 minutes from downtown

To experience the Canadian Rocky Mountains in all their splendor, take a scenic trip along a four-lane highway to Banff National Park, which covers about 6,500 square kilometers (2,500 square miles) of breathtaking mountain landscape. Banff townsite (population about 8,000) is 16 kilometers (10 miles) west of the park gate.

When three railway workers stumbled on a hot spring bubbling from the base of Sulphur Mountain in 1883, Banff National Park was born. Canada's oldest national park is also its busiest, attracting 3 million visitors annually from around the globe, providing them with over 60 hotels, campgrounds, bed and breakfasts, and backcountry lodges, as well as 100 restaurants and cafés, plus numerous shops. Whether you like to downhill or cross-country ski, golf, hike, kayak, canoe, white-water raft, horseback ride, bird-watch, or mountain bike, Banff has it all.

To see Banff's birthplace, walk or drive to the **Cave and Basin Historic Site**, just 4 kilometers (2.5 miles) return from Banff Avenue. Then follow an interpretive boardwalk that leads to a marsh rich with waterfowl and fish.

DAY TRIPS FROM CALGARY

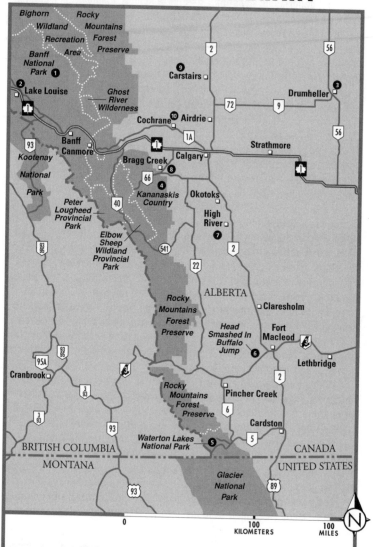

Day Trips from Calgary

1 Banff National Park and Banff Townsite
2 Lake Louise
3 Alberta Badlands and Drumheller
4 Canmore and Kananaskis Country
5 Waterton Lakes National Park
6 Head-Smashed In Buffalo Jump and Fort Macleod
7 Bar U Ranch National Historic Site
8 Bragg Creek
9 PaSu Farm
10 Cochrane

Banff Avenue and Bear Street are lined with intriguing shops, museums, and galleries. Many shops specialize in high quality outerwear, giftware, and local artwork. Numerous museums tell of the natural history of the area. The **Whyte Museum of the Canadian Rockies** on Bear Street houses a collection of art, historical displays, and research archives while the historic **Banff Park Museum** at the corner of Banff Avenue and Buffalo Street displays wildlife specimens from as far back as the 1860s. It also houses a Discovery Room for kids. For a look at the area's fossils and evolution of the Rockies, check out the **Natural History Museum** on Banff Avenue, while the **Luxton Museum** on Birch Avenue features life-sized dioramas of Natives' daily lives before the arrival of Europeans. Traditional dress, tipis, and ceremonies are depicted in the scenes.

Winter sports abound in the snowy playground of the Canadian Rockies. There are numerous downhill skiing and snowboarding events to watch throughout the winter and spring, but you should also try some of the fine slopes yourself. **Sunshine Village**, known for its 100 percent natural snow, is a 15-minute drive west of Banff townsite and is 2,730 meters (8,954 feet) at the summit. Runs range from gentle slopes to Free Fall, one of North America's most challenging runs with a pitch of 83 percent. Sunshine provides on-mountain accommodation at **Sunshine Inn**, and a day lodge where you can relax with a meal after a day on the slopes. **Mount Norquay**, a ten-minute drive from Banff townsite, offers beginner terrain as well as intermediate and advanced slopes. **Cascade Lodge** is a new facility offering accommodation, cafeteria, lounge, and restaurant.

Winter or summer enjoy unparalleled vistas from **Sulphur Mountain Gondola** or **Mount Norquay Sightseeing Lift** with dining, guided hikes, displays, and spectacular views at the top.

With more than 50 species of mammals, including elk, deer, bear, bighorn sheep, and mountain goats, as well as about 300 varieties of birds, the area offers some of the finest wildlife viewing around. Evening wildlife walks around Banff are offered June through September.

If culture is what you're after, the **Banff Centre for the Arts** lets you explore the arts in performances, concerts, and exhibitions. Numerous events held throughout the year attract audiences, artists, and performers from around the world.

For a self-guided walking tour, pick up a booklet at the **Information Centre** on Banff Avenue. It includes a route map and introduces visitors to

T I P

A useful visitor's magazine called *WHERE Rocky Mountains*, available at tourist information centres, gives up-to-date information on events, accommodations, dining, and shopping in the Rockies.

Banff National Park

Banff's heritage buildings and its long and colourful history as a resort community. From mid-May to the end of October, **Banff Transit** offers service to downtown shops, restaurants, Banff Avenue hotels, Banff Springs Hotel, and Tunnel Mountain hotels and campgrounds. For a more leisurely pace, hire a horse-drawn carriage to take you around to the sights.

After a day of soaking up the scenery, soak in a natural hot pool to relax tired muscles. Since the 1800s, the **Upper Hot Springs** pool on Mountain Avenue has been one of Banff's most popular attractions. The spa is fed by naturally heated springs on Sulphur Mountain and offers steam room, mineral water plunge, and access to the outdoor pool. There are also exhibits describing the history and geology of the hot springs and interactive touch screen computers.

The south end of Banff Avenue is crowned by **Cascade Gardens**—a complex of gazebos, waterworks, and flower gardens set around the Banff National Park Administration Building.

No trip to Banff would be complete without a visit to baronial **Banff Springs Hotel** and its world-renowned 27-hole golf course. During the early 1900s wealthy travelers came to this mountain castle to enjoy the mineral baths and therapeutic treatments. Today the hotel's $12 million resort spa features cascading waterfalls that spill into soothing, mineralized whirlpools. Enjoy some luxurious pampering.

A note of caution: Although the park animals may behave in a mild manner, please remember that they are wild animals. It is wise to keep your distance.

Getting There from Calgary: *From downtown Calgary take Centre Street north until it intersects 16th Avenue N (Highway 1). Turn left and travel west along 16th Avenue past the city limits and continue on until you reach Banff National Park.*

DAY TRIP: Lake Louise

Distance from Calgary: 2 to 2½ hours (but you'll no doubt make stops along the way); 175 kilometers (110 miles) west of Calgary

Lake Louise is 55 kilometers (34 miles) west of Banff on Highway 1. It is the most famous glacial lake in the Canadian Rockies and certainly one of the most beautiful. Named after Princess Louise Caroline Alberta, daughter of Queen Victoria, it is flanked on one end by **Mount Victoria** and **Victoria Glacier**, with world-famous **Chateau Lake Louise** at the opposite end. Melting glacial silt lends the startling turquoise color to the lake and also contributes to its frigid temperature. No skinny-dipping here!

Professional parks interpreters lead two-hour **Lake Louise Lakeshore Strolls** and six-hour hikes onto the awesome **Plain of Six Glaciers**. There are also hikes through the pristine wilderness of the **Moraine Lake** area. The **Valley of the Ten Peaks** surrounds the lake. To the north, **Mount Temple**, with the glacier on its summit, is the third-highest mountain in Banff National Park.

Winter or summer, take the **Lake Louise Gondola** to the top of the ski area for panoramic views of mountains, valleys, and glaciers. Another way to drink in the views is to rent a canoe and paddle the waters of Lake Louise or Moraine Lake. Alternatively, you can follow the trails on horseback or hire a horse-drawn sleigh for a one-hour ride from Chateau Lake Louise to the other end of the lake in winter months.

Cross-country skiing, downhill skiing, and snowboarding are popular winter pastimes at Lake Louise. You can even rent a helicopter and try the sensational experience of heli-skiing. **Lake Louise Ski Area** is Canada's largest ski resort, with 1,620 hectares (4,000 acres) of downhill ski terrain. It was rated as one of North America's top five ski areas and first for scenery by *Snow Country Magazine*.

At the base of Lake Louise, **Whisky Jack Lodge** has recently added an extension incorporating a full-service restaurant and bar. For a backcountry experience you can cross-country ski to **Skoki Lodge**, a rustic log lodge with handmade pine furniture and cast-iron stove. Nestled deep in the Rocky Mountains, it takes about three or four hours to cross-country ski to it from **Temple Lodge**.

Getting There from Calgary: *From downtown follow the directions to Banff (see Day Trip: Banff, above) and continue along Trans-Canada Highway (Highway 1) for another 55 kilometers (34 miles).*

DAY TRIP: Alberta Badlands and Drumheller

Distance from Calgary: Drumheller is 90 minutes northeast of Calgary; Dinosaur Provincial Park is 138 kilometers (84 miles), or about 2½ hours, east of Calgary

This "day trip" in fact includes more dinosaurs than you could possible pack into 24 hours. You could likely do it credit in two days, however.

The moon-like landscape of Alberta's badlands near Drumheller reveals more than 70 million years of geological history. Gouged out by ancient rivers and ice, this area was once the domain of the dinosaur and is rich in fossils. The first dinosaur remains were discovered in 1884 by Joseph Burr Tyrrell and paleontologists are still discovering new specimens today. In the world-famous **Royal Tyrrell Museum of Palaeontology** you can view ancient treasures harvested from the earth. This is a major exhibition and research centre and one of the largest palaeontological museums in the world. It features stunning reconstructed dinosaurs stalking the exhibit space and interactive displays that occupy visitors for hours. During October and November and January to May, there are camp-in opportunities for you to bring along a sleeping bag and sleep among the dinosaurs. Evening activities include digging for fossils and meeting scientists. There are also day camps in summer for youth and adults to dig dinosaur fossils from a nearby quarry.

Dinosaur Trail is a 48-kilometer (29-mile) circular route starting in Drumheller. It passes through breathtaking viewpoints and includes stops of interest along the Red Deer River Valley. You can also travel down the Red Deer River aboard a hovercraft and view rock formations from a unique vantage point.

The hamlet of Rosebud on Secondary Highway 840 is home of the **Rosebud Dinner Theatre**. People drive from all around to take in this popular theatre because of its reputation for professional productions, old-fashioned service and home-style food. Meals are served in the old **Mercantile building** and live theatre follows at the **Opera House**. Stay the night at the **Rosebud Country Inn and Tea Room** and you can set out the next day for the second leg of dinosaur investigations.

Royal Tyrrell Museum of Palaeontology

Calgary CVB/Alberta Economic Development & Tourism

Dinosaur Provincial Park, proclaimed a UNESCO World Heritage Site in 1979, is 48 kilometers (29 miles) north of Brooks on Secondary Highway 544. You can learn about the geological and natural history of the area through daily interpretive programs by park staff and self-guided walks. The **Royal Tyrrell Museum's Field Station** features fossil displays and a view of palaeontologists at work.

Getting There from Calgary: *To reach Drumheller, from downtown Calgary take Centre Street north to 16th Avenue N. Turn right and drive east on the Trans-Canada Highway*

(Highway 1) until it jogs south and Secondary Highway 591 continues east. Follow 591 for a short distance until you reach the Secondary Highway 840 intersection, then turn north onto 840 and drive on until you reach Rosebud. Continue north on 840 until it intersects Highway 9. Turn east and follow it to Drumheller.

DAY TRIP: Canmore and Kananaskis Country

Distance from Calgary: 106 kilometers (66 miles), or about one hour, west of the city.

Referred to as "God's Country," Kananaskis Country encompasses 4,250 square kilometers (1,641 square miles) of outdoor recreation space. K-country includes three provincial parks and some of Canada's most spectacular terrain, ranging from grassy plains and rolling foothills to Alpine meadows, rocky cliffs, and icy glaciers.

At the northern edge of K-country, the picturesque town of Canmore nestles at the base of **Three Sisters Mountain**. In winter, the **Canmore Nordic Centre** (site of the 1988 Winter Olympic Nordic events) attracts outdoor enthusiasts as does the International Sled Dog Races. There is also an 18-hole public golf course to challenge you in summer, and museums, galleries, and shops to peruse year-round. If you're traveling to Canmore in the late summer, the **Canmore Highland Games** take place at Centennial Park. It's a two-day event with Scottish music, dancing, and heavy sports competitions.

Return east on the Trans-Canada Highway to where it joins Highway 40, then head south to the **Nakiska Ski Area**, site of the Alpine ski events of the 1988 Winter Olympics. It features 732 vertical meters (2,400 feet) of slopes and several day lodges. Continue along Highway 40 to **Kananaskis Village**, a picturesque resort centre with hotels and other amenities.

Kananaskis Country Golf Course, designed by Robert Trent Jones, boasts 36 holes incorporating lots of sand traps and water hazards. It has numerous tee off positions so golfers of various abilities can enjoy this facility.

Further south is **Fortress Mountain**, an uncrowded downhill ski facility featuring rugged scenery, day lodge, and on-hill chalets.

The newest Canadian Pacific mountain resort is the **Kananaskis Lodge**, built for the 1988 Winter Olympics. Set in one of the most breathtaking valleys in the Canadian Rockies, you can hike or cross-country ski virtually right from your door. For a change of pace, sleep in a tipi! **Sundance Lodges** rents handpainted tipis at sites along the Kananaskis River. They come with wooden floor, beds, heater, and lantern. Or stay at **Rafter Six Ranch Resort** for a dude ranch experience. It offers bed and breakfast, horseback riding, heli-tours, and white-water rafting.

Getting There from Calgary: *From downtown take Centre Street north until it intersects 16th Avenue N (Highway 1). Turn left (west) on 16th Avenue and continue on until you reach the town of Canmore.*

DAY TRIP: Waterton Lakes National Park

Distance from Calgary: 270 kilometers (150 miles), or about three hours, southwest of Calgary

While this trip can be done in a day, it is more enjoyable spread over two. The approach to Waterton Lakes is startling and spectacular with towering mountains rising straight up from the prairie. Located in the southwest corner of Alberta, it is bordered on the west by British Columbia and the south by Montana's Glacier National Park, with which it shares an international peace park. Waterton is also part of the Trail of the Great Bear, a scenic corridor that links Yellowstone National Park in Wyoming with Banff National Park in Alberta. Additionally, Waterton Lakes National Park is a designated UNESCO World Heritage Site.

In the heart of the park is the town of Waterton, jutting out into the lake. It is a full-service alpine village community with wilderness at its doorstep. It offers backcountry hiking and well-groomed Nordic ski trails, horseback riding, cycling, golf, and tennis. Step aboard a scenic shoreline cruise that takes you across the border into the United States. A full range of accommodation is available, the most spectacular of which is the **Prince of Wales Hotel** overlooking the lake from a perch high above. While the park is open year-round, not all facilities are.

For a different dining experience, try the game features on the menu at remote backcountry **Kilmorey Lodge**. Choices may include bison, caribou, elk, venison, and even ostrich.

Make a stop at Cardston on your way to or from Calgary and take in the **Remington-Alberta Carriage Centre** for an authentic experience of nineteenth- and early twentieth-century horse-drawn transportation.

Waterton Lakes National Park

Calgary CVB/Alberta Economic Development & Tourism

The centre's interactive galleries tell stories of the turn-of-the-century carriage industry.

Getting There from Calgary: *From downtown head south on 1st Street SE, which becomes Macleod Trail and then Highway 2 as it leaves the city limits. Continue along Highway 2 until you reach Cardston, then turn west on Highway 5, which takes you to Waterton.*

DAY TRIP: Head-Smashed-In Buffalo Jump and Fort Macleod

Distance from Calgary: 165 kilometers (102 miles); or about 1½ hours

A UNESCO World Heritage Site, Head-Smashed-In Buffalo Jump documents the buffalo hunting culture of the Plains Indians. For some 6,000 years, they hunted buffalo by driving them over cliffs to their deaths. Head-Smashed-In is among the oldest, largest, and best-preserved of hundreds of buffalo jump sites across the western plains. The unique Interpretive Centre is built into the side of the hill that was used as the actual buffalo jump. Siksika (Blackfoot) guides explain their culture through events such as storytelling and an annual powwow. There are also exhibits and artifact replicas on Plains Indian history, and several times a day the theatre presents a ten-minute film featuring a re-enactment of a buffalo hunt. Don't forget the outdoor interpretive trails and archaeological excavations.

Fort Macleod is home of the first North West Mounted Police (NWMP) outpost in Western Canada. The **Fort Museum** in the heart of town offers a glimpse of what life was like in 1874 for these early lawmen. The museum features extensive displays of artifacts from the NWMP, settlers, and Native peoples. A mounted patrol performs a musical ride four times a day throughout the summer.

Wildlife Viewing

Traveling around Alberta affords visitors myriad opportunities to view an amazing variety of wildlife. Watch for Alberta Watchable signposts along highways. They feature an image of a person looking through binoculars and alert you to prime wildlife viewing spots. You can purchase an Alberta Wildlife Viewing Guide in local bookstores or by calling 403/422-1053.

Getting There from Calgary: *From downtown head south on 1st Street SE, which becomes Macleod Trail and then Highway 2 as it leaves the city limits. Continue along Highway 2 until you see signs for the Interpretive Centre just before Fort Macleod. Turn west on Secondary Highway 785 and travel 14 kilometers (9 miles) to the site. To visit Fort Macleod, travel back along Highway 785 and turn south on Highway 2, which takes you into town.*

DAY TRIP: Bar U Ranch National Historic Site

Distance from Calgary: 90 kilometers (54 miles) or about one hour

Established in 1882, Bar U Ranch preserves and commemorates the contribution of ranching to the province's history and growth. Experience the spirit of the Canadian West at the visitor centre, which incorporates interpretive displays with a video of *The Mighty Bar U*. Enjoy a guided tour of the original ranch site and mosey amongst the buildings and corrals of a working ranch. The **Bar U Ranch Roadhouse** offers homemade soups and stews, sourdough biscuits, and buffalo burgers, or drive into nearby Longview for a unique dining experience at **Memories Inn**.

On your return trip to Calgary, stop in at Okotoks, a thriving town nestled in the valley of the Sheep River. Explore the coulees or spend an afternoon climbing **The Big Rock**, the largest glacial erratic in North America. In the town itself visit the **Station**, home of the Visitor Information Centre, which also houses an interpretive display, art exhibitions, and live theatre. Antique hounds especially enjoy the shops in and around Okotoks. Lunch at the **Ginger Tea Room** is worth the time. It incorporates a lovely gift shop with work of local artisans under its roof.

Getting There from Calgary: *From downtown travel south on 1st Street SE, which becomes Macleod Trail and then Highway 2 as it leaves the city. Continue along until you come to the Okotoks turnoff, which is Highway 2A. Follow Highway 2A through Okotoks and past High River to Secondary Highway 540. Turn west on it and continue to the Bar U.*

QUICK TRIP: Bragg Creek

Distance from Calgary: 40 kilometers (24 miles) or about 40 minutes

Head west to the hamlet of Bragg Creek just southwest of Calgary to find downhill skiing or golf at Wintergreen, biking, trail rides, rafting, and canoeing. For a less strenuous pastime, browse the local galleries, boutiques, and antique stores. Accommodation includes myriad bed and breakfasts and campgrounds, and dining opportunities abound. The **Bragg Creek Steak Pit** hosts a Native dinner theatre on Thursday nights, or, on the way to or from the city, you can stop in at **Priddis Greens** on Highway 22X for a meal at their clubhouse. They offer an especially nice Sunday brunch complete with champagne and orange juice.

Early mornings are the best viewing times for catching sight of wildlife.

Getting There from Calgary: *From downtown travel south on 1st Street SE, which becomes Macleod Trail. Continue south until it intersects Highway 22X at the south end of the city. Turn west on 22X until you reach Secondary Highway 66 and then turn north. Continue into Bragg Creek.*

QUICK TRIP: PaSu Farm

Distance from Calgary: 75 kilometers (45 miles) or about 30 minutes
A working sheep farm setting north of Calgary, PaSu features a beautiful restaurant and tea house with gourmet cuisine and attached gift shop featuring Canadiana. Bring the whole family one weekend in September when they hold sheepdog trials, or attend Medieval Night. Owners Patrick and Sue DeRosemond also operate a bed and breakfast on the grounds.

Getting There from Calgary: *From downtown travel west on 5th Avenue S until it intersects with Memorial Drive. Continue west on Memorial and then take Deerfoot Trail north, which becomes Highway 2 as it exits the city. Take the Carstairs turnoff and follow signage along Secondary Highway 580 until you encounter PaSu Farm.*

QUICK TRIP: Cochrane

Distance from Calgary: 40 kilometers (24 miles) or about 30 minutes
Located just north of Cochrane on Highway 22 is the $15-million **Western Heritage Centre**, which celebrates Alberta's ranching heritage. It is an interactive interpretive facility commemorating the ranching, farming, and rodeo life of southern Alberta. After a few hours of being a "virtual cowboy," cool off with one of the many flavors of hard ice cream at **MacKay's Cochrane Ice Cream Shoppe** on 1st Street. Calgarians often drive out from the city for this summer treat.

Getting There from Calgary: *From downtown travel north on Centre Street until it intersects Banff Trail. Head north and it becomes Crowchild Trail and then Highway 1A. Continue west to Cochrane for an outstanding panoramic view of the Canadian Rockies from the hill high above the town.*

IMPORTANT PHONE NUMBERS

Emergency
Police 911
Fire 911
Ambulance 911
Avalanche Hazard Information
    247-1910

Major Hospital and Emergency Medical Centres
Alberta Children's Hospital 229-7211
    Emergency 229-7070
Foothills Hospital 670-1110
    Emergency 670-1315
Peter Lougheed Centre 291-8555
    Emergency 291-8999
Rockyview General Hospital 541-3000
    Emergency 541-3449
Colonel Belcher Hospital 541-3600
Tom Baker Cancer Centre 670-1711

Time & Temperature
263-3333

Weather
299-7878

CITY MEDIA

Newspapers
Calgary Herald
Calgary Sun

Magazines
Avenue
Cityscope
Western Living
WHERE Calgary

Radio Stations
CBC 1010 AM current affairs;
    102.1 FM stereo music
66CFR AM oldies and Flames Games
CHFM Lite 96 FM lite rock
CJAY92 FM classic rock
CKRY 105 FM country
CKXM 1060 AM oldies
KISS FM 96.9 pop, rock, and country
POWER 107 FM pop, rock
QR 77 770 AM and 88.9 FM news, talk,
    and information station

Television Stations
Channel 3 CFCN
Channel 5 RDTV
Channel 6 CBC
Channel 7 CALGARY 7
Channel 8 the A-Channel
Channel 11 CBC (French)
Channel 12 KREM - CBS
Channel 14 KSPS
Channel 15 CBC Newsworld
Channel 16 NBC
Channel 20 YTV
Channel 22 ABC
Channel 23 Women's TV Network
Channel 25 TSN
Channel 26 A & E
Channel 27 Nashville Network
Channel 32 Showcase
Channel 34 FOX
Channel 35 Discovery Channel
Channel 36 BRAVO
Channel 52 Much Music

VISITOR INFORMATION

Calgary Chamber of Commerce
    750-0400
Calgary Convention & Visitor's Bureau
    262-2766
Travel Alberta 800/661-8888

CITY TOURS

BREWSTER TRANSPORTATION & TOURS
808 Centre St. SE
221-8250
From May 15th to October 15th, Brewster offers tours of Calgary City Sights. Tours last approximately 3.5–4 hours, daily departures. Fare: $42 adults, $21 six–15 years, free for under six if sharing a seat with an adult. In December, Brewster traditionally runs 2.5-hour Christmas Light Tours. Fare: $10 adults, $8 seniors/children.

EXCLUSIVE MOUNTAIN TOURS
32 Hudson Rd. NW
282-3980
Their 2.5-hour City Tour costs $25 per person (admissions extra).

RAINBOW BALLOONS
7136 Fisher St. SE
259-3154
Float over Calgary's skyline in a hot air balloon for approximately 1.5 hours. These tours are weather-dependent. Fares: $150 one passenger; $145 each if two passengers; $140 each if four or more.

BRAGG CREEK TOURS & TRAVEL
P.O. Box 980
Bragg Creek, AB T0L 0K0
403/949-3400
They organize various year-round day tours in and around Kananaskis Country. Prices vary according to package.

Walking Tours
For self-guided tours of Calgary's historical buildings, pick up booklets including maps and information from the Municipal Building (800 Macleod Trail SE). They include: The Connaught-Beltline District Heritage Walking Tour, The Mission District Heritage Walking Tour, The Stephen Avenue and Area Historical Walking Tour, and The Union Cemetery Interpretive Tour.

CAR RENTAL

Avis, 269-6166
Budget, 226-1550
Dollar, 221-1888
Hertz, 221-1300
Thrifty, 262-4400

PUBLIC HOLIDAYS

New Year's Day - January 1
Family Day - third Monday in February
Good Friday - varies
Easter - varies
Victoria Day - third Monday in May
Canada Day - July 1
Heritage Day - first Monday in August
Labour Day - first Monday in September
Thanksgiving - second Monday in October
Remembrance Day - November 11
Christmas Day - December 25
Boxing Day - December 26

BANKING

There are numerous bank machines located throughout the city at malls, banks, etc.

Major banks and main branch info:

ALBERTA TREASURY BRANCH
239 - 8th Ave. SW
974-5700

BANK OF AMERICA CANADA
#1900, 855 - 2nd St. SW
269-4909

BANK OF MONTREAL
340 - 7th Ave. SW
234-3620

BANK OF NOVA SCOTIA
240 - 8th Ave. SW
221-6401

CANADIAN IMPERIAL BANK OF COMMERCE (CIBC)
309 - 8th Ave. SW
221-2422

CANADIAN WESTERN BANK
441 - 5th Ave. SW
262-8700

CITIBANK CANADA
4210 Canterra Tower
261-5100

FIRST CALGARY SAVINGS
#200, 510 - 16th Ave. NE
230-2783

ROYAL BANK
339 - 8th Ave. SW
292-3311

POST OFFICE

There are more than three dozen postal outlets in the city with most located in malls, drug stores, or 7-Eleven Food Stores. The main post office downtown is at 207 - 9th Ave. SW (974-2078).

BABYSITTING/CHILD CARE

As there are myriad daycare facilities throughout the city, call the following for recommendations:

For pre-school age children—Alberta Family and Social Services Licensing & Subsidy (541-6400)

For school age children—City of Calgary Community and Social Development Department, Community & Childcare Standards Unit (268-5111). Check the yellow pages of the phone book for members of the Alberta Association Family Day-Home Services or Calgary Regional Association for Quality Child Care.

DISABLED ACCESS INFORMATION

CALGARY HANDI-BUS ASSOCIATION
276-8028

ALBERTA ASSOCIATION FOR DISABLED SKIERS
286-8050

ALZHEIMER SOCIETY OF CALGARY
290-0110

CANADIAN WHEELCHAIR SPORTS ASSOCIATION
453-8687

CEREBRAL PALSY ASSOCIATION
253-5955

DISABLED SAILING ASSOCIATION OF ALBERTA
238-0689

INDEPENDENT LIVING RESOURCE CENTRE
263-6880

MULTIPLE SCLEROSIS SOCIETY
250-7090

RESOURCE SERVICES FOR PEOPLE WITH DISABILITIES, CALGARY PARKS & REC
268-5213

SOUTHERN ALBERTA BRAIN INJURY SOCIETY
521-5212

MULTICULTURAL RESOURCES

AFRICAN COMMUNITY ASSOCIATION OF CALGARY
5th floor, 900 - 6th Ave. SW
263-4522

ALLIANCE FRANÇAISE DE CALGARY
#301, 902 - 11th Ave. SW
245-5662

CALGARY ABORIGINAL AWARENESS SOCIETY
#360, 1207 - 11th Ave. SW
296-2227

CALGARY CHINESE COMMUNITY SERVICE ASSOCIATION
#203, 197 - 1st St. SW
265-8446

CALGARY FEDERATION OF FILIPINO ASSOCIATIONS
54 Whitlow Cres. NE
280-3021

CALGARY ITALIAN CLUB
416 - 1st Ave. NE
264-4133

CALGARY JEWISH CENTRE
1607 - 90th Ave. SW
253-8600

CANADIAN HISPANIC CONGRESS OF CALGARY
883 Abbeydale Dr. NE
569-0332

GAY AND LESBIAN COMMUNITY SERVICES
#205a, 233 - 12th Ave. SW
234-8973

GERMAN CANADIAN CLUB OF CALGARY
3127 Bowwood Dr. NW
288-2255

INDIA CANADA ASSOCIATION - CALGARY
826 Edmonton Tr. NE
277-0206

BOOKSTORES

AIRDRIE BOOK STORE
Towerland Mall
505 Main St. S, Airdrie
948-9531

BLUE CASTLE BOOKS
B-1941 Oxbridge Dr. NW
289-6881

THE BOOK COMPANY
Bankers Hall
315 8th Ave. SW,
237-8344

CHAPTERS
9631 Macleod Trail South
212-1442

Dalhousie Shopping Centre
5005 Dalhousie Dr. NW
202-4600

West Hills Town Center
350 Stewart Green
217-2779

CLASSIC BOOKS
Southcentre Mall
100 Anderson Rd. SE
271-1011

COLES BOOK STORE
Market Mall
3525 Shaganappi Trail NW
288-1611

Deerfoot Mall
901 64th Ave. NE
275-3550

330 7th Ave. SW
263-7333

North Hill Shopping Centre
1632 14th Ave. NW
282-5668

Calgary Int'l Airport
2000 Airport Rd. NE
291-3540

Chinook Centre
6455 Macleod Trail SW
252-6727

Sunridge Mall
2525 36th St. NE
285-2077

Southcentre Mall
100 Anderson Rd. SE
271-7331

Northland Village Shoppes
5111 Northland Dr. NW
286-4079

Bow Valley Square
205 5th Ave. SW
233-0252

COOKBOOK HOUSE
722 11th Ave. SW
265-6066

FIFTH HOUSE
9-6125 11th St. SE
571-5234

GUITAR CONNECTION
8234 17th Ave. SE
233-2058

LOGOS BOOKSTORE
129-5403 Crowchild Trail NW,
247-1155

MAP TOWN LTD
100-400 5th Ave. SW
266-2241

MARK MY WORDS
216 -10816 Macleod Trail S,
278-5133

OWL'S NEST BOOKSTORE LTD.
815A 49th Ave. SW
287-9557

PAGES ON KENSINGTON INC
1135 Kensington Rd. NW
283-6655

POSITIVE CONCEPTS
1115 1st St. SE
262-3800

REIDS STATIONERS
710-17th Ave. SW
229-4400

SELF CONNECTION BOOKS
4004 19th St. NW
284-1486

SMITH BOOKS
166 Toronto Dominion Square
269-9202

Marborough Town Square
1425-3800 Memorial Dr. NE
273-9807

Chinook Centre
6455 Macleod Trail SW
259-2051

Brentwood Village Mall,
3630 Morley Trail NW
282-4144

Sunridge Mall
2625 36th St. NE
280-1758

Southcentre Mall
100 Anderson Rd. SE
271-1011

SOCRATES CORNER BOOKS
315-555 Strathcona Blvd. SW
242-8042

TREEHOUSE BOOKS
West Hills Town Centre
236 Stewart Green SW
246-4654

**UNIVERSITY OF CALGARY
BOOKSTORE**
2500 University Dr. NW
220-5937

WESTLANDS LTD
118 2nd Ave., Box 116, Cochrane
932-3030

A WOMAN'S PLACE BOOKSTORE
1412 Centre St. S
263-5256

INDEX

You'll Feel Like a Local when You Travel with Guides from John Muir Publications

CiTY-SMArT™ GUIDEBOOKS

Pick one for your favorite city: *Albuquerque, Anchorage, Austin, Calgary, Cincinnati, Cleveland, Denver, Indianapolis, Kansas City, Memphis, Milwaukee, Minneapolis/St. Paul, Nashville, Portland, Richmond, San Antonio, St. Louis, Tampa/St. Petersburg*

Guides for kids 6 to 10 years old about what to do, where to go, and how to have fun in: *Atlanta, Austin, Boston, Chicago, Cleveland, Denver, Indianapolis, Kansas City, Miami, Milwaukee, Minneapolis/St. Paul, Nashville, Portland, San Francisco, Seattle, Washington D.C.*

TRAVEL✦SMART™

Trip planners with select recommendations to: *Alaska, American Southwest, Carolinas, Colorado, Deep South, Eastern Canada, Florida Gulf Coast, Hawaii, Kentucky/Tennessee, Michigan, Minnesota/Wisconsin, Montana/Wyoming/Idaho, New England, New York State, Northern California, Ohio, Pacific Northwest, South Florida and the Keys, Southern California, Texas, Western Canada*

Rick Steves' GUIDES

See *Europe Through the Back Door* and take along country guides to: *France, Belgium & the Netherlands; Germany, Austria & Switzerland; Great Britain & Ireland; Italy; Russia & the Baltics; Scandinavia; Spain & Portugal;* or the *Best of Europe*

ADVENTURES IN NATURE

Plan your next adventure in: *Alaska, Belize, Guatemala, Honduras*

JMP travel guides are available at your favorite bookstores. For a FREE catalog or to place a mail order, call: 800-888-7504.

John Muir Publications • P.O. Box 613 • Santa Fe, NM 8750

Cater to Your Interests on Your Next Vacation

Frances Purslow

ABOUT THE AUTHORS

Frances Purslow has resided in Calgary for over 14 years and knows the area well. A former teacher, she is now a writer/editor with publishing credits in numerous publications across Canada and the U.S., including the *Chicago Tribune*, *Calgary Herald*, and a children's magazine called *Kid's World*. While much of her editing experience is of a corporate nature, she has also developed a Children's Activity Calendar and has been a contributing writer to such books as *The Calgary Gardener* and *The Calgary Science Fun Guide*.

Frances and husband Neil have four teenagers: Grant, Joel, Todd, and Teresa.

Jacqueline Louie is a Calgary-based freelance writer with a keen appreciation of Calgary's dynamic culinary scene.